A SECOND LOOK AT JESUS

The Perspective of Experience
JOHN EVANS

A Second Look at Jesus, the Perspective of Experience

Copyright © John Evans
ISBN: 978-0-578-14954-7

All rights reserved.

No part of this book may be reproduced by any means, nor transmitted, nor translated into a machine language, without the written permission of the publishers.

Condition of Sale
This book is sold subject to the condition that it shall not, by way of trade or otherwise, be lent, re-sold, hired out or otherwise circulated in any form of binding or cover other than that in which it is published and without a similar condition including this condition being imposed on the subsequent purchaser.

Disclaimer
Every effort has been made to ensure that the information in this book is accurate and current at the time of publication. The author and the publisher cannot accept responsibility for any misuse or misunderstanding of any information contained herein, or any loss, damage or injury, be it health, financial or otherwise, suffered by any individual or group acting upon or relying on information contained herein. None of the opinions or suggestions in this book is intended to replace medical opinion. If you have concerns about your health, please seek professional advice.

John Evans is a pilgrim of the spirit. His book is a pilgrimage
searching for spiritual truth. He has found that truth in many
places, landing in the embrace of The Episcopal Church. I
think readers will find it stimulating and inspiring."

-*The Rt. Rev. Peter James Lee, Bishop Provisional, Diocese of East Carolina*

Acknowledgements

It is hard to know where to begin acknowledging my indebtedness concerning this book. I originally intended to title my book "Credit Where Due." I must therefore guard against writing another book under the guise of acknowledgements.

My parents were interesting, thoughtful and loving people. They set the tone in my childhood. Without their early influence upon my development, I would not likely have been suited for this kind of work.

My early exposure to Christian values was also key. I especially want to credit those teachers for their part in promoting the habit of acknowledging my faults and shortcomings and the working, with God's help, to become a better person.

My Guru Maharishi, my mentor Robert Pritchard and my spiritual guide Pir Vilayat worked long and hard to purify, inform and strengthen me. Their efforts were not always appreciated at the time, but I would be a lesser man now without the challenges they posed then.

All of these strong and insightful men have prepared me to better appreciate the excellence of Jesus and the religion he inspired. Without the life and witness of Jesus, the world would be a more brutish place. I am deeply thankful for His willing sacrifice.

My family and the disciplines of parenthood forced me to grow up and become more responsible than I would have liked. My children, beginning with the mystery of their birth, have also transformed me. They have gone on to become admirable human beings in spite of my shortcomings as a parent. I pray that they flourish.

A large number of friends and supporters who have consented to read early drafts of my book and this has influenced the outcome. They offered questions, corrections, and suggestions. My stepson, Sam and my wife, Alice feature prominently among them. Among these volunteers were a number of generous priests and pastors along with a Rabbi and an Imam. Even my very accomplished Bishop, Peter James Lee, has found time to lend his advice and support.

The support of my friends at my church has been an important part of my story. They allowed me to play an early leadership role among them. They engaged me in an honest and loving manner. They provided me with all kinds of support including financial help for the professional editing and design services that improved my book.

I thank my friend Jean Jones who encouraged me to believe that I could write poetry. That poetry led to the prose, which became the balance of this book.

The Editing of this book has received a professional upgrade through the effort of Expert Subjects LLC. I thank my copy editor Jennifer and cover designer Marija for their excellent work. I insisted upon having my own way on some matters. My astute readers will likely identify some of these decisions as errors. Please do not blame Jennifer or Marija.

The enduring love of my wife Alice has been a constant source of refreshment and balance for me. She has also been my personal ambassador of Wisdom in all things. Her feedback on my writing has been of the highest quality. Through the years, she has provided me with every kind of help and support. No praise is high enough for her.

Introduction

Restless
Does
your breath rise and fall
with the aspirations of the whole creation?
Does
every particle of creation ravish you
with an insane love for the creator?
Does
nothing shake your passionate gratitude
for the simple gift of life?
If so,

keep

doing

whatever
brings you
to this blessed pitch
of intensity.

If not,
if every moment of your life
does **not** resemble
one prolonged, wet kiss
with the Divine,
it is your right,
your sacred duty
to be dissatisfied
and
restless.

John

In the summer of 1978, I took a summer course in Biblical Hebrew at Harvard Divinity School. One of the questions that interested me was the Hebrew name of God. This word was clearly a central part of Hebrew theology and practice for more than 2000 years. I wanted to try it as part of my daily spiritual practice. The first thing my instructor told me was that no one is sure how to pronounce that Name today. He said that while the King James Bible used the word Jehovah, this pronunciation was almost certainly wrong.

Looking further, I found that a few hundred years before the time of Jesus the use of the Hebrew name of God became more and more restricted until only the high priest was allowed to use it. He did this only once a year, during the High Holy Days, while standing alone within the innermost room of the temple. How and why did this disappearing act occur?

I looked further still into this question and I found an interesting statement by Jesus: The Bible has evidence in John 17:26 that Jesus took a different path concerning the name of God. He said; "And I have declared unto them *thy name,* and will declare *it:* that the love wherewith thou hast loved me may be in them, and I in them."

This quote clearly shows that Jesus, acting contrary to the trend of his time, not only knew how to pronounce this name of God and used the name himself, he taught this name of God to his disciples. What has happened since? Why were we not taught this name and its proper use in the catechism of our youth?

I found more information in Acts 2:1-21 where I read; "When the day of Pentecost came, they were all together in one place. Suddenly a sound like the blowing of a violent wind came from heaven and filled the whole house where they were sitting. They saw what seemed to be tongues of fire that separated and came to rest on each of them. All of them were filled with the Holy Spirit and began to speak in other tongues as the Spirit enabled them." Peter's speech goes on for some time and then ends with the phrase: "and everyone who calls on the name of the Lord will be saved."

With further research, I found more that provoked my curiosity. What is the explanation for the mysterious blessing of Jesus found in John 20:22? Here we read; "With that he breathed on them and said: 'Receive the Holy Spirit."

There is more. Paul, when agitated by dissention within the church of Corinth, refers to "the fourth heaven" in second Corinthians 12:2. This leads one to ask; exactly how many heavens are there? Why have we not received a clear explanation on this topic?

Jesus warned us in Matthew 7:6 we read "Give not that which is holy unto the dogs, neither cast ye your pearls before swine, lest they trample them under their feet and turn again and rend you." Well enough. I understand that certain teachings should not be given to the unworthy, but certainly losing these precious teachings altogether is *not* a desirable outcome.

Questions like these are answered to the best of my ability later in this book. I could give some quick answers here and now but it is not likely that anyone would appreciate them or understand very well. Instead, I will start my story near its beginning and let you discover some of these truths as I have. Only then will you be able to properly appreciate new insights concerning who Jesus was and what he taught.

I was raised as a traditional Roman Catholic. I was fully engaged from an early age with the sacraments, parochial school and, service as an altar boy. The religion of my youth taught me right from wrong and gave me an approximate explanation of my relationship with God. However, the result was not entirely satisfactory.

During my first year of college, I learned to meditate. A few months later, in the summer of 1971, I was transformed by what I can only call an irresistible force that delivered a peace that truly passes all understanding. The transformation of that spiritual breakthrough has never left me. Its significance only becomes more vivid as time passes.

I have tried to follow up on that event and, along the way, met some fascinating people. I learned to teach meditation. My meditation teacher then sent me to India to teach and represent him there. Returning home, I worked with a courageous Civil Rights' activist, Robert Pritchard, who was locked in a struggle to turn back a resurgent Ku Klux Klan.

This kind and wise man took the time to befriend me and counsel me. One day Robert took me aside and recommended I "take a second look at Jesus." I respected Robert and took his challenge to heart. To a great extent, this book is the result.

Traditionally, Christianity has not recognized the validity of spirituality if it is not closely tied to its own doctrine. This attitude was simply not an option for me. The ongoing miracle of the surging life that was and is animating me *could not be denied.* Instead, I have closely re-examined contemporary and historic Christianity. I searched for evidence that my experience and the methods that triggered it were consistent with my Christian heritage. I have found what I was looking for. I think that you will find these discoveries interesting.

What I uncovered convinces me that Jesus intended we all partake in the ongoing miracle of life with an intimacy and intensity far exceeding contemporary Christian standards.

With this book, I intend to make three points:

First, I am an ordinary example of my time and its influences. I have had both mundane and inspiring life experiences. I am aware of and responsive to the peculiarities of our time. Here, I am telling a personal story, so I have tried to keep my human perspectives clearly in view.

Second, at a relatively early age, I was led to a decisive spiritual experience. I was permanently transformed within the context of my ordinary human life. I intend, by various means, to tell enough about the details of those deeper dimensions of my experience to *raise your expectations* of what is spiritually obtainable.

Third, I will make some very specific recommendations of what *we can all* do to achieve something similar within our own spiritual lives. The purpose of this book is to open the door for many to achieve a more spiritually significant life here and now.

It took me some time to arrive at a satisfactory result in my rediscovery of Jesus and his message. The sequence of my thoughts and pacing of my book reflects this. I needed to learn in context and you will too. Please be patient! The details I report along the way are intended to make my story more clear, complete and helpful. I aim to be useful.

The Archer

I am an archer. I have selected the finest materials for close grain, straightness, and resilience. My bow, of ancient design, was formed under the guidance of master craftsmen. I have learned and practiced technique until I have become broad and thick. A worthy target has come into view and I have drawn the bowstring back and back with the strength of my entire being. The bowstring is poised by my ear. My arrow was born to fly true. I am aiming, aiming and the moment of release has arrived.

John

Table of Contents

A Distant Thunder

Chapter 1. Early Days... Page 3

Chapter 2. Venturing off to the Revolution .... Page 21

A Cool Drink

Chapter 3. Initiation .... Page 29

The Deluge

Chapter 4. A Quickening .... Page 35

Dredging the Channel

Chapter 5. Meeting the Guru...................................... Page 45

Chapter 6. Hindu Missionary School .... Page 58

Chapter 7. Ripening Fruit .... Page 75

Chapter 8. An Apostle to India .... Page 81

Chapter 9. Coal to Newcastle? .... Page 91

Chapter 10. Holy Men (and Women) .... Page 97

Chapter 11. Klan Business .... Page 105

Chapter 12. Taking A Second Look at Jesus .... Page 120

Chapter 13. Seeking Jesus the Jew .... Page 133

Chapter 14. Love in My Life .... Page 146

Chapter 15. The Islam Few Know .... Page 151

Merging Tributaries

Chapter 16. A Graduate School for Mystics .... Page 165

Chapter 17. Preparing to Launch .... Page 180

Chapter 18. A Friendly Southern Invasion .... Page 185

Chapter 19. Working the Ground .... Page 195

Chapter 20. Harmlessness .... Page 204

Chapter 21. Child Takeover .... Page 208

Chapter 22. Ripening Crops .... Page 213

The Delta

Chapter 23. Returning Home .... Page 233

A Taste of Salt

Chapter 24. Answering the Cynical Revolt .... Page 275

Chapter 25. Something Old, Something New .... Page 288

Index of Key Terms .... Page 299

Index of Poetry .... Page 301

A Bibliography of Suggested Readings .... Page 304

Yahuweh Reference Material .... Page 323

A Distant Thunder

Striking Sail

I am becalmed in the harbor of salvation.
The thrill of the voyage yields to something else.
It is fineness too subtle for my canvas.
I have dropped sail and rest at peace.
A final comprehensive sigh leaves my frame,
A release from my beginning till now,
An ending without end.
I was born for this.
I rest easy, grateful.
Thank you Jesus.

John

Chapter One

Early Days

Mystic /ˈmɪstɪk/
A person who tries to become united with God through prayer and meditation and so understand important things that are beyond normal human understanding.

Oxford Learners Dictionary

In the summer of 1967, when I was fifteen, my father moved our family to an old farmhouse on the north shore of Lake Oneida, New York. The forty-five acres of land that came with our house were mostly forested and I would often wander the woods behind my home.

If I went straight north, the land sloped gradually upward through a neglected apple orchard and past an old, abandoned railway bed. From there the land slowly sloped downward and eventually culminated in a spring-fed pond and wetland.

This was my favorite destination. The spring breathed a transcendental perfume of new life. Two small streams emerged on opposite sides of that wetland and each meandered and grew as they found their way back around toward Lake Oneida.

A Second Look at Jesus

The western stream was narrow enough that I could easily stride over its course as it emerged from its source. This brook wandered for about eight miles, growing as it progressed. Trout were found in its lower reaches, as the stream approached the lake near Jewell, New York.

The eastern brook flowed past a small cemetery a short distance from my home at it too sought the lake. That cemetery held the remains of a number of Revolutionary War veterans. Our land more or less marked the outer edge of colonial settlement at the time of the Revolutionary War.

The Oneida tribe had lived east of us and allowed a few white settlers to reside among them. A sizable number of the Oneidas had embraced the teachings of Jesus and they were not unfriendly to the Colonials. They were the easternmost tribe of the Iroquois Confederation that, with its allies, stretched south to Virginia, west toward the Ohio valley, and north to Canada. When war broke out, the Confederation initially voted to remain neutral in the white man's fight. Their neutrality persisted for some time, but eventually the British convinced the Confederation to join forces with them and support the advance of General Burgoyne from Canada. In exchange, the Crown promised the united tribes a strict prohibition of further westward settlement.

There was a dissenting vote. The Oneida tribe chose to break with the Confederation and join with the Continental cause. The remaining tribes soon invaded the Oneida land, killing many Colonials and Indians and driving the survivors east. The Iroquois Confederation went on to prey upon isolated settlers, sparing neither women nor children, all along the frontier.

Later in the war, George Washington ordered the Continental Army to destroy the hostile Iroquois Confederation. Their major villages and the supplies stored there were put to the torch by the late fall of 1779. When winter came, cold and hunger took a great toll among these people. After the war, the land of the Iroquois Confederation was largely vacant and parcels of it were offered

Early Days

to Revolutionary soldiers, in lieu of back wages, for their war service. This accounted for the Revolutionary veterans buried near my home.

The land was reasonably rich, although often rocky. When the Erie Canal was built a few decades later, it passed right through Lake Oneida and heightened the prosperity of the entire region. Then, as better farmland became available further west, this part of upstate New York was largely abandoned and much of the marginal farmland reverted to forests. This history influenced the temperament of the land and our presence upon it.

I loved the solitude of that land. The solitude was a healing balm for the troubles of my adolescence. The toxic residues of petty insults, anxieties and disappointments seeped out of me as I made my way deeper and deeper. The bright conversation of the birds, the subtle wind, the unbroken song of running water, and the perfume of freshness pervading the community of nature reoriented my soul towards the dawn of life.

My mother was not as charmed as I was. I remember her softly weeping in the living room on the day we saw our new home for the first time. Her husband had bought this farmhouse, which lacked any aesthetic merit, in an uncultured and economically blighted region of upstate New York. She had not been consulted. From this vantage, between Jewell and North Bay, New York, she saw her bleak future with sudden clarity and wondered how it all had come to this.

She was a gifted artist, born in Connecticut. Only fifteen years before she had graduated from Syracuse University with a Fine Arts degree. Syracuse, only forty miles away, might as well have been in another continent.

My father was born in 1923 and grew up a child of the Depression. He lived on a farm just outside of Rochester, New York. Their farm was a large and prosperous enterprise. However, everyone in his family worked **very** hard. Grandfather grew forage, vegetables, and grain. They had a sizable herd of milk cows.

A Second Look at Jesus

They also bought and sold horses. I am told that my grandfather once purchased a herd of wild horses from the west that was on their way to slaughter for meat. When he took them off the freight car, they were underfed and in poor health. He saw that these horses were fed, exercised and trained. Many became proficient dressage jumpers.

Expedient training methods were used. For example, to get the horses to tuck their feet high when they cleared a rail, my father was told to swing a 2x4 at their feet while they were air-borne. This method was harsh, but it worked. Sometimes, if a horse was a little lame in one leg, the opposite leg would get a measured blow to "even them out" just before a buyer came. Grandfather was a hard man. He was also a survivor. He protected and provided for his family. Not all Depression-era farmers succeeded in this respect.

My grandfather's child-rearing methods were similar to those he used with his horses. Sometimes, force was part of the program. When it was time for my father to learn how to swim, he was literally thrown into the nearby Barge Canal until he figured out the fundamentals of fluid dynamics.

My father had the job of milking the cows. That meant getting up at four am every day. This chore had to be completed before he was *allowed* to walk to school. He also delivered wagons of manure to gardens all around town. His friends called him Farmer John. In spite of a certain amount of derision because of his earthy home life, he was socially active. He always had some money in his pocket. I am also told that, as a young man, he ran with fast women!?

My father, once he had passed beyond grandfather's control, showed he was generally a more gentle and compassionate soul. He did not inflict his children with most of his father's methods. I did not know it at the time, but my parents had an agreement about me. My mother could raise her daughters as she saw fit, but I was my father's son.

Early Days

Now and then my father and I would talk about right and wrong and wisdom and foolishness. I remember that in my mid-teens I became quite proud of my persuasive powers. I once told my father that I could take either side of an argument and usually prevail. My father looked me in the eye and said that he was disappointed to hear that. I have considered the import of what he said over the years and I now agree. His point was not evident to me until later when I had gained more life experience. Not every side of an argument has equal value in practical life and we do wrong if we use intellect to argue against wisdom.

My father was possessed by a restless, inquisitive intelligence. By inclination, the bulk of my father's attention was focused on the study of human nature. My father treasured friends and acquaintances as others might collect wine or rare coins. He valued interesting life stories and unique human perspectives. Above all else, he valued authenticity both in and with his friends.

Many of my father's friends and acquaintances were primitive to the point of crudity. My more refined mother did not approve of them and they did not come to our home. Instead, we visited them where they lived or worked.

I remember a reclusive bachelor who lived in a tarpaper-covered shack deep in the woods. He sold us raw milk and fresh eggs. My father delighted in him and others who led a simple and rustic life. These "primitives" showed us how little was needed to live well.

Once, my father took me to visit an old man who lived across the road. He was in the grip of emphysema. Between rasping breaths and a violent hacking cough, his conversation was filled with poisonous racial epitaphs. Every other sentence referred to "lazy coons," or "ignorant niggers." As we walked away, my father observed some people refused to change and all we could do was to wait for them to die. I saw his point. This man was beyond persuasion. He was most likely going to die as he had lived; agitated by hate.

A Second Look at Jesus

On the other hand, The Reverend Orelious Bounds was an example of my family's cultured friends. He and his wife, Marie, had retired to a piece of land a few miles east of us. With the help of their church friends from Rochester, they had put up a garage. They lived in that garage as they slowly built their retirement home. They were two of only a few dozen black people in the entire county at that time. Reverend and Marie Bounds were consistently kind and helpful to us. My parents enjoyed the wisdom this couple had acquired over their many years of service.

Mrs. Bounds taught me a valuable lesson one day. She had planted a pretty, flowering bush along her driveway. She had a persistent problem with people backing up over her bush when they were trying to turn around in preparation for departure. Then she directed her husband to acquire a sizable boulder and place in front of that shrub. From then on, she warned all her guests to be careful not to damage their car on the big rock as they backed around to leave. The bush thrived. Years later, when I introduced her to my girlfriend Alice, she took me aside and told me to marry her without further delay. This was sound advice and that girl has become my life companion.

During that period, one of my adult friends was New York State Trooper, Paul Pratt. Under Paul's guidance, I learned the value of antiques and the stories that came with them. I was shown artfully crafted Hepplewhite nightstands that were an enduring testament to simple function with grace. I became a *picker*. To this day, I find meaning in the ability to identify and acquire the valuable, the significant among the detritus of life.

Paul taught me to appreciate a weathered, crusty patina finish that was a sure sign of authenticity, even as it concealed some of the object's original beauty. It was here, in the appreciation of antiques, I had the first inkling that my ancestors may have been every bit as alive and intelligent as I was. These antiques carried an aroma of the hopes and aspirations of their original makers and owners. Such objects, for the observant, can punctuate and guide an accurate reading of history.

Early Days

It was around this time I first acquired my life-long appetite for the wit and wisdom of my predecessors. Benefitting from lessons previously learned just made sense. For example, how could a lost person find his way back to civilization without a map and compass? One should travel downhill until reaching a stream. That stream should be followed as it grew and joined with tributaries. Eventually you will find a settlement. Civilization is always found along reliable water sources. The answer was simple and elegant.

During my high school years, I made my pocket money buying and selling antiques. On weekends, I moved a collection of furniture, art glass, wooden duck decoys, bronze bells, muskets and other merchandise out of the garage and displayed them along the highway that ran in front of my home. I sold no modern trinkets. I could usually double any investment I made, since I knew what I was buying. I also had many opportunities to keep items I found interesting.

I especially appreciated old rifles. As far as objects went, I considered them significant. I saw them as a focus of what, in their time, their owners considered worth living and dying for. Such tools were a way to decisively say **no** to oppressors and predators of all kinds. At about age fourteen my father bought me a deer rifle that had been originally forged as an American weapon of war. It was a model 1898 Krag rifle with a shortened barrel and deep brown walnut stock. That stock became lustrous and alive when I rubbed it with linseed oil. That Krag also had a bright, rifled bore and an incredibly smooth action that responded with deft precision when handled by someone who understood it. This was a fully functional relic of an earlier time. I remember thinking this rifle, or one similar, may have seen service with Teddy Roosevelt's Rough Riders as they stormed San Juan Hill in Cuba.

Newspaper magnate William Randolph Hearst and some of his influential friends had conceived that war. They believed it was

A Second Look at Jesus

time for America to join the family of great nations by acquiring colonies and naval bases overseas.

The opening move was a series of compelling and mostly truthful newspaper stories about atrocities committed by Spanish forces as they tried to suppress a long-running liberation movement by Cuban patriots. By the time the American Battleship Maine blew up in Havana's harbor early in 1898, the average American was more than ready to join the Cuban people in their struggle for freedom. Ejecting a foreign power from our neighborhood was just a bonus. In the end, we got our bases in Cuba, the Philippines, Guam and Puerto Rico. As a nation, we have sometimes looked back, questioning the wisdom of all this ambition. I know that I have. Today, I imagine that our nation's power and our influence has probably grown beyond anything conceived by Hearst and his friends.

My dog was a gun enthusiast too. We had an old basset hound, Coco, who simply lived to hunt. Every day he would meet me as I got off my school bus. Then, he would rush off toward the woods behind our house, stop and look over his shoulder to see if I was following. Next, he would rush part way back and start the process all over again. All of this time he would keep up a steady cadence of deep throaty howls and piercing yelps. If he saw me carrying a shotgun or even a broom, he would triple his enthusiasm, spinning around a few times and then heading back out to the fields and woods that were always ready to host an adventure.

To get a proper perspective on this canine display, you would need to know that the lower parts of a Basset Hound; ear tips, jowls, belly and an outsized male organ all travel about an inch above the ground. This breed's great dignity and enthusiasm are untouched by the mirth they inspire. Bassets are very effective rabbit hounds. The rabbits invariably treat the slow pace dictated by the short Basset legs with contempt. You see, rabbits always circle back to the place where they are "jumped" to put the trailing hound on an endlessly circling scent trail. Then, they jump wide to leave their simple-minded pursuer behind to follow an

Early Days

endless trail. If the dog is fast, they make a very large circle and the chase becomes very long and tedious for the hunter who is waiting for the rabbit to return to his starting point. A basset, however, is treated with such disdain that the rabbit circles back in just a few minutes. Then the rabbit becomes stew. To me the joy and triumph of my dog was more important than dinner.

One day, everything was unfolding in my rabbit hunt as usual, but this time, my prey screamed when I shot it. Until then, I did not even know that rabbits had a voice. This cry pierced my heart and made me nauseous. Now, I knew this was not just a game. My sport and sustenance was purchased at a high price.

I tried to avoid causing harm. Eventually, however, I concluded that complete avoidance of destruction was neither possible nor desirable. Part of my job on Earth was to cause some destruction now and then (albeit mostly in the realm of ideas). Instead, I have grown in gratitude for the contribution all creation is making towards my life. I will become food myself someday. We all will. In the meantime, I focus on **not wasting this precious opportunity to live meaningfully here and now.** I have tried to live in a way that reflects well the unseen source making this display of life possible. Then, when the time comes, I aspire to die well, too, reflecting both that source and the lessons I had learned along the way.

My father always encouraged me to learn the lessons nature offered. A few years before, while living in Wisconsin, my father looked into the idea of operating a soapstone and asbestos mine, which was located in the northern part of the state within the Menomonee Indian Reservation. He took me there on several occasions and we had an opportunity to learn some nature lore from our hosts.

Ice fishing is very popular in Wisconsin. The usual method was to construct a shed and drag it onto a lake. These huts were often fitted out with numerous creature comforts. They had lanterns, wood burning stoves, radios, plenty of food, coffee, beer and whiskey. There was an opening in the floor where holes were

A Second Look at Jesus

cut in the ice and a fishing device was placed over the hole. These fishing contraptions were spring loaded and if a fish took the bait they would trigger the device, which would jerk the line upward to set the hook and display a flag to announce it was time to reel in the fish. I thought this contraption trivialized the life and death of the fish.

Our Indian friends showed us a better method. In the first place, they never bought bait. There was a local bug that laid eggs within a certain weed. During the late summer, those eggs matured into a larva and the weed grew a round, pulpy knob around them about the size of a large grape. This housed and fed the grub living inside all winter long. If undisturbed, the grub would burrow out in the spring and get on with its life cycle. Our Indian friends showed us where to gather these knobs and demonstrated how to cut them open and get to the grub. The fish loved those grubs.

The Indian method of fishing involved chipping a hole in the ice and then putting a simple baited hook and line into the water. Next, we would lie down with a blanket over our head and gaze into the water. The result was magical. The light that penetrated the ice around us softly illuminated the water. The blanket removed all the refracted light that usually prevents us from seeing beyond the surface of water. As a result, I saw with perfect clarity, straight to the bottom of the lake. The underwater foliage and the different kinds of fish at various depths were as clear and intimate as if I was swimming with them. It was simple matter to lower the bait so it was free of the weeds and close to the fish while we watched. The Indian method was so effective, it was almost unfair. It also made the entire process a soul-transporting revelation.

Some of my most profound moments came while I hunted. Once, at about age twelve, as I sat very still in a wintery Wisconsin clearing, a wren landed on my rifle barrel and looked me over carefully before flitting away. Just a few years ago, a large hawk landed in a tree adjacent to my hunting tree stand in North

Early Days

Carolina. He was not more than twenty feet away and gazed intently at me. Not satisfied, he shifted to a nearer branch and looked me up and down for a long time.

From these experiences and others, I have concluded keeping very still allows interesting experiences to come near. Then, if we are paying attention, we can experience the lessons they have to teach us and incorporate them into our life.

The subtle approach of a cautious deer can be a life transforming experience:

A Good Hunter Knows
We are best advised to rise before dawn
and
observe a remote clearing.

Only the naïve look for plain view of the whole animal.
A true hunter knows better
They look for a brown eye, a black nose,
a twitching ear
or tail amidst the brush.

Then, in a sparkling instant, comes the revelation:
The parts reveal the whole.

Sometimes sound or sight is elusive.
Then, we need to open our focus deeper,
feeling with our whole being.

What does your solar plexus detect?
That doe is standing in and on your being.

Do you feel it?

In this realm each of us are at once observed and observing.
Steady, don't flinch at the moment of recognition.

A Second Look at Jesus

Embrace it like your beloved
who rolls under the quilt
and then...
draws you in for a deep, moist embrace.
Or
like the time that we first ruptured my shell
and
I flowed out beyond the stars.

John

School was generally less soul satisfying. I was a moderately successful B student. My greatest weakness was math while my strengths were in the sciences. More important to me were the relationships I formed with my friends and teachers. It was my good fortune that a few teachers singled me out and made a personal commitment to helping me approach adulthood with more confidence and competence. For me, the foremost example of this personal intervention was my French teacher, Georgiana Landry. She was a slight, self-possessed spinster who had overcome polio. She had been left with only a limp thanks to good fortune and an iron will. She found the time and interest to listen to my hopes and fears. I remember she told me I was not alone. She encouraged me to hold true to my ideals. Concerning religion, she counselled me not to take doctrine as anything but an opinion. Significantly, she said the mystics were different; they were "God's own." *That* sounded interesting.

One winter day, there was a new girl on my bus. She had been sent by her family in New York City to stay with country relatives. I began to sit with her on our long morning bus rides. Her favorite topic was her Guru back home. She explained that Guru means *dispeller of darkness* in Sanskrit. She clearly loved what this man was offering and treasured what he had taught her. She told me just a little about what that teaching was and I made a mental note to follow up on this topic when I found

Early Days

an opportunity. I had no idea what a meaningful turn this encounter was for me.

Another important person in my life during these tender years was my football coach, Mr. Kleinhammer. Under his leadership, I trained hard and took pride in my fatigue, aches and bruises along with the skills that I learned.

I started and played throughout most games. Early on, I did my part as an "end", but eventually the coaches determined I had "stone fingers." This meant balls tended to bounce off them rather than "stick" when I tried to catch a pass. Eventually it was decided since I ran very hard and did not shrink from impact, I would become a running back. I was given the job of fullback. This is supposed to be a position for a player of great power and drive. At only 156 pounds, I lacked the strength and momentum normally expected. As a result, even when I ran very hard, I bounced off my opponents as often as I penetrated their line.

Our team did not win many games. In fact, one year we had a nearly perfect record of losses tempered by only one tie. Still, we fought hard and I never lost heart. I had the satisfaction that can only come from holding nothing back. Most important, I learned that the opportunity to become strong and resourceful was within my control and, in the end, this endured long after the outcome of the games was a distant memory. Football was an important opportunity to learn about overcoming obstacles. I am thankful for such an opportunity.

My father encouraged me in my sport. He too had played in his high school years. He was apparently a very effective offensive tackle. He was proud to have been named as an "all county" best in that position. He told me, with some regret, that his father had never attended one of his games. He and my mother did not make that mistake. They did attend some of my games.

My father's past held some surprises. During the summer between junior and senior years in high school I was able to participate in an opportunity to take a summer class at Colgate College, about 30 miles from my home. My father drove me there on the

A Second Look at Jesus

first day and reminisced about the football rivalry that existed between Colgate and his college, Syracuse.

He told me a story about one of his high jinks that centered upon the color orange. This was the Syracuse College color. If fact, the football team was often referred to as simply "The Orange."

As we entered the beautiful Colgate campus for the first time that summer, we paused next to the large pond that was near its entrance. The story began with my father's acquisition of some military marker dye of the type used to assist in the rescue of aviators shot down over the ocean. My father and a friend rented a small Cessna aircraft at the Syracuse airport. Then, they proceeded to Hamilton, New York and executed a die-bombing mission on that pond. In this way, they turned it a brilliant orange color on the day of the big, annual grudge match between the Syracuse and Colgate football teams. My father was the bombardier!

I tended to be less daring. Socially, I was especially reserved and introverted which made it more difficult to meet girls and cultivate romantic friendships. There were two notable exceptions; one was a sweet girl I met in Ohio shortly before my move to upstate New York. I still remember what it was like when I first kissed her, under a full moon and on the banks of the Wabash River. I had the clearest sensation of my inner world spinning.

Later, I had an unexpected summer romance with a delightful girl from southern New York. Many letters passed between us and we visited each other's homes for a few weekends. Her kisses tasted as fresh as a mountain spring. I was in love. Alas, our romance did not last. She settled on a local boy instead.

My parents remained an important source of guidance for me as I tried to master love and life. I did not always agree with their assessments. However, I had no real complaints against them. They were reasonable up to a point and well intentioned.

I will note, however, that my mother sabotaged my plans to go to Woodstock in 1969. She was the one who first suggested I attend when she saw an ad in *The New Yorker* magazine. The

Early Days

event would not be far away and I had a driver's license. Then, as the time to leave came near, she insisted I finish a painting project for her that *had to be done* that weekend. In fact, as she confessed years later, she was afraid I would encounter casual sex and dangerous drugs along with the rock and roll at Woodstock. She wanted to delay my exposure to such things.

I shared my parents with three younger sisters, Sharon, Elizabeth and Catherine. Sharon was close enough to my age that we would play and contend with each other. In many ways, she was my first true friend. About two and a half years younger, Sharon was almost able to keep up with me and was game for just about any adventure. She was a scrappy and energetic companion. In many ways she has influenced the kind of feminine relationships I came to appreciate later.

I remember when young, Sharon was as skinny as a rail. In fact, when she tried to learn to swim she could not float very well. I can still remember her setting off with a furious Australian crawl stroke. She could go only a few feet on the surface before turning into a submarine.

I most clearly remember my sisters from the earlier years I spent in Wausau, Wisconsin. We were there from the time I was about five years old until I was thirteen. We spent most of our years in a large, Victorian house on Franklin Street, a very good part of town. My parents bought it for a song and we renovated it ourselves.

I did not know it at the time, but that house had fallen into decline after it was used as a "cathouse" during WW2. The house was abandoned for years. Its reputation profoundly depressed its value and created a wonderful opportunity for us a dozen years later.

My three sisters and I were good friends. One Easter, our parents gave my sister Sharon and me a couple of live chicks. I remember their downy feathers may had been dyed, one blue and the other pink. Those birds grew into a red rooster and a white hen. My bird, the rooster, was named Road Runner and Sharon's

A Second Look at Jesus

was called Fluffy. Later that year, we entered them into the chicken livestock category at the Marathon County Fair. I remember they won prizes, one a white and the other a red ribbon. Back at home, we would chase them around the house for sport. This fun ended when our roosters started to crow at dawn *every* morning. Our suburban neighbors complained. Soon thereafter, my father then took off their heads. My mother advised me not to look, but I felt I should stand by my friends to the end. Those birds made a miserable meal too. Not only were we unhappy about eating our pets, but all of that chasing around the house had made them nearly as tough as leather!

The chickens were fun, but my homing pigeons were more impressive creatures than the hens. I built a coop for them on the high side of our lot. I learned pigeons have a highly developed sense where their home is located. You can release these birds dozens or even hundreds of miles away from their coop and they will always find their way back. They need not have travelled that route before. Homing pigeons are bred to display this ability to a maximum degree. Some people use their pigeons to compete in races.

When racing, each "homer" released is assigned a clock in a box that is activated as the race begins. That clock runs until the bird lands back at its home coop. Then, a small, numbered metal band is removed from the bird's ankle and placed in a compartment within the clock box. Then, in the act of stopping the clock the metal band that proves that the pigeon has made the flight was sealed within the box. Later, the race organizers evaluate the times and distances involved before declaring the winner.

To this day, scientists are not entirely sure how pigeons can fly so unerringly over terrain they have never seen before and consistently arrive back home. I did not bother with the timed races, but my father would occasionally take my pigeons on his business trips and release them. They usually came home, although a few were lost, most likely to hawks.

Early Days

Pigeons are remarkable creatures. They have a brain the size of a small peanut. Considering the elegance and sophistication of the life form humans have been blessed with, it is not right we have a low opinion of our potential. I believe that this includes our own ability to find our way back home.

Human relationships were, of course, more challenging than relationships with pets. There were times when Sharon would annoy me and I, in turn, would tease her. We developed an undercurrent of mutual antagonism that surfaced from time to time. Sometimes my father would apply his belt if we went too far and significantly disturbed the peace of the family home.

Our games were fun, but they were not entirely safe. One time, Sharon was captured as part of a fort game. Then, she broke her collarbone in a daring leap off the high porch to escape custody. A few years later, she broke her arm in an accident involving a tree, a steep hill and a rope with a section of ladder that formed a very unstable seat. I pushed her too hard, the ladder tilted and, for a moment, she flew. Then, she landed. This time her arm was broken in three places and her jaw too. I confess, I was reckless. I am sorry about the harm I caused. She healed and carried on as my good friend.

Liz was considerably younger than Sharon was and was gently treated by me. She was tender, quiet and conservative when young. She later showed some irreverent artistic talent. I remember one of her sculptures had the creative name "Kentucky Fried Snake." In her teen years, she was a terror. Conflict with my parents reached an alarming threshold. Liz has since gone on to become a first-class mother and has accomplished a resounding success as a military wife and volunteer.

Catherine was the baby of the family. She was and is strong, flexible and gentle. She has definite aptitude for deep spiritual experience.

As I approached college age, I took my mother's counsel and applied to a New York state college, Harvard University and

A Second Look at Jesus

Antioch College. Since I was no more than a B student, Harvard was not interested in me.

The personal interview for the New York state school was memorable. For some reason, I gave a wildly unexpected answer when asked what I wanted to get out of a college education. I said, "I want the truth and I don't care if I die to get it." I do not know who was more shocked, the interviewer or me. I was quite earnest. He implied his school was not prepared to handle that degree of idealism.

Fortunately, Antioch College was willing to accept me. I entered that summer, immediately after graduation from high school.

Chapter Two

Venturing Off to the Revolution

Antioch College was a trip. I remember being picked up at the airport by a scruffy looking Antioch student who drove a small, rounded Volvo that dated from the 1950's. He counselled me on the way to campus. He said that, if I wanted, for the first year I could "just kick back and smoke grass." It was the summer of 1970 and he assured me that I would not be expelled. With a war on, no professor was going to flunk me out, causing me to be sent to Vietnam. I did not take that advice to heart, although some may have.

At the time, I was fascinated with the idea of exploring the mysteries of the mind. I took some entry-level classes including Psychology and I remember reading The Teachings of Don Juan, A Yaqui Way of Knowledge and Be Here Now with great interest.

I also enjoyed the freewheeling culture that prevailed at Antioch. There were no team sports, although a spirited game of Frisbee football was organized from time to time. There was regularly scheduled skinny-dipping at the pool. The professors

A Second Look at Jesus

were first class and clearly loved their jobs. The buildings were clean and the staff was efficient. At all times, grass and music were flavoring a heady mix of fresh ideas, freedom and opportunity for adventure.

Most of us were sampling the culture of the day (sex, drugs, and rock and roll, along with radical politics). The exceptional Antioch students were the studious and responsible. This tribe tended to live in Mills dorm. Those students were the ones who constituted our volunteer fire department and worked as student security guards. The Mills dorm was like a ghetto of diligence and responsibility surrounded by a city of playful indulgence and not a little chaos.

The culture of the time and place encouraged every kind of experimentation and exploration. Politically, to balance the self-indulgence of hippie culture, I decided to spend some of my spare time helping at the Black Panther Party headquarters in nearby Dayton, Ohio.

On Saturday mornings, a sizable number of children would show up for a free pancake breakfast at the Panther headquarters. Afterwards the Panthers would teach the children about self-respect and looking out for each other. I think the management enjoyed having some Caucasians doing the step and fetch work. I know I appreciated the opportunity to learn from the experience.

I remember teaching one young Panther how to drive in an ancient, mint-green Plymouth. I was the only one in our small group who could handle a manual transmission. On another occasion, we volunteers were called into the back room and the "brothers" showed us the pistols they kept concealed under their belts. I suppose they wanted us to know they were properly serious revolutionaries. We were suitably impressed.

Other outings included anti-war protests and filling out union picket lines. I remember yelling at the "dirty scabs" stealing union jobs. Back at school, I could listen to nearly endless passionate debates between the devotees of Mao or Trotsky. They would

Venturing Off to the Revolution

hold forth for hours with references to "stalking horse" this or "paper tiger" that. I did not care to take part in those discussions. I was mindful that the Beatles had warned us "People carryin' pictures of Chairman Mao, ain't going to make it with anyone anyhow." I found tightly focused political junkies to be rather boring.

After a few years, the Vietnam War wound down, but our resistance to militarism continued. There was a bomber base for the Strategic Air Command nearby and it was rumored they were using the twin towers of our administration building as an aiming point for mock bombing runs. One of our tribe went to a flat-roofed building in line with the traffic flow of the bombers and spelled out SAC SUCKS in toilet paper. In due course, the college got a complaint from the Air Force. That was political fun for us. We were merry pranksters.

In contrast to this heady new-age mix, my first campus job was helping at the horse stables associated with our school. I learned about handling and grooming the horses. More importantly, I was the top guy for mucking out the stalls and piling the manure outside. The contrast between my far out friends at school and the no nonsense widow who ran the riding school was instructive and stabilizing.

Antioch was a work-study school, which meant after every three or six-month study period we were expected to get a job that interested us and related somehow to the classes we were taking. It was all self-directed. We chose our jobs through a very effective employment department Antioch ran.

In the fall of 1970, my first "co-op" job was working as an attendant at the training ward of the Bronx State Mental Hospital. It was a revelation. There were some mixed-up people in that hospital. I remember one man my age who was convinced the Scientologist cult was controlling his thoughts and movements. Now and then, he would walk around with mock-robotic movements. He came to us after his unseen controllers told him to jump off a roof. He did as he was told. Some patients would

A Second Look at Jesus

spend hours in the shower if we let them. Others were sociable to a limited degree. Our job was to be friendly and engaging. This was the best part of my job. In hindsight, I think this simple availability of friendship may have had the greatest healing impact we had among the patients we were able to engage.

I helped oversee the everyday activities of the patients, such as taking medications, attending to personal hygiene and interacting wherever it seemed to be helpful. We broke up a few fights and sometimes helped to deliver someone to the padded restraint room. Usually the drugs the patients took kept them low-key.

I remember the chief psychiatrist for the unit was a man of some influence. Whenever he walked into a room, several of the patients would straighten up and stop acting crazy as long as he was around. Then, after he left, they would revert.

One remarkable outcome of my job was how exhausted I would become. Sometimes I would lie down intending a short nap after work and not wake up until it was time to go back to work the next morning. These people were in a struggle with me as to whose reality would prevail in our relationship. This was a soul-challenging job.

Some have observed that the mystic swims joyously in the same ocean, which drowns the insane. All the while, most look on from the safe shore. In this job, I saw how fragile and perishable the human mind is. It is formed in love and is best repaired with kindness and tenderness.

Now and then, I would take the subway to Manhattan. My discretionary budget was slender. I remember a macrobiotic restaurant on the Lower East Side called The Cauldron. They served a big bowl of brown rice, a bowl of miso soup and and a pot of tea for about a dollar. I did catch some monumental concerts at Fillmore East and later at Fillmore West with Frank Zappa, The Grateful Dead, Big Brother and the Holding Company and others. More commonly, I heard intimate concerts that some inspired, but undiscovered musicians would hold in their apartments. They posted classified ads in *The Village Voice* and

Venturing Off to the Revolution

collected a few dollars at the door. Everything was low key and everyone had a good time.

One evening, I was returning home after a date on the Lower East Side, next to Roosevelt Park. Suddenly, someone leapt out of the shadows, grabbed me around my neck and put a large knife to my throat. He used a serrated kitchen knife. For some reason I handled the situation in a completely unconventional manner. I pretended to be drunk and unable to understand the mugger. As he struggled to communicate to me that he was going to take my money, I kept walking, talking, and making no sense whatsoever. He walked with me with his arm around my throat and talking all the while. Eventually we got the intersection of a busy street and I said, "Look, everyone can see you." He let me go and ran. Perhaps, this was not a safe or rational response on my part, but this *is* what happened.

A Cool Drink

Chapter Three

Initiation

Back at Antioch, in the winter of 1971, I shifted my interests somewhat. I no longer thought Western psychology had the answers I was looking for. Concluding that something more profound was needed, I became very open to the idea that something more spiritual might work better. Therefore, that winter when I saw a poster inviting me to learn Transcendental Meditation (TM); I acted. At thirty-five dollars, the course of three sessions seemed unnecessarily expensive, but I paid the price. Once initiated, I was not impressed. My TM teacher, Marty Milligan, seemed like a nice enough guy. I did not want to believe I had been bilked, although it appeared this might be the case. Outside of an odd, stirring sensation at the crown of my head there were just random thoughts, along with this odd sounding word, a mantra, which I repeated over and over.

TM had something special going for it: this meditation was about experience, not theory. I was a little surprised that TM was presented without much of its cultural context. Words like *Shiva*, the *Upanishads* and *Samadhi* were not used. Instead, the TM teachers offered a culturally neutral explanation. We were told effective meditation amounted to following a carefully chosen thought, a mantra, as we perceived it emerging in our mind.

A Second Look at Jesus

This thought, like any other, emerged from an unlimited source in creative intelligence. Due to the simplicity and innocence of the inner situation, the mantra did not lead to rational thought. We were not even told the meaning of the mantra. For us it was just a sound. Instead, we perceived the *process* of thinking as we viewed the emergence of this particular thought in earlier and earlier degrees of its development. We experienced thought *vertically* in meditation rather than *horizontally* as with the logic and emotion of every day interaction. This theory made sense to me and I was more than willing to try it. I persevered in my twice-daily meditation practice. That time became an island of peace and certainty within the sometimes-chaotic ebb and flow of my life.

Later that winter, I engaged Antioch's very efficient job placement organization in a new job search. There were hundreds of well-maintained index cards organized for job type and location. This was a tremendous resource and it did much to strengthen my confidence that life is a manageable adventure. I arranged to work the next spring and summer at Planned Parenthood in San Francisco. I chose this particular job because I regarded the Bay Area as something of a cultural holy land for our generation's optimistic movement to reshape the world.

While in the Bay area, I lived in the flat lands of Berkeley a couple of blocks from the police station. Berkeley University was further up the gentle slope that began at San Francisco Bay. The wealthy folks lived on the surrounding hills and had a view of the bay. On the other hand, we lowlanders had a *point of view* and dreamt of revolution and our part in it.

One day, I could not get home because the police were dealing with several cases of dynamite found in a rented garage two doors from my house on Roosevelt Street. That caused me some thoughtful moments. Why would someone focus on destroying buildings and killing people rather than removing obstacles in minds and hearts? It was utterly crude and likely to harden the resolve of the ones we sought to transform.

Initiation

In these times, there were plenty of unique characters walking around. One acquaintance always sang his sentences in an odd pentatonic melody. Others had the appearance and manner of hippies, but were solid, responsible people with serious jobs. I rented a room in a house owned by a woman who was a violinist for the local symphony orchestra. Our next-door neighbor was a doctor.

Sometimes a word of explanation was needed for newcomers like me. I once went to a local motorcycle repair shop that posted their basic services in their waiting room. I puzzled over the fact that an Acid Tune cost five dollars more than a Basic Tune Up. I asked the clerk about it and he explained the finer sensitivities required for that particular service came at the cost of a tab of acid. He said the discerning customer who desired the very best service rightfully covered this added cost.

When I first came to the Bay area I had no vehicle, but that was not any sort of problem for my morning commute to my job in San Francisco. I seldom stood more than a few minutes on University Boulevard with my thumb out. One longhair or another would soon stop. After a few courtesies, they would typically produce a joint to share on the ride. We had no doubt we were the archetype for a new society to save the world from its barbaric ways. One world, one people, stoned and in love.

I came across an interesting thread of discontent among some of the women I met. They were coping with the withdrawal of their men from perfectly good relationships with plenty of sex and no real cause of complaint. Their men were headed to India to seek enlightenment and the women were profoundly annoyed. One such woman came over to our group home and talked with great animation to our informal leader. She wanted to know if there were any "real men" present because she was looking for one. They gave a brief look where I sat, next to the spacey guy who lived in the attic. "No," he said, "we just have a couple of boys." Judging from her ferocity, I think he may have done me a favor. I was probably not up to the job and I do not think she was looking for a trainee.

The Deluge

Chapter Four

A Quickening

I was nineteen in the spring and summer of 1971 and spent many of my weekends visiting California communes. These rural settlements were a reaction to the unsustainability of the 1967 Summer of Love in San Francisco. These communes were an attempt to live our ideals away from corrupt urban culture. Usually, I went north from my Berkeley home along the Coastal Highway. Early one summer day I followed a friendly suggestion and found a place known as Wheeler's Ranch. I remember as I rode my Honda twin across their property line, the air became tangibly thick with animation, as though all of us were all suddenly breathing the same vibrant air. The people I met welcomed me like a prodigal son.

As I arrived, many were gathering around a low hut made of limbs and covered with sheets of plastic. The residents invited to join in as they shed their clothing and crawled into the "sweat lodge." This casual nudity was exotic wild life to one raised as a Catholic. Still, in I went. Everyone was densely packed into the small space. Soon, steam erupted from water ladled over the glowing hot rocks piled in a central pit, penetrating through every pore and bone in my body. The air became more alive in every way. My breath seemed to originate from the middle of

A Second Look at Jesus

my being, a thousand miles inside. The leader called upon the Great Spirit to purify us and teach us to love each other. Minutes passed like hours. The heat was oppressive and then liberating. As I passed through a number of personal barriers, I just kept breathing.

I remember that I emerged feeling as fresh and weak as a newborn. A few yards away some of us gathered around the fire. One of the tribe offered me a joint. I said no thanks. He insisted. I said no. He said I *had* to try it. I took a small puff. A token toke so to speak. You see, I had lost my taste for marijuana. Now, after a few months of regular meditation I had noticed that grass stopped making me high. Instead, it started to make me feel dull, as though someone had drawn a damp, grey blanket over my mind. That was not very appealing experience. As a result, I lost interest in drugs of all kinds.

A little later, I left the fire and sat cross-legged on a large stump to meditate. I was still practicing as I had learned six months before. Mantra, mantra, mantra, *thought*, mantra, mantra, *thought*, mantra then.. then… In a flash, insight asserted itself. From the base of my spine there was a seismic shift followed by an eruption of irresistible energy that rushed upward. This energy penetrated the crown of my head, exploding the substance of my mind far and wide in a prodigious rush. I was skewered by a tremendous, vital power. Facilitated by my meditation practice, a root of my being had fractured my shell and wedged itself through a fissure at the crown of my head. The pressure differential there was tremendous. As a result, my human qualities were rushing into freedom and a balm of stellar proportions replaced them as an abiding presence.

I found myself expanding into the one and only being, while simultaneously I noticed my human form was recoiling in shock. My human limitations stood in raw, naked contrast to a vast splendor. The distorting elements of my human condition glared in sharp contrast. These constraints of my identity were hopelessly shattered and abruptly shoved out of the way by the reality

A Quickening

I had stumbled into. My dream life of isolation had been dealt an unrecoverable wound. *My life* became simply *life*. My personal thoughts were swept away as a vast, new purposefulness surged through me. All this was taken in with a single glance from a new perspective, beyond and utterly untouched by the events unfolding on that tree stump.

I was profoundly alarmed. I found myself spontaneously praying for time and grace to survive and accommodate the overwhelming stream of raw force that had shattered my world and now thrust me so irretrievably beyond every limit. Slowly, slowly the intensity of this experience seemed to moderate a little, though my body remained quivering and bolt upright on that stump.

Later, I gathered my wits. I stirred and walked off, marveling. My whole being was galvanized and resonating. I had suddenly become porous. There seemed to be something like a rustling breeze blowing gently through my body. My ears hummed with a deep inner resonance that pressed from inside, even as I heard others talking casually as though nothing had happened. After my experience on that stump, my outer life went on more or less as before. I had dinner, spent the night and rode home the next day. Inside, I was simply perplexed by the wonder unfolding within.

Over the years, I have reflected often on this turn in my life, which had decisively changed me. Why did this experience happen, when it did? It was the culmination of my life at that time. This phenomenon was something like that found in the Century Plant. This spiny bush, the *agave parryi*, flowers once in its lifetime. Until that big event, it lives a modest existence and stores its resources. Then, based upon environmental conditions and its own inner sense of timing and preparation, the plant sends out a huge stalk full of glorious flowers. The flowers produce seed and then, having fulfilled its mission, the plant dies. Perhaps we are all essentially like the century plant. We change when we are ready; we fulfil our destiny and then depart.

A Second Look at Jesus

It was as though an inversion had occurred. Until that moment, I perceived myself as a human being having a spiritual experience. Thereafter I lived as a spiritual being having a human experience. The experience was not entirely pleasant. Neither was it unpleasant. The view from my new perspective was too clear, too raw for comfort. I was uncertain about what exactly I should do with my life. A different set of values and motivations had come into play. All I could do was begin to assess the emerging new order and adjust as necessary.

Owner

Owner and inventor of the great enterprise that we call creation, we former doubters greet you. We have stumbled onto the shore of your eternal existence and fall prostrate in awe at the grandeur of your surging unity. The unexpected humility of your existence at the basis of our being both slays our pride and exalts us. Thank you for the kindness of cutting short our time caught in the thrall of this world of appearance and calling our attention to you.

John

The lead-up to this experience reminds me of the way young children are taught to dive into a body of water. Perhaps you remember, too. First, we were told to stand with our toes at the edge of the dock that extends into the deeper parts of a body of water like a river. Next, we put our arms straight up in the air and join our hands. Then we lean forward with our hands still reaching above our head. We lean forward more and more until our hands and our body are pointing toward the water. At some point, gravity takes over and we get wet. We reach a tipping point. Once in the river, the current carries us forward and, in due time it delivers us to the ocean of God. This is the life path of a mystic.

In a similar fashion, an effective meditation technique helps us create an inner condition where the mind begins to find its

A Quickening

spiritual basis and leans more and more upon the animating spirit of life. At a certain point, the attraction of the spirit gains the upper hand and we *fall forward* into a living, breathing relationship with the author of life. From there we are carried progressively toward a full and unconditional relationship with our Creator.

This reminds me of the Parables found in Matthew 13:44-46 that Jesus used to illustrate commitment to the "kingdom of heaven." Here, Jesus said; "The kingdom of heaven is like a treasure hidden in a field. When a man found it, he hid it again and then in his joy went and sold all he had and bought that field." "Again the kingdom of heaven was like a merchant looking for fine pearls. When he found one of great value, he sold all he had and bought it." At this time I was "all in" to God as I was experiencing him.

When this experience emerged, I had been meditating for six months, twice a day, for twenty minutes. That was all. Anyone could have done this type of meditation. We all have the same basic makeup. I am sure that results would vary somewhat, but I testify that it is well worth the effort to cultivate and explore such an opportunity.

After four months in the Bay Area, I felt thoroughly at home there. Life seemed brighter and clearer while, deep in my inner life, the burgeoning flow of life rushing up through me and out the crown of my head was steadily flushing me out. It was like a spring flood pushing mud, trees and boulders out of a stagnant and polluted watercourse. Little by little, I was growing to accommodate what I had discovered. Increasingly, I was becoming a hollow vessel open to new aspirations, broader and clearer than before. As this inner process continued, day and night, my ability to function in the here and now was working well enough, although I was perhaps a little distracted. Overall, I had more insight than before, but for all practical purposes, I was no one special.

A Second Look at Jesus

The Rabbit
Born aloft by an unseen force,
the fleshy cloak squirms
as my soul soars.

I am remembering the words of my weathered leader
He had told me:

"There is more to life than turning green grass into
little brown pellets."

Now I see and tremble.
A moment ago I was a timid creature,
tentatively confident in my powers of ear, nose and haunch.
I had edged out from the shadows and into the clover.
Now, the mind gapes at this new realm.

Yes,
sometimes,
prayer
is
like
this.

John

While all of this revolution was going on inside, I continued to pursue many of my previous interests. Weekend trips to various communes remained a part of my life. One day, I picked up an unusual woman who was hitchhiking. She needed a ride to a commune further north. She assured me I would be welcomed to spend the night at her destination. She was wearing very provocative clothing. She had very short cut off jeans, sandals, and on top, just a couple of crisscrossed silk scarves. Her natural beauty was fully on display. She also had a serious sheath knife strapped

A Quickening

to her right thigh. She was truly a flower with a thorn. She told me she wanted her weapon visible to deter a bad outcome while hitchhiking. We arrived to the commune on my motorcycle without incident. She enjoyed the hospitality of the alpha Hippie in his tepee. I slept with the stars and had no complaints.

Back in Berkeley, I found an opportunity to buy an excellent motorcycle. It was a single cylinder BMW. The owner agreed to hold it while I went to the bank for the money. When I got back a short time later, my motorcycle was gone and I was not a little put out.

A few days later, I saw a poster for a meditation teacher-training course in northern California. This course happened to cost about the same as the motorcycle. I took this to be a sign and sent in an application. When I was accepted, I left my job early and thumbed my way to Humboldt College on the northern coast of California where Maharishi had rented facilities for a month. I wanted to have a clearer idea about what was behind this spiritual practice that had transformed my life.

Dredging the Channel

Chapter Five

Meeting the Guru

*H**ayah* is an ancient Hebrew word. It is a verb that means "to live" or "to exist," and is from the same root as the famous Hebrew name of God revealed to Moses on Mount Sinai (Exodus 3:1-22).

I am telling a story about spiritual unfoldment. I want you to know what all the fuss is about. To make this book more meaningful perhaps you would like to start something, within yourself, that will complement my story as I tell it. I recommend you try meditation with the word *Hayah*. This is discovery prayer and it will provide a vehicle for you to begin to perceive a fuller scope of your *own* story. Then we will be able to talk together about a similar experience. If you want to make a start, close your eyes now and take five minutes to sample the flavor of *Hayah*.

In the 16th century, there was a wonderful Saint by the name of Theresa, from the Spanish town of Avila. She was a learned woman and a profound mystic. This is a poem about her spiritual life. It describes her manner of opening to God by calling on her Lord's name.

A Second Look at Jesus

Every Prophet's Name
*I found completeness
When each breath began to silently say the name
Of my Lord
That name, my conception of him, extended to me
A hand that led me to a place
Where even your divine name could not exist
Why?
Most thoughts express discontent, longing or negotiation.
The teapot may whistle out an ecstatic cry,
but even that I learned to control
until everything I knew burst
in a glorious symmetry.
I have no seams, no walls, no laws.
My frontiers and God's are the same.
One Divine Being is existence
All the forests on this earth combined are
But a tiny wood fiber-a particle of one spoke
on the Wheel.*

What is the relationship of form to the unseen parts of God?

*What percentage of God is unseen?
What percentage of the Truth of Him do we know?*

*He led me to a place where only Light existed.
Only in us is God so lost that He asks questions.*

*The soul outside all walls
Never troubles Him, never wonder things like,
"Where are You,
Beloved?"*

*For then your arms and God's
are intertwined.*

Meeting the Guru

I said to my Lord,
"This Holy place I have entered –
Is your name the only key
to this?"

And my Lord responded,
"How old do you think is existence?
For eons of time souls have been entering Me;

Every Prophet's name is a key,
as is every heart full of forgiveness and love."

Theresa of Avila (1515-1584)[1]

This poem reminds me that, for some, meditation, or a very focused form of prayer, has always been a part of the Christian spiritual path.

On the appointed day, I saw Maharishi (whose name means *great seer*) for the first time. He was small and brown with a straggly head of long hair and a neatly trimmed beard. He wore wood-soled sandals and a pure, white draping of spotless silk. Around his neck was an orange coral bead rosary strung in gold wire links. He moved slowly and with a gentle dignity toward the dais on the stage of the cavernous assembly hall. He paused now and then to accept fresh-cut flowers from various well-wishers. He delicately added them to a growing collection gathered inside his left arm. With each gift, he would solemnly intone "Jai Guru Dev." I later found out Jai meant victory and Guru Dev meant divine dispeller of darkness. This expression was a way of saying we shared the hope that the teachings that had transformed our lives would, in turn, help others. Now and then, he would choose one of his flowers and give it to a devotee standing the swelling line.

This outer spectacle was complimented by an extraordinary inner reality. His presence formed something like a low-pressure

A Second Look at Jesus

depression around which all of us joyfully and spontaneously organized into spirals of rotating strands of reflective matter. The experience was very subtle and pervasive. I had never perceived such a dynamic before. I was simultaneously struck with love and awe. We all were.

What followed was nearly a month of meditation and teaching. The meditation time was thoughtfully organized. First, we would do a breathing exercise called *pranah yama*. *Yama* means control or regulation. *Pranah* refers to the subtle energy associated with the physical act of breathing. *Pranah Yama* was about increasing and balancing our spiritual energy with the technique of breathing slowly and deeply through alternate nostrils. This was followed by twenty to thirty minutes of meditation. Then, we would do about a dozen yoga stretching-exercises called *asanas*. Taken together, these three activities constituted what we called a *round*. We started out with just a few rounds a day between meals and lectures, but soon we were doing perhaps six or more rounds a day.

The effect was not unlike turning up the heat on a cooker. In my case, it was clear that my kernel had already popped. Regarding the others, it was hard to say. However, something similar was clearly going on for everyone. While our paths may have been different, we were clearly moving parallel to each other.

Maharishi would started lecture with an invitation to report on experiences that had emerged that day. Usually the reports were about torrents of thoughts and feelings. Sometimes tedium was the dominant experience. Some people reported spontaneous physical movements such as twitching necks or arms. These latter symptoms were termed *physical stress* release. We were told that all these thoughts and movements were the result of our meditation and came from the loosening and release of *stress*. We were counselled that it was not useful to dwell on the specifics of these experiences, as they were simply blockages in our nervous system that were on their way out. They all indicated something

Meeting the Guru

good and useful was going on. All of it was a side effect of necessary purification. That was all.

Occasionally, there would be a more inspiring description of an inner vision. Mostly the reports were not very grand. For some reason, it never occurred to me to report my experience from a few months before. Maharishi invited us to report the experiences of that day. In fact, I never found an occasion to tell about my experience on that commune tree stump to Maharishi or anyone else in the TM organization.

We meditators formed close community that month. Clearly, we were converging on a common goal.

You and I
We appear as two clods of earth,
you and I,
nearly as inert as rocks
but...
with a secret.

We each embrace an eternal seed.
It has been softened by our tears of joy and sorrow.
Now, it stirs and begins to sprout, root and branch.
Drinking our muddy substance, it grows.

Rooted beyond time, it consumes our limitations and prospers.
In due season, it bears fruit
that ripens and yields to the touch.

And so, we become the Tree of Life.

In time, our earthy identity is consumed,
used up but,
what remains is so grand, no one will care.

No one will care.

John

A Second Look at Jesus

Sometimes the explanation of experiences associated with meditation would lengthen into a detailed lecture about the nature of creative intelligence or the natural tendency of the mind to move in the direction of greater satisfaction and bliss. The explanations would remain in conventional, English words. Now and then, someone would ask what a technical Sanskrit word like *Samadhi* meant. Maharishi would usually accommodate. For example, Samadhi means "steady intellect"; intellect that does not waver due to its rootedness in our eternal being. Then he would always steer us back to a blander, western formulation. I was too dense to realize it at the time, but Maharishi was denying us the raw materials to trivialize his teaching by making it into a mere religion. Genuine experience and transformation were our goal.

One explanation struck home. Maharishi said that inviting God into our life was akin to inviting an elephant into our modest hut. The inevitable result was a certain amount of destruction. Then it was necessary to build a larger and stronger structure. This process of destruction and reconstruction continued over time until a vast palace was constructed and the elephant was in a properly proportioned and durable environment.

In overview, the system was to alternate deep and alert restfulness through meditation with normal, daily activity. The meditation would uncover new sensitivities and abilities that would then find application in the normal course of living. By integrating these new qualities, little by little in our lives, we would evolve incrementally into a better mode of life. Some waypoints along the path of growth were described, but we were advised not to pay much attention to individual experiences whether pleasant or not. Instead, we were simply to return to the meditation process so that our evolution would proceed.

No personal effort was to be used during meditation. Instead, we were to trust the natural tendency of the mind to gravitate toward greater charm and beauty. Certain inner vistas were more attractive, profound and full of life. Then, finding delight, we would naturally focus on them.

Meeting the Guru

This contrasted with the common assumptions on meditation. If you asked the average devout person, his method would likely involve trying to recreate a pre-conceived experience of a historic scene or a truth as described by either another person or a book. This we termed "mood making," which is another way of saying autosuggestion. This would just amount to reorganizations of the realizations we already have. It was not our method to affirm, "I feel great," "God is great," or "God is love." This method begs the question. Who *is* this I? What *is* feeling? What *is* greatness? What *is* Love? Moreover, what *is* God? Instead of conformity to preconceived patterns of thought, we were looking to discover whatever the mystery of our being was ready to reveal to each of us *at that moment*. We were seeking the fresh, the new and the unexpected.

Our method did not depend upon our understanding of words or interpretation of scripture. This natural and incremental approach was, we believed, more authentic. We aimed to base our lives upon genuine experience, not descriptions of the experiences of others. We were intending to unfold from within, integrating divine qualities within our life as they emerged. We were all unique and our unfolding would likewise need to be unique. Our evolutionary progress would also be naturally sustainable because it was integrated, little by little, into our everyday reality.

Parallel with this growth experience was an evolutionary refinement and strengthening of our human form as a suitable instrument to sustain these experiences. We were creating a continuity of experience between our outer form and our innermost subjective state. There is a reason that it takes time to arrive at a profound result. The body lags and drags. For example, proper conditions and time are required to grow new neural pathways. We matured slowly in our ability to sustain this inner experience. However, with patience and persistence, everything adjusted as necessary.

Apart from the meditation teaching, many of us were shocked and horrified to find that Maharishi was a conservative. He

A Second Look at Jesus

insisted that anyone associated with him be clean-shaven and dressed in a suit or a modest dress. We were expected to respect our parents, our government, and the religion of our birth. He believed in peace through strength. Government authority in all its forms was also to be respected. Along with meditation, hard work and discipline were considered the only way to make our lives better. We were taught that success was earned and deserved before it was achieved. Eventually it became clear the only change to our culture Maharishi intended was a restoration of the missing ingredient of steady inner growth. In due course the long hair, beards, sideburns, and mustaches disappeared from the audience.

All too soon, that month passed and I was headed back home and then to college. I had set my sights on completing the process of becoming a TM teacher. This required a second course of at least three months. That winter such a course was offered on the island of Majorca, Spain. Through Antioch, I was able to arrange for a six-month teacher-training course as a semester abroad *and* get college transfer credits from Maharishi International University. I was thrilled.

To me, this semester at Antioch preceding my TM course was a time of transition and full of paradox. I was neither fish nor fowl. I was a clean-shaven New-Age citizen. Drugs held no interest for me. Neither did politics. I continued to attend the folk dancing events on Friday nights. I enjoyed my friends, but we had less and less in common.

I did find the time to take a trip out west during a school break. This was the golden age of hitchhiking. I set out with a Danish girl who I knew. We got from Ohio to Colorado in just a few days. Rides were always easier to come by if a girl was present.

One day, as we were hitching in the sparse interior of the Colorado plateau region, we were stopped and arrested by a state trooper. Apparently, hitchhiking was a crime in Colorado. I called my father and he told me never to tell my mother about my arrest.

Meeting the Guru

His older brother, my uncle William, who intended to hunt pheasant that day, executed my rescue the next morning. First, he bailed us out. Then, he drove us to a truck stop and paid a trucker to take us at least as far as the New Mexico border. From there, my Danish friend continued west to see California and I looped through the Texas panhandle and went back to Ohio through the rural south.

My uncle William was an interesting man. He was a B24 bomber pilot during WW2. One of his stories involved bailing out of his damaged bomber in the winter of 1944. The local resistance forces took him in. Then he was passed from hand to hand until he was near the American lines. Once there his guide told him to hold in place, under cover. Then, suddenly, he was told to go **go GO**. He jumped up and started to run. He was amazed to see all around him many other flyers were emerging and running simultaneously toward freedom. Until that moment, he had thought that he was alone!

My father started with a less than distinguished military career. Like his older brother, he entered flight school. Early on, however, he had crashed his trainer when he stalled and "landed" his aircraft while it was still twenty feet in the air! They washed him out of the flight-training program after that crash. He told me his skull was repaired with a silver plate. For the recovery of his pride, it was especially important to my father that he eventually earn his pilot's license after he left the service.

My father served out most his military career in Alaska. While there, he amazed his friends and officers by never being bitten by mosquitos. These pests were simply not interested in him. At one point he was shipped off to Texas with others from all over the services for medical tests to see what about their body's make-up made them unattractive to those insects. The doctors wanted to see if they could create a similar effect for all soldiers. The scientific basis of this phenomenon proved elusive however and no actionable medical insights were gained.

A Second Look at Jesus

Near the end of the war, my father become a weatherman. He then volunteered to be part of a small group that would parachute into Manchuria and provide weather data in preparation for the anticipated invasion of mainland Japan. This was a very hazardous assignment. My father told me he never regretted the Pacific war was cut short with the use of atomic weapons.

Not until much later in my life did, I come to appreciate the sacrifices and hazards my father and his generation faced during those years. In some ways, I will never be their equal. I can only be thankful for their dedication and try to meet the challenges that I face with similar bravery.

Back at Antioch, I continued to learn in and out of the classroom. Sometimes we had to run a gauntlet of Jesus freaks who would try to buttonhole us as we entered the student union to pick up mail or eat a meal. They would invariably thrust a small tract toward us and ask if we "accepted Jesus Christ as our personal savior." The truth was I had done my very best to find God through the Christian path. These well-meaning hucksters maintained that their formulation was the last word in correct approach to Jesus. They were sure they held *all* truth. Of course they did. No one except for them really understood spiritual truth and they were getting fantastic results. The other so-called Christians had it all wrong and anything outside Christianity was madness. They wanted us to drop everything we valued and follow them. We were to believe exactly as they said. Then and only then, would Jesus fill the void. I was just guessing, but I did not think Jesus would have approved of such an approach. He was humble, subtle and personally engaging. He loved people as he found them. Then he worked to help them improve their condition. These evangelist jokers were as subtle as muggers were and made no effort to get to know my situation or me. They were just hunting weak souls.

I should explain the term "Jesus freak" was not intended as an insult. You see, all of us, who had stepped outside the established norms, were more or less considered freaks by those who

Meeting the Guru

"colored within the lines." We embraced the term "freak" even though it was intended by "straight" people as an insult. We further invested it with our own meaning. For us it signified fearless and sincere action within the realm of our own conscience and without regard to the opinions of a culture that had clearly lost its soul. So "Jesus freaks" were freaks like the rest of us, but they had settled upon Jesus as the essential truth they cared about. That was cool with us so long as they refrained from the practice of religious assault.

I could not help reflecting on my youth as a Catholic. I had memorized the Catechism and believed it implicitly. Our Dominican nuns required we attend Mass each day before school. Confession was once a week and no impure thoughts were allowed to pass without weekly confession and absolution. We spent long stretches in the choir loft learning Gregorian chants that we performed on special Sundays. To this day, I can recite much of the Latin Mass learned as an altar boy.

Once, as I waited to enter a new school on the first day of eighth grade, one of the nuns swept in like a hawk, grabbed me and gave me a good shaking. She said, "I saw what you did young man, I am going to keep my eye on you!" To this day, I have no idea what I did wrong.

I have since learned the Dominican order came to play a key role in the Inquisition that began under Pope Innocent III. Through efforts of the Dominicans many Cathars, Lutherans, Hussites, and others were identified as heretics and met a fiery end between 1125 and 1826. I do not know if the church has ever expressed regret or contrition over these activities. Perhaps our teachers were drawing upon that fierce aspect of their heritage in their dealings with us. I do not doubt that they loved us, but the rod of correction was always at hand. Perhaps, in their view, all children were born as heretics and in need of conversion. Perhaps, they were not entirely wrong.

To be fair, once our teachers had established their dominance over us they were genuinely focused on giving us a

A Second Look at Jesus

quality education. I am thankful for the ethical values they tried to encourage in us. They also shared the beauty of sacred music. I fondly remember the many hours spent learning Gregorian chants and other hymns of great beauty.

In hindsight, I can see my teachers were driven by love and used discipline toward that end. They also surprised us from time to time by showing sensitivity to our state of development and the issues of the day. This was an exception to the rule, however. Most time was spent on the fundamentals of reading, writing, math and science.

Religion class was at least once a week. There was no ambiguity in *that* curriculum. They taught and we responded, carefully. Correct answers were always a repetition of what we read in the Baltimore Catechism.

The result of this doctrinal approach to religion formed much of my childhood. For example, my mother had to defy the parish priest in order for me to become a member of the newly built YMCA in our hometown of Wausau, Wisconsin. As I recall, the religious reason given for the YMCA prohibition was that some of our Y membership dues might end up paying for the purchase and distribution of "Protestant Bibles" in Africa.

I have since learned that Catholic Bibles are full of marginal notes telling the reader the exact meaning of what they have just read. The Protestant practice of printing their own version of textual notes or just the text alone was considered dangerous since an unauthorized interpretation might result! As further evidence of my nearly complete programming, I clearly remember telling my sweet grandmother she was going to go to hell since she was a Baptist and not a member of the one and only *true* church. I made her cry. I was truly sorry, but I felt I had to be honest! Of course, today I am ashamed of my performance, but I have learned from it.

I have given further thought to the concept of loading up converts with doctrine. I am now convinced that it does more harm than good, especially if the doctrine in question is a convoluted

Meeting the Guru

effort to justify something that ought not to be justified. There is an important concept popularly known as Ockham's razor that needs to be acknowledged here. Ockham observed "the simplest answer is generally the right one."

There is a world of difference between understanding a concept and knowing from experience or insight that it is true to life. It seems it is unhealthy and counter-productive to have too much unprocessed and unverified opinion of any sort in our mind at any one time. If a program of meditation were designed to accompany each concept, the result might be better. In addition, if each student had all the time he or she needed to progress, then the teaching would have a deeper identification and function within the life of each believer. Spiritual growth happens in God's time.

Chapter Six

Hindu Missionary School?

Spending some time with *Hayah* will begin to cultivate fineness and simplicity in your life. It is important to get the pronunciation right. *Hayah* sounds like the American slang greeting "Hiya" with a slight aspirant *h* sound at the end. If you want to appreciate this book, close your eyes and spend a few minutes with *Hayah* before you begin each chapter. This will begin to awaken your appreciation of the majesty of the creative process unfolding within you. It will open a growing, subjective appreciation of what I am trying to describe.

You can, of course, opt out of my suggestion that you experiment with this practice. I believe that this book will still be worthwhile as a source of information and intellectual stimulation. I just want you to know that by doing so you will miss something important without the parallel of a spiritual experience. Therefore, I will place the word *Hayah* at the beginning of each remaining chapter of this book as a gentle reminder of the opportunity it offers.

Hindu Missionary School?

That winter of 1971, my TM teacher training continued in Majorca, a Mediterranean island off the coast of Spain. The Transcendental Meditation organization had leased the mostly abandoned beach hotels during the off-season at bargain prices. Summer courses were held at empty ski lodges in the Swiss Alps. There were few tourists and the resulting solitude was ideal, since we spent most of the days sitting inside with our eyes closed. We slowly increased the proportion of time we spent "rounding" each day until we were meditating ten to twelve hours a day. Simple vegetarian meals and talks filled up the balance of our time. We did not socialize much. In fact, many of us observed total silence for most of our time there. We were intent upon making the most of this opportunity to transform our lives. We were aiming for nothing less than Cosmic Consciousness. This goal amounted to the ability to maintain unbroken awareness of our source in God as we went about our everyday life.

Maharishi's teaching summarized human experience as follows: We each have our source in unlimited creative intelligence. This creative intelligence, through our human form, experiences objects outside of ourselves either through our senses or, more intimately, as thoughts through our minds. Meditation is a process of experiencing a progressive refinement of thought, as we perceive it in more subtle forms, near its source in creative intelligence. As this process of inner discernment progresses, the objective world becomes less and less oppressive and the subjective side of our life is able to assert itself with greater strength and clarity. In essence, the subject gets larger and clearer as the experience of the object (our mantra) diminishes. With practice, meditation leads us to the ability to be aware beyond objective experience altogether. This is awareness of awareness itself without an object. We called this Transcendental Awareness, a fourth state of awareness beyond and yet overlaid by the transient states of waking, dreaming and sleeping. Cosmic Consciousness, a significant milestone of progress on the path of spiritual maturity, is characterized by the ability to sustain the inner experience

A Second Look at Jesus

of transcendental awareness along with waking, dreaming, and deep sleep.

Fortunately, experiencing life this way is more instinctive and natural than trying to explain it. True understanding follows experience not vice versa. Gaining the experience only requires putting one foot in front of the other. You just need to have a simple method to allow the refined perception of thought and have that experience on a regular basis. Under the influence of these experiences, we expect to grow over time and evolve into the ability to sustain the cosmic view along with daily experience.

I remember a test that showed how far I had progressed at that time. Since we were there in Majorca in the off-season, we also had to contend with construction activity. For a while, the construction crew next door was dealing with some bedrock under the sand to prepare for the foundation of a new hotel. Jackhammers and dynamite were their tools. First, someone would sound a horn that sounded like an oversized party favor. Then, after an interval of half a minute or so, there would be a loud KABOOM. The first time I heard this I nearly levitated. Over time, however, I was able to treat both the horn and the dynamite as just another thought and go back to my mantra. After this, ignoring mere jackhammers was easy. Since then I have always enjoyed peaceful surroundings, but would not shrink from meditating on a New York subway if necessary. This is a useful ability.

I remember one day, I perceived that my mantra seemed to be repeating itself. Upon closer observation, I discovered the harmonious sweetness and subtlety of its enunciation was far beyond any sound I had ever uttered. I described it as angelic. From this point onward my sacred word was more or less repeating itself 24/7 and meditation consisted in simply paying attention to it. I remember expressing some of this to Maharishi at one of our meetings. At the time, he was looking elsewhere. I clearly remember as I filled in the detail of this experience, his head pivoted around and he gazed at me intently.

Hindu Missionary School?

There is a verse in the Bible found at Matthew 6:7 which says, in the King James translation: "But, when ye pray, use not vain repetitions as the heathens do for they think that they will be heard for their much speaking." I have two observations to make concerning this valuable statement by Jesus.

First, Jesus is talking here about prayers of petition, asking God for guidance and blessings. Jesus goes on soon after this to recommend that we pray in private and that we consider the "Our Father" prayer as an ideal form of petition to God. This masterpiece asks for only a minimum of worldly sustenance and a simple reorientation toward a proper, humble relationship with our creator. Point taken.

Second, the form of meditation or prayer that I was engaged upon was of a different sort. I believe that it can best be described as a "discovery prayer." Here, we are not asking to "be heard." We are not asking for anything. There is no agenda at all. Instead, we are simply exploring our connection with our Creator with the help of that same Creator. Having found a renewed and clarified appreciation of that connection, we would be in a perfect position to appreciate the wisdom contained in the "Our Father" prayer. Further, I testify that Discovery Prayer is far from "vain repetition." I have found that it yields a very rich return on my investment.

Discovery prayer allows for the free play of the Creator in our lives. Too often, we are convinced to reduce our spiritual life to a "paint-by numbers" exercise. Why do this when the Creator is willing and able to complete us as an original work of art, each one a masterpiece?

We TM meditators were a diverse group, although we tended to be quite young. Most of us were college age; one girl down the hall had, at one time, made her living as a Playboy Bunny. I met some members of the famous Beach Boys band. Some of the older people had been involved in serious jobs with broad worldly responsibility. We were mostly white and included participants from all over the world. There were French, German,

A Second Look at Jesus

English people in large numbers, while Americans made up the majority. I talked with people from troubled spots like Northern Ireland and Lebanon. All of us were setting aside our pasts for better futures. The future was in our hands to work out.

After about three months, we all moved to a new location in Fiuggi Fonte, Italy. Fiuggi was a town of health spas built around some famous springs. Its water was valued for special health-giving qualities. It was bottled and sold all over Europe. Normally, tourists would bathe in the spring-fed grottoes. Not us. We were still spending many hours a day in meditation.

After another six weeks, our daily meditation time started to taper off. Then we had a little time to discover that the town of Fiuggi was a delight. As spring progressed, the numerous almond trees around town came into flower. The people were friendly, although a little tempestuous.

We had to endure an election in the Italian style, which included little Fiats that, for a few weeks, circled around town blaring unintelligible slogans from enormous loudspeakers. They were like boisterous mice. The gelato (ice cream) was a pleasure enjoyed by many until we found out that it was possibly made with beef fat. Then sales went to about zero. We were nearly all vegetarians.

Maharishi's talks continued daily, although, if he were busy elsewhere or not feeling well, we would get his video instead of a personal visit. We missed him if he was not present. During much of this time, Maharishi was suffering from a violent hacking cough. His illness was painful to witness. I yearned to see him free of this malady.

Sometimes he also surprised us by lapsing, without warning, into gales of laughter. Sometimes they were deep, throaty belly shakers and sometimes there were light-hearted giggles, sometimes cascades of sweet middle-ranged peals of joy; all imaginable forms of laughter rolled on and on. These eruptions would suspend the lectures without apparent reason and then taper off just as mysteriously. Then Maharishi would pick up his narrative

Hindu Missionary School?

and masterfully carry on with the point he was making. I took some lessons from this; the first was that all of us had human limitations. Enlightenment did not necessarily prevent all disease or other obstacles. The second was that laughter was a perfectly acceptable part of dealing with oppressive limitations and generally was more effective than endless intellectual analysis.

For the last month, our meditation time tapered off further and we spent more time learning to teach meditation. First, we were taught how to instruct new students in effective use of their mantra. We were taught verbally and we took notes of the exact wording that Maharishi wanted us to use for instructing students in the manner of using their mantras. The whole point was for people to close their eyes and then, after a few minutes, they were asked to open them again. We would next ask them if they noticed thoughts while their eyes were closed. Next, we asked if they noticed, those thoughts came naturally and effortlessly. Finally, we said they should repeat their mantra just as effortlessly.

Another element in our training was learning to recite an invocation of the succession of teachers that had brought us the technique of meditation. There was a brief summation of spiritual cosmology according to the Vedic system, a reference to the sacred books that summarized our path and a longish list of teachers including Vashistha, Vyasa and Shankaracharia, his four disciples and finally our own Guru Dev. Our branch of this tradition came from one of those disciples, Trotica. We were told that he was not an intellectual, but he served his teacher with a willing heart and spirit. The entire invocation, in Sanskrit, was set to a beautiful melody. This was recited before each new person was taught meditation and was not so much for them as for us. It helped us to open up to the source of our teaching so that we could be more vital and effective.

The last element of our becoming TM teachers was learning the sacred words themselves, the mantras shared at the time of initiating new meditators. In this trade, they were commonly

A Second Look at Jesus

known as "seed mantras." Because there were so many of us at these courses, Maharishi decided, for the first time, he would do this teaching in batches of about a dozen. We each had headphones and the mantras were repeated several times along with the simple guide (age of the student) for choosing who got what mantra. Then, we came to Maharishi one at a time and repeated the mantras. He corrected our pronunciation as necessary and sent us on our way.

Around this time, Maharishi announced he was seeking to recruit a small group of 108 people who would join him full-time in spreading his teaching around the world. We had to be willing to work hard and be financially able to pay our way while we taught. I was able to arrange with Antioch College to let me pay my way for some time. Maharishi interviewed me and said I should join him later that fall at Lake Tahoe.

I went home by way of Rome and enjoyed several days touring the Vatican and Roman ruins. After a further three more months of study at Antioch, I arrived at Lake Tahoe, California.

Our days at Tahoe were spent with more time listening to the opportunity TM offered to make our world a more harmonious and healthy place to live. Our effort was conceived as a mass program to create an uplifting influence of worldwide proportions. Maharishi had a theory that, long before even a majority of people took up meditation, a sizable minority of strong meditators could have a galvanizing effect for the betterment of humankind, as though each of us were becoming mobile lamps. With more *light*, society could function with fewer bumps and bruises because people could *navigate* better than they otherwise would.

Maharishi used medical tests and the theoretical model of quantum mechanics to demonstrate that: 1: Transcendental Meditation created a healthier body and more orderly brain wave pattern and 2: the orderliness of the transcendental field of subatomic particles could extended through us to the world at large. This was the basis of Maharishi's World Plan to bring widespread peace and harmony. Our job was to teach enough people

Hindu Missionary School?

to meditate so, collectively, our influence would usher in a new, better age. Immediate action was taken to bring TM to countries willing to receive us.

From Tahoe, we, The 108, went on to spend some more time with Maharishi in Seelisberg, Switzerland. Here, teams were chosen to go to various locations around the world. I, along with a few others, was chosen to go to India. Our time with Maharishi at Lake Tahoe and Switzerland gave us an opportunity to interact more intimately with him.

During this time, we adopted the practice of sharing stories about the personal observations Maharishi would make from time to time. These comments were traded like treasure among us. We discovered, for example, that Maharishi had a sense of humor. One time there was a clear need for legal advice and Maharishi said to get a lawyer. However, he pronounced the word "liar." Now, Maharishi had a strong Indian accent and it was assumed he was simply mispronouncing the word. Someone tried to correct him. "No," he said, "I meant what I said. Where is the liar?"

Another time he told us just about the first person he met when he visited a new country was a representative, acting under cover, from that government's intelligence service. They invariably wanted to know about Maharishi and TM to determine if they were going to be a destructive or destabilizing influence. Maharishi said he always looked forward to these encounters because these people were, in fact, extremely intelligent and he was delighted to brief them.

Maharishi was not above making occasional derogatory comments. Once, when he was unhappy about a person who came from a city famous for foggy weather, he observed that people from that place were always "in a fog." In a similar vein, Maharishi had a vivid expression used when he was angry with someone. He would say, "I will be wild on him." None of us wanted that!

In contrast, Maharishi always expressed the most profound love and gratitude for the role his teacher, Guru Dev, played in

A Second Look at Jesus

his life. Their tender bond was clearly the conduit through which flowed all the spiritual values we perceived in Maharishi. He displayed pure and utter devotion to his teacher.

Maharishi also introduced us to a concept I still consider valid and useful. He said a certain amount of superficial ignorance continues to play a part in the life of an enlightened person. The term he used is "*lesha avidia*," which meant residue of ignorance. The way he put it is that attaining enlightenment is like throwing away a ball of butter. The ball is gone, but the hands are still a little greasy.

Maharishi also told us it was entirely possible, in spite of good intentions, we might someday encounter misbehavior in some part of our organization. He said if that happened, we should not lose sight of the overall effect of what we were trying to achieve. This concept was tested more than once in the coming years.

Slowly, a more realistic picture of Maharishi emerged. He had a gentle heart, but also a will of steel. He was very much a chief executive. As much as we would have wanted him to just be with us and help us realize our personal goals of self-development, this was not at the top of Maharishi's agenda. One day, he looked over our group of fifty or so and said; "I want you to know that when I look out at all of you I do not see individuals; I see means of accomplishing the World Plan." The world plan was, of course, to bring TM to every part of the world. This was hard to take. We all craved a more personal touch, a more personal caring from him.

This was not to be. When you talked to Maharishi, it was strictly business. He wanted large numbers of new TM meditators. By this time, he had thousands. Individually, he wanted to know what you accomplished, what you were going to accomplish and how were you going to do it. All the while, he gave off the most intoxicating spiritual essence. My heart softened and the energy flowing through me intensified to a degree that was hard to bear. I was being stretched powerfully in two directions at once. My heart and mind were centered on the human enterprise, with all its pain and aspirations, while the impersonal,

Hindu Missionary School?

up-rushing, energy animated extended me more and more each moment. All the while, Maharishi wanted practical results. This experience was at once indescribably sublime and excruciating.

As nearly as I could tell, having offered an effective program of meditation, Maharishi wanted people to accept responsibility for their own lives. Any other approach would have been unworkable. Maharishi had caught the attention of millions of needy people. There was not enough time in the day to do much more than teach and try to be a good example. Maharishi made a practice of carefully managing who had personal access to him. He did not want to let people become too dependent or complacent. Every now and then someone close to him would be given the heave ho, sent home or on a protracted mission out in the field. Exceptional personal attention was exceedingly rare. The only common exception was the brief, formalized greeting he gave people who offered him flowers on his way into the speaking halls. Flower sales were brisk.

While teaching, Maharishi was a great one for formulating brief maxims. One of his favorites was "Established in yoga (union with God) perform action." The idea here was action, without taking into account the rest of creation, is likely to cause harm. Likewise, enlightened inaction is not helpful. Drawing on both poles of human existence was the way we were to proceed.

Akin to this was the concept that all growth is achieved in complimentary periods of rest and activity. Meditation provided for a unique state of *restful alertness* while the activity that followed provided an opportunity to actualize the gains discovered in meditation.

He was also fond of saying, "Water the root to enjoy the fruit." It might seem childish and simplistic. Perhaps it was. However, it was also true. Abundant nourishment at the intake side of life is mandatory for a rich harvest.

Another concept was "See the job, do the job, stay out of misery." There is a great deal of posturing and hyperbole associated

A Second Look at Jesus

with the concept of virtuous action. He counselled it is best to avoid such tangles and just get on with what needs to be done.

Maharishi took the time to clarify a point about the limits of human ability. A God-realized person *can* accomplish *anything* because of the power of God he or she can draw upon at the root of his or her existence. In contrast, God *does* accomplish *everything*. This is the difference between being a fully realized child of God and the being God. We can optimize the function of our human existence through good spiritual and personal practices, but our physical form is mortal. Our physical form limits our focus, the scope of our life. The job of a mystic is to make that limitation minimal.

"Knowledge is structured in consciousness. Without that consciousness what good is knowledge?" Consciousness is the container of knowledge. If the container is not large enough, then at best a truncated version of truth can be accommodated. With enough inner capacity, truth is easy to come by and it can function freely and without cramping. Knowledge then becomes a more useful part of our everyday life, not an appendage or an embellishment.

Then there was the observation that "The teacher always teaches from his consciousness and the student always learns from the perspective of his consciousness." Sometimes, growth is required before comprehension is possible. However, without recourse to fresh spiritual insight, knowledge is subject to copying errors not unlike reproduction degradation with a Xerox machine when copies are made of copies repeatedly.

Maharishi used to lament the necessity of putting "unripe fruit (us) on the market." He was correctly observing we were not up to his standard. To overcome this perverse dynamic he wanted us to cleave to the exact words and procedures he prescribed. We did so.

Maharishi commented that, when he designed the TM meditation program, it was not formulated for the spiritually gifted. Rather, it was designed so that even the "most ignorant" person

Hindu Missionary School?

could arrive at the desired goal so long as he stayed with the program.

The recommended approach to life was on a "highest first" basis. Having achieved that pinnacle of transcendental consciousness, all other goals were more easily within reach.

Any one of these insights can save a lifetime worth of wasted time or misdirected effort. Taken together these teachings went far towards simplifying our internal thought processes. They helped us to cut through the clutter of conventional thought that otherwise would have bound us, allowing us to be more effective and joyous.

Once Maharishi inquired about one of his disciples, he had not heard from in some time. He was told the disciple had left the organization and gone his own way. With a wistful, faraway look on his countenance, Maharishi commented: "that was the way things go. They come, they meditate and their mind begins to clear and then I don't hear from them anymore."

Around this time, Maharishi reported to us a meeting that had intrigued him. He had recently met with a Sufi teacher, a Pir. He said that he was deeply moved by the power and authenticity of both this Pir and his teaching. Maharishi was puzzled, however, by the *wazaif* (sacred words) this Pir used for meditation since they were somewhat different from the mantras Maharishi used and yet they seemed to be effective. Maharishi speculated the arid climate associated with the Middle East might have had some influence.

Another topic of discussion around this time was an effort by some Christian priests to consult with Maharishi and to research our methods as far as they could without actually being initiated. They likely had scruples about appearing to stray from their church to the point of disloyalty. Necessarily, the information they were able to gather was somewhat sketchy and theoretical. It was as though they stood at a threshold and saw what they could without actually entering the room or touching anything.

A Second Look at Jesus

For example, when talking about the meditation process we always said in our introductory TM lecture that any thought could be traced to its source in unlimited creative intelligence. Our visitors apparently took this to mean that the choice of the word used for meditation was not important and that any word could be used with equal results. This is simply not the case.

The missing information here is the way the sound of the word chosen interacts with the subtle, inner architecture of the human form. Consider this example; if the doctor wants to get a good look down your throat, he asks you to say aaaaaahhh. The reason is that in the act of forming that sound, you reconfigure your mind and body to make the sound and in the process open your throat.

In a similar fashion, the sound of every word we form causes us to reorient our mind and its subtle connection with our body in order to form that word. We can observe spontaneous examples of these phenomena in the sounds we spontaneously make to express degrees of pleasure, revulsion, insight, ecstasy, contemplation, awe and more. When used intelligently and purposefully, this aspect of speech can provide an exceptionally powerful and efficient way to reorient and reposture our inner life. In everyday life, the sound value of words is not very important. The effect is random and diffuse. In conversation, we commonly use words for the meaning they represent rather than the sound they make. Our soul, however, has a resonant potential and sacred words are an effective way to capitalize on this. With repetition, the sound of such a word becomes cumulatively powerful in its effect upon the subtle underpinnings of our life. In order to cultivate this effect, a careful, informed choice of the focus for meditation is desirable. With the use of a sacred word, we are able to rediscover the sacred experience that originally inspired that verbal expression.

Ah is such a sacred word. It is the sound of us as we open ourselves. It is the expression *alpha* out the expression "I am the *alpha* and the *omega*." Related to *Ah* Is the expression *Aha*. It reflects the subtle interplay between opening, breath and spirit.

Hindu Missionary School?

These words are not commonly associated with religious systems, yet they are associated with human expression across all cultures.

Sacred words are different from representational words. Their sound is directly linked to their effect upon us. Any meaning derives from that effect. We use them for the response they bring from our soul, which is the interface between the unity of God and our outer individuality. These sacred words function as the language of the soul. When we use sacred words correctly, our human life-form functions as a God-homing device.

Consider now the word *abba*. It is pronounced with a long "*a*" *sound*, as in *fa*ther. Jesus uses this interesting word in Mark 14:36 in his prayer to God at Gethsemane and elsewhere. Apostle Paul also mentions it several times. Christian literalists note that *abba* is the intimate name for father (daddy), and move on to another fact. A mystic observes something else, an opportunity to access depth. They recognize that *abba* is an ancient word. *Abba* and *amma* (mother) come from a simpler, more intuitive time. With correct use, these sacred words can do us a world of good.

There are areas of spiritual sensitivity, subtle energy substations, which correspond to various locations along our spine. Each specializes in bringing forth an important quality or function within our life. As they are fed by our attention and an increasing flow of spiritual vitality begins to bring them more alive with wonderful results.

The "*a*" sound is the animating sound for the energy in the heart area. Consonants direct and control the energy galvanized by the vowel sounds. Among the seven major "substations," or spiritual centers in the human form, the heart is in the exact middle. According, the heart plays a pivotal role at the center of our human form. The "*a*" sound is the sound that initiates all creative impulse. It is also the sound of opening.

What "*abba*" actually does, for those who pay attention to it, is reinitiate the entire process of creation. The "a" sound is the dawn of creation and summarizes the full arc of that enterprise

A Second Look at Jesus

in seed form. The "*b*" consonant sound is a full stop to that energy of creation and is both death and the end of the entire creative impulse. "A" is alpha and "B" is omega; first activity and then rest. It is the experience of life. Within us, it is the divine perspective born within perishable, human life. The most interesting part of this word, "*abba*," is the ending. That final "*ba*" is rebirth or resurrection, a new creation.

The image that comes to mind is of a ball that is thrown down. When it impacts the earth it distorts, flattens. Then, if the ball has resilient integrity, it will bounce back to the thrower with almost the same force. If, on the other hand, the ball is lacking the necessary characteristics, then it will not bounce back. *Our* job is to develop the necessary qualities of resilience so that we rebound to our source. It is not very hard.

Amma is a little different. As with *abba*, the beginning "a" is opening, extroversion. However, the middle consonants, "mm," guide the user toward, not death, but introversion or introspection. This is resonance within containment (like the womb). The final "a" of *amma* is, like *abba*, rebirth. Can you see the value of this as a sacred word? With it memory, *continuity* is not lost, it is emphasized. Such a perspective cultivates the perspective of Wisdom.

These are examples of what makes a sacred word sacred. When we repeat these very special words we are reviewing the gist of the entire story of life again and again and again. It becomes, in the most instinctive and fundamental way, the operating code for one's life. Most importantly for us, it is done consciously. This is a link between our everyday consciousness and the mystery of life at the origin of thought and existence.

Initially, *abba* and *amma* pertain to the impulse control and the limitations of life. They make a good first lesson on inner reflection and adjustment. Upon further exploration, much, much more is revealed.

I strongly suspect that Jesus and his disciples used the name of "*abba*" more or less as I described in this book. They may or

Hindu Missionary School?

may not have taken the trouble to analyse the word as I have, but that is not what counts in getting a good result in our souls. With such sacred word, practice and experience count. Getting the process to function optimally is like learning to whistle. When we get it right, the result is music on a cosmic scale. This result is available at all times.

In fact, the entire creation is recreated anew each moment. This provides for the continuity we experience as change over time. This is the secret of forgiveness, and miracles too for that matter. It reflects the reality of fresh starts. If we can appreciate the opportunity this fact offers, we take advantage of the entire power that moves the universe to put us on the optimal path for our life and, it works through us, to be effective factor in creation at large.

There was much to learn within the TM organization. We also had a deep curiosity about the inner and outer life of our teacher. Maharishi never talked much about himself. However, over time I gathered bits and pieces from various sources and gradually built a broader picture of Maharishi's story. He was born into a family of modest means in the (Kshatriya) leader/warrior caste. He had gotten some higher education. One day, he approached a renowned spiritual teacher by the name of Bramahnanda Saraswati in the Himalayan village of Jyotir Math. He asked to be accepted as a disciple. Instead, he was sent home to complete his undergraduate degree. He returned after graduation and it appears he never again left his teacher. Among his students, Brahmananda was affectionately known as "Guru Dev" (divine dispeller of darkness). We were told that Maharishi had a gift for producing an "apt phrase" so he was appointed to handle Guru Dev's correspondence. After the passing of his beloved teacher, Maharishi retired to a remote part of the Himalayas and was alone for some time except for a few other ascetics.

One day, he conceived of an idea to offer the benefits of the spiritual life he knew to the masses. When he shared his idea with one of his spiritual friends, he thought Maharishi had lost

A Second Look at Jesus

his mind. In response the friend pointed to a small stream that ran through a valley near their caves and said, "We don't even like to think about what lies beyond that river." Maharishi replied, in the opinion of his reclusive colleagues, he had "planted himself deep in the mud of this world."

What followed, between 1955 and 1957, was a series of tours around India. Then, beginning in 1958 these tours extended throughout the West. In the beginning, Maharishi taught in the name of the "Spiritual Regeneration Movement." When I met him, he was in the midst of transforming his appeal to the more common and accepted vernacular of western science. With the Beatles and others, he had gone through the roller coaster of publicity that came from association with celebrities. He resolved, in the future, celebrities would not receive special treatment.

Instead, the effects of meditation came to be scientifically measured. Blood chemistry, brain waves and other objectively verifiable criteria were analysed and interpreted. People were encouraged to learn meditation for practical health reasons. If students of meditation gathered a more profound harvest along the way, that would not be a bad outcome. The point, in my opinion, was to bring spiritual regeneration to people who did not even know they wanted it or needed it.

Chapter Seven

Ripening Fruit

Hayah

I am going to pause in my narrative to give a clearer view of what was going on in me because of the meditation I had been doing. At this time, as I was about to go to India, it had been less than two years since my first spiritual breakthrough on the stump at Wheeler's Ranch. I had been meditating for at least thirty to forty minutes, twice a day for a little more than two years. Within that span, I had also spent six to seven months in a meditation retreat during which I was meditating most of my waking hours.

The meditation had the effect of bringing my attention to the root of my existence and allowing me to spend extended periods there. I had acquired a distinct taste for that inner life. I craved more and more of it. Under the influence of such attention, I was progressively discovering and awakening the basis of my body, mind and soul. My inner resources were responding, much as a garden of fruit-bearing trees responds to abundant sunlight, rich soil, air and water.

The energy that first rampaged through me at Wheeler's Ranch had more or less settled into a channel that passed through the middle of my being and at intervals along the course of that flow, there were areas or centers of subtle sensitivity and competence

A Second Look at Jesus

that fed upon elements in the flow. They were somewhat like vibrant cities of light along an animating river. Those centers were converting elements from that energy flow into functions, corresponding to various aspects of my human life. Roughly speaking, these areas were top of head, forehead, throat, heart, kidneys, genitals, and the base of my spine. The aspect of human spirituality is beautifully expressed in Jeremiah 17:7-8. There it says: "Blessed is the man who trusts in the LORD and whose trust is the LORD, for he will be like a tree planted by the water, that extends its roots by a stream and will not fear when the heat comes; but its leaves will be green and it will not be anxious in a year of drought nor cease to yield fruit."

My human mechanism was becoming an instrument of introverted observation. In its own way, it was more subtle and powerful than an electron microscope. In fact, I had come to believe scientific understanding and technological devices are only approximate reflections of the more perfect functions and mechanisms found within us.

The first mantra given me by my TM teachers appeared to be stimulating the crown of my head. With further practice and some additions to my initial TM technique I found an efficient focus upon my heart along with those areas of my brain associated with my pineal and pituitary glands. Over time, those areas began to resonate with increasing vigor and clarity. They were stimulated by each repetition of my mantras. Over time, the effect of those mantras became as direct and repeatable as striking a bell.

Over time, the other centers also began to resonate with each other in sympathetic harmony. I was told this is a normal result. The teaching metaphor commonly used to explain this phenomenon is that of a table with a number of legs. If we grasp one leg of the table and draw it toward us, the whole table and all of the legs come along too.

Ripening Fruit

There are plenty of reports in the historical record of similar experiences among students of meditation. The only unique thing here was it was happening to *me* at *this* time and place.

It would be a mistake to make too much of the experiences I am reporting. After all, the reality of God is more common than dirt and seekers have been finding him since the beginning. A more healthy response to such reports is to take heart and discover the same capacity within one's self.

There is no reason to believe *my* description of *my* inner experience is going to be the same as you might report someday. The topic under discussion is, after all, experience beyond the limits of human understanding. When approaching that reality we just have to see what happens.

When faced with a glimpse of the true expanse of the creator, the brain ceases to be gregarious. After the shock of being put in its place, the mind resorts to a different mode of thinking and becomes a more humble servant characterized by truthful reporting up to the limit of the logical mind. Thereafter the mind reflects poetic or symbolic impressions until the absolute limit of our personality is reached. After that, there is only silence. We all have natural variations we are born with, as well as a diversity of early programming during our youth. As a result, the sensations and poetic images that make up our experience must vary somewhat. When comparing reports of people who have experience in these realms, the most we can hope for is that those reports will rhyme with or resemble each other. It is unlikely they would be identical.

A poem is
A poem is an address,
a minimal set of markers
set around an important junction in my soul.

A Second Look at Jesus

*Defined by each turn,
the direction taken,
and the distance travelled,*

*these words suggest the border that defines a vibrant reality
of the soul's prime real estate.*

Too many words distract.

Too few and you get lost.

A poem is not the words.

*It is your soul
finding a portion of mine
staked out plainly
for your examination.*

John

Beyond human prerogatives and articulation, there is the underlying spiritual architecture of our soul. There are spiritual centers and each has a different signature tone. All of them resonate as if they were tuning forks set for different pitches. The higher frequency resonances are near the top of the body and the lower frequencies nearer the bottom. All possess a compelling vitality and all have their signature beauty. Over time, their resonance becomes less distant and less abstract until the effect is very tangible indeed.

Associated with this resonance is something akin to combustion or room temperature fusion. Each center combusts and consumes its share of everyday experience and the substance of our daily lives, converting it into what we could call a fragrant essence. From the worldly perspective, the essence I am referring to would most commonly be called wisdom. These fragrances, the

Ripening Fruit

diverse richness yielded from the creative enterprise of our lives, are what endure when human frame is long gone. Spiritually, we could call this God's memory of us.

There is also the sense of a powerful conversion of energies as the centers whir, hum, and resonate like power transformers or substations. Over time, it begins to become clear that the vigor and the intelligence of this ongoing process of unfolding life are daily exceeding our previous assessments of what was involved in living.

The overall effect is a revelation of a purposeful, ravishing beauty. Within ourselves, we are each a part of a celestial choir of incomparable ecstasy. Love of others emerges in this context. When you perceive how lovely people are there can be no other reaction.

Resonance

I'll tell you a secret
Before we were fleshy we were a single vibrant syllable
Then a song
And then a collection of songs
Behind every morsel of flesh is a symphony,
Each one unique
We speak words, but the real communication is something else
It is the resonant interweaving of our theme with others
It is all about the points of sympathetic resonance
Blue notes responding to major chords
*A thrilling riff that makes everyone **stop** and pay attention*
Deep, throaty and complex harmonies binding us together

The Composer wishes his work to be appreciated
So instructors are provided from time to time
Teaching ascending and descending scales, harmonies, melodies
Remedial lessons for those who forgot

Remember.

A Second Look at Jesus

We are of one substance with the original chorus of praise
You were made for this performance
Come now,
Join in

John

These experiences incrementally change our sense of identity. Each sets the stage for a further insight. For example, in relationships we see others as we see ourselves. If we see ourselves as a body, we see other people as bodies too. If we are mostly mind-bound, then we relate to others as minds. If souls, then souls, etc.

With human experience, of the intensity I am describing, we seem to be a collection of interrelated and harmonious spiritual attributes. Within, we are like a crystalline garden of exuberant fruit and flowers. The shape of the garden layout recedes in importance as things progress. Outer circumstances begin to lose their grip on our attention. Instead, when we meet someone new we naturally focus the content of his or her soul. We are enraptured by the "perfume" associated with the flowering of their personality. We love people not out of duty but because they are essentially *lovely*.

Chapter Eight

An Apostle to India

Hayah

Finally, in the spring of 1972, our small group was released to proceed to India. I went alone, preceding most of the others. Nothing can prepare you for India. This country is a harmonious riot of millions of souls scrambling with verve and playful dignity to make a life where little is easy. It nearly swamped my mind.

I landed in New Delhi at dawn and was immediately assaulted by a cacophonous chaos of baggage handlers, taxi drivers, and police armed with vintage Lee-Enfield rifles. Beyond all of this tumult, the new air seemed to possess an extraordinary ability to pierce deeper than usual into every particle of my being. The sun was just emerging as a fierce ball of fire on the horizon. Somehow, it seemed much nearer than normal and it clearly announced it would be dominating my days here. Inside, I was focused on destiny and the challenge before me. I was a dedicated soul, under a self-imposed vow of celibacy. I gathered my thoughts about the

A Second Look at Jesus

path ahead. Soon after we got on the road my taxi driver asked, "Would you be wanting a pretty woman? We can stop along the way. I know just the place." I was shocked. This was not the India I had imagined it! It was too real for comfort!

The western culture is clustered around its middle, the sweet spot where personal freedom, political moderation, a strong work ethic and a moderate set of values churn out material prosperity. India explodes these boundaries. It is a land of genuine saints and rogues, wealthy and poor, subtle and vulgar, beauty and squalor. All these opposites and modest middle strata jostle against each other with distressing intimacy. The emphasis was on humanity. As a result, material success is deemphasized and hard to come by, but intercourse with spiritual inspiration and human nature is vivid and constant.

The Indian traffic ethic takes up where the Italians leave off. Their relatively low death toll is an ongoing miracle. Swarms of motorized rickshaws, taxis, motorcycles, scooters, domestic sedans, and a few colonial relics careen around traffic circles like a populist version of the Imperial Roman chariot races. Horns are essential equipment and are used so aggressively that lesser noises are crowded out. Faith in the preserving power of God becomes not just a virtue. It is a necessity.

Only a handful of us were sent by Maharishi to be his representatives in India. We carried business cards identifying us rather grandiosely as "International Director, World Plan Executive Council." We were initially buoyed up by the organization of devotees who were left behind from Maharishi's early years. We went in pairs. A very fine married team went to Bombay. Another pair of guys went south to Bangalore. Howard Hansen and I stayed in Delhi. Initially, we were taken into the family of M. N. Seth. We lived with them in their mansion in the posh Golf Links development.

Mr. Seth, a successful industrialist, took us in hand and explained how Indian society functioned. We could have wasted years learning what was taught to us over a few short weeks. Over time, I added more detail and a picture emerged.

An Apostle to India

In India, he explained, class still mattered greatly. The caste system may not have been as absolute as it once was, but most personal assessments began there.

The youth of India was not comfortable with this reality, although they had to contend with it daily. As westerners, we were uniquely able to mix with all sorts and types while representing our message in a culturally neutral context. We were outside the social order we interacted with. With this advantage, whatever we taught was judged on its merits to a greater degree than might otherwise have been the case.

In addition to class, race was and still is a factor in India. The Aryans (yes, the same Aryans that the Nazis idealized), swept into northern India many centuries before and carried their Vedic religion with them as they conquered and dominated the darker Dravidian people who were largely Animist (like their African ancestors). A great deal of creative melding has taken place over the centuries, but at one time the lighter skinned Vedic pundits, meditators and philosophers ruled over northern India while the dark-skinned Animists ruled the south.

Upper class women tend to stay out of the sun and sometimes use special creams to lighten their skin color. Marriages are usually arranged. The matchmakers minutely consider class and wealth along with personal appearance.

Today the religious/spiritual culture of India is extremely rich and full of vitality. India is a vibrant market of spiritual diversity, surrounding a core of deep and genuine unity. Sure, there are problems, but overall, I saw a vision of how Indian spirituality functions and interacts as a vast blessing.

Over this basic structure of traditional culture, there was an overlay of colonial era British reforms. There are thirty official languages spoken by at least one billion Indians. Hindi is the dominant language for government interaction, while English is the secondary language most people hold in common and use to reach across regional, cultural and national borders. The English legal system, that holds all men equal before the law, helps to

A Second Look at Jesus

establish a level-playing field and is likewise critical to Indian national identity. Personal property is generally well respected these days, although a strong influence of socialism prevailed while I was there. The British bureaucratic system was likewise retained and so were the English military traditions. In matters of personal conduct and decorum, something like Victorian expectations prevailed.

In the crisis that accompanied their national birth, Indians discovered their path to national unity in the humble disciplines of tolerance and respect espoused by Mahatma Gandhi. Apparently, every time there is departure far from Gandhi's example, trouble ensues.

One thing all Indians seem to agree upon is the best of all aspirations is God realization. There is one more thing. The people have an irrepressible cheerful optimism, especially the young. These qualities are the ones to which we appealed. I suppose my love for the Indian culture is plain. The people possess a combination of virtues hard to find anywhere else in the world.

In this context, Howard and I were novelties. We were a reflection of one of their native sons who had found success in the new world. In India, Maharishi was commonly known under the more humble name of Mahesh Yogi (purifier yogi). We carried color videotapes of Maharishi for teaching purposes. These tapes were an exceedingly rare medium at that time and an object of much fascination in India. With this advantage, it was relatively easy to assemble a decent crowd to hear Maharishi's teaching. The teaching itself was somewhat novel, although the more scholarly listeners could find precedent for our approach. Soon we were initiating a number of new TM meditators.

After a few months I got a new partner, David, and we worked with the Indian press to get our message out. We were still very green, however. On one occasion, we sent out several dozen finely printed invitations to all of the major press outlets in Delhi for a big press conference. We purchased nearly one hundred hors

An Apostle to India

d'oeuvres. At the appointed time, only one reporter showed up. He kindly helped us to consume some of our food and counselled us that invitations needed at least two follow up calls. It turned out that hard work was necessary if we were to succeed! We tried again and did much better. Some favorable articles followed.

At age twenty, entrusted to represent something very large that I truly believed in. I had carte blanche authority on how to proceed. There was a willing and appreciative market and plenty of support in every way that mattered. I once addressed the entire student body of a women's college in Delhi. Another time I spoke to a Vedic Culture study group. We spoke to dozens of Rotary Clubs. We kept to the same basic script no matter where we spoke. Our constant theme was that effective meditation is without individual effort. The invincible force of evolution worked on its own behalf to bring an effective result. This same power moved the universe. If we kept out of the way and let the evolutionary force of nature work for us the results would be profound.

Sometimes our hosts would try to bring us with them to view some of the more famous saints and gurus who were then in circulation. One in particular was famous for making ashes appear from his outstretched palms. The ash symbolized the residue of sins and ignorance consumed in the fire of yoga. He had a huge following. Maharishi had told us to avoid such wonder-workers. In his view, such showmanship was unworthy of a serious spiritual endeavor. We were there on a "one pointed" mission to represent him and Transcendental Meditation.

Once, I was more or less tricked by one of the monks in Maharishi's organization to visit a private home where someone was talking about spiritual life. When I came in, he wrote something on a scrap of paper and asked me to hold on to it. After we spoke for a while, he asked me to name a number and then look at the paper. The numbers were the same. The point, well-made throughout the east, was that the spiritual realm was real and imminent. The wonder workers would then follow up with a direct appeal for the audience to make a commitment to engage that

A Second Look at Jesus

greater reality. There was the rub. Too often, the follow-through was lacking. In India, the visiting of gurus had become something of a national hobby, an entertainment. Access to the spiritually accomplished was so widespread in the east that often it was not properly appreciated and acted upon.

One of the very great pleasures of serving in India was the opportunity to meet with Maharishi's disciples. There were exceptions. Our banker had sticky fingers. One of the local teachers complained bitterly that it was not right that westerners were permitted to teach Indians. In general, however, Maharishi handed us a bag of golden nuggets and jewels in the form of his contacts. His Indian monks, of whom I met four or five, were all sober and dedicated although most enjoyed a good joke as well as the next person. They travelled in more traditional circles, which would generally not be open to us. His "house holder" (married) devotees were happy to devote considerable time and resources to make sure we were as successful as possible.

Not all was sweetness and light. I once had occasion to go to a police station to report something missing. While there, I saw two policemen bringing in a prisoner who vigorously struggled and resisted. His captors paused and held him firmly while a third police officer executed a rifle "butt stroke" against the side of his head. Now, thoroughly sedated, he was dragged upstairs between a pair of policemen to a holding cell. Okay, I understood. This was a new place and new rules prevailed. Rough justice is part of the program. I got it. I did not want to approach this particular reality closer than necessary.

On another occasion, I found myself at the Indian Department of Revenue and talking to an official of rather high rank. While I was there, an applicant and his assistant came into the room. Perhaps I should term him a supplicant based upon his demeanor. His helper had a two- wheeled mover's dolly with tax records in boxes stacked more than three feet high. The assistant to my tax official took a document off the top of the stack, opened to a signature page and positioned it under the hand of

An Apostle to India

my official. The official signed it without taking his eyes off me or missing a beat in our conversation. Pages were deftly flipped, more signatures were applied and the supplicant rolled on out of the room. This experience remains, for me, a model of low-tech efficiency.

Once I had occasion to visit a small bank far out in the country. They had a guard. He was ancient. He possessed a huge "handle bar" mustache and was armed with nothing but a spear. It was a perfect example of appropriate technology. I am confident that he had the necessary effect of keeping peace within that bank.

That summer was extremely hot. New Delhi is just east of the immense desert of Rajasthan. In the summer there were sometimes weeks in a row when the wind would blow from the desert directly over Delhi. There was a special name for this wind. It was called the *Loo*. True to our instructions from Maharishi, we faithfully wore full suits every day. One of the taxis we frequented was an enormous American Buick that had originally served as a staff car during World War II. The vehicle was painted black and still had four bright chrome stars, the insignia of the General who had once used it, on each of the front fenders. I remember spending some very uncomfortable time in the back of that taxi. Then, one day, in the back of that taxi, there was an opening.

Delhi 1972
The Loo, is a scorching hot wind,
fresh off the Rajasthani Desert.

It is baking me, at 120 degrees
like a slow roast chicken
inside the suit,
inside the taxi,
inside a lusty traffic tangle.

I am enthralled by what I have just discovered
Just behind my nose, reaching back to the center of my brain,

A Second Look at Jesus

someone has turned on the freezer.
Very odd.
I am numb, frosted.
A little behind my forehead, crystals refract inner light –
pure,
unborn,
uneverything.

What now?

John

My meditation had taken up the attributes of archaeological exploration. I would probe and search for openings to new rooms. Once inside I would feel for the "switch," illuminate the interior and gape as new mysteries were revealed. In fact, I was discovering and activating latent sensitivities and abilities that previously seemed to be nothing but legend or fantasy. Little by little, I was rounding out my life.

I have always been a reader. By the time I was nine or ten, I often gobbled up a book a day. I especially liked science fiction. My favorite author was Isaac Asimov and I had an especially high regard for his Foundation series. While in India, I consumed the spiritual classics of that great culture. The Vedic culture books included the Upanishads, the Mahabharata, the Valmiki Ramayana, the Yoga Sutra of Patanjali, the Shrimad Bhagavantam, and the Vivekachudimani. I also read from a category of literature called shastras which amount to "how to" texts on specific subjects. These covered subjects such as mantras, their uses and their effects. They also offer teaching about the effects of planets, herbs and gems upon human life. Among Buddhist texts, I especially remember one titled <u>The Inconceivable Liberation of Vimalakirti</u>. I found this material and much more through the venerable publisher/distributer Motilal Banarsidass in Old Delhi. I have continued to patronize them for many years.

An Apostle to India

Sometimes my colleague and I got a little nostalgic for our western culture. Then we would visit the American embassy library or attend an event held there. I found considerable pleasure and comfort in just reading a *Time* magazine now and then. We made friends with some of the diplomatic staff around town.

Once I was having a discussion with one of the American diplomats concerning the possible availability of some restricted funds that America jointly controlled with the government of India. I wanted to fund the teaching of the "Science of Creative Intelligence" on a wide scale. I had just handed him one of my "International Director" cards when my partner completely spoiled the effect by handing him one of his too. The official looked at them side by side and said, "Would the real International Director for India please stand up?" We all had a good laugh. Nothing ever came of the money.

I was struck with the good cheer that animated the poorest among the Indian workers. I remember seeing a construction crew of very slender men and women excavating for a sewer project. They were carrying the dirt in wicker baskets. I was told they got just enough money to cover a sparse diet. They lived in the culvert pipes not yet placed in the ground. They did it all this with grace, dignity and joy. In a similar fashion the loading and unloading of ships was intentionally done with inefficient quantities of manual labor. The point was not to save money. It was to save lives.

It seemed to me many of the "poor" in America compare poorly with those in India. Perhaps the poor of India are too complacent, but the resentfulness and jealously among some of the American poor is not helpful either.

While on the topic of money, let me say, in India, we did not collect money from the people who came to learn meditation. In the west, Maharishi had a strict policy requiring everyone pay to learn meditation. Maharishi said he had found that unless westerners paid for something they would not place much value on it.

A Second Look at Jesus

This was a clear violation of the tradition and culture of India. Guru Dev prohibited the practice. He said it made the teacher share in the sins of the student. I understand it was actually quite hard to give a substantial sum to Guru Dev's organization. If he did not like your motivation, he would turn you down.

Chapter Nine

Coal to Newcastle?

Hayah

After about four months, I moved to Madras, an important port on the southeastern coast of India I was with a new partner, Stephen Shimer. An attorney and his family took us in. Initially, we lived in a guest apartment on the upper floor of their home. Our host took care to see that our understanding of India grew under his supervision.

One day, our hosts took us to see Mahabalipuram, a seventh century port city and international trade center. Both Roman and Chinese coins have been excavated there. This is the place where numerous bas-relief statues and monolithic temples were found in nearly perfect condition. My host told me that the temples I could see along the ocean shore were the outermost of seven groups spaced some distance apart and extended into the middle of that ancient city, now under water.

Back at home, he introduced us to his friends and contacts. Once he made us wait in the living room until the top of the hour

A Second Look at Jesus

passed. "Why?" I asked him. He said, "We were waiting for the auspicious time to start out." I was puzzled, but followed his lead. He was deeply committed to astrology.

On another occasion, we met the Cultural Minister for the state of Tamil Nadu, who pointed out that aircraft were invented in India. This had been reported in one of their scriptures. Apparently, cultural pride lives everywhere.

Cows freely roamed the city and they were treated with kindly deference wherever they wandered. They were universally regarded as both a symbol and a practical expression of God's benign generosity. The relationship between cow and man was benign and symbiotic. Cow milk is also especially important to the diet of vegetarians, as Hindus generally are. For these reasons and others cows are revered and protected.

Holy men (and women) also were found here, there and everywhere. We were taught it was considered a great spiritual blessing to feed or give shelter to such a man or woman. Such acts allowed one to share in the merit of these holy beings. It was like stoking a holy fire and receiving some of the heat and light in return. There was one such holy man who took up a station at the end of our residential street. He had the three vertical, white stripes painted on his forehead, showing he was a devotee of Vishnu, the sustaining aspect of God. One day, we had a closer encounter.

The Lord in Rags

We had passed him many times as we took a taxi from home
Regally upright, he wore vertical white stripes on his broad,
mahogany forehead
A sovereign holding court along a Madrasi road
His clothing was elemental
His presence an unexamined mystery
I came and went
He stayed
One day, as we approached, he rose with grace
and gazed earnestly at me

Coal to Newcastle?

His noble intelligence swept over my pathetic façade
clearing all before it.
His intent invincible,
He was recognizing the Sovereign within me
To this moment,
I have not recovered.
The taxi passed by.
I have not.

John

I have had a handful of similar encounters with great souls, often without words. Their inner stature dwarfed their fleshly presence. One was an Antioch student whom I briefly noticed as he was preparing to load his belongings into a car at the end of a semester. Some friends were helping him with his luggage outside the Mills dormitory. The remarkable thing about him was he was both vast and utterly unmoving inside. He was like a separate universe untouched by the activity that washed around him. I never expected to find someone of his stature so close to home. At the time, I expected all great souls to be exotic foreigners. In practice, I found that is not the way life works.

On another occasion, while waiting for a visa renewal at an Indian government building, I saw a Buddhist monk in a pale yellow robe. Inside, he was an angelic being, dancing in perfect freedom.

We never know when a passer-by might have such a blessing for us. I often wonder how many Christians would be able to recognize Christ if he walked by them in blue jeans, or a suit or a skirt. How does such recognition occur? Like recognizes like. There is no other way. Our soul simply recognizes other great souls if we are open enough for that inspiring recognition to occur. This is how souls recognize each other. It is a direct recognition of co-existence.

Stephen and I sometimes ate at local restaurants. They were very different from Indian restaurants in the west. In Madras,

A Second Look at Jesus

the food was often served on banana leaves. Waiters would put scoops of rice, lentil stew, vegetables and flat bread in front of us. They would playfully serve us more and more until we put both of our hands over our plates and said "bas" (enough). This wonderful food, along with the gift of loving treatment, was very inexpensive. Usually, this feast would cost less than a dollar.

Fresh snacks in Madras were generally of two types. Here and there, you would see a man with a large machete next to a large pile of green coconuts. For a modest sum, he would chop the outer husk off the top of one, pierce it and serve it with a straw. Then when we had finished drinking the rich, sweet juice he would cut the nut in half, scrape the soft, gelatinous meat into a half shell and serve it with a husk chip for a spoon.

The other quality snack, found in both Delhi and Madras, was freshly squeezed sugar cane. For this treat, a great heap of fresh sugar cane was stacked next to an iron wringer with a big crank and fed into the machine, usually by a youngster while a husky fellow worked the crank. The result was ambrosia. Now, to appreciate it, the consumer had to be a little relaxed about sanitation. There were flies about and everyone shared a few glasses that were only given a perfunctory rinse between customers. Akin to the juice was the crystalline raw sugar that is called *gur* which is common in India and, strangely, unavailable in America.

Madras is the home of one of the most ancient Christian communities in the world. It claims to have been founded by the apostle Thomas himself. They were "discovered" by Portuguese traders in the 16th century. Unfortunately, there is evidence that some of the unique characteristics of this ancient community were intentionally erased over time. Eventually, most of them were brought into full conformity with the Church of Rome, at least on paper.

The Catholic Bishop of Madras saw me, without an appointment and was the soul of hospitality. He politely listened as I described what we were trying to accomplish. We had a very friendly and cordial conversation and then he prayed for me

Coal to Newcastle?

and wished me success. I left there refreshed and amazed at his humble kindness. This was not what my experience with "The Church" had led me to expect.

Stephen and I had taken an informal vow of celibacy. We wanted to focus on spiritual growth. At that time, the effects of meditation were more than a handful. Truthfully, I could not have done justice to a relationship along with our work and the changes going on within. Nonetheless, we were apparently judged by many mothers to be fully qualified to marry their daughters. We endured not a few receptions with tea and biscuits, featuring a strong emphasis on the virtues of pretty daughters along with our usual spiel on the benefits of regular meditation.

Once we were invited by our neighbor across the street to come over for "refreshments." This was a household of a widowed mother and two teenage daughters. The mother had gained some renown as an Indian classical dancer and she had once performed in Japan. She had endured a disease, leaving her face deeply pock marked which only served to bring more attention to the beauty of both her form and her inner countenance. She shared a traditional dance that was achingly beautiful and full of playful spirit.

Then the purpose of our visit entered the room. Her teenaged daughter came forward with a tali tray. These common serving utensils were made of stainless steel. They were about twenty-four inches in diameter and had an edge about one inch high. The tray in her hand had a flat surface around the edge, extending the circumference a little more than an inch and a half. She put the tray on the ground and stood on the edge. Then she began one of the most amazing performances I have ever seen. She made that tray shimmy, walk on opposite edges, and do some other things that I am at a loss to describe. Every bit of the energy to move the tray came from her lower regions, so to speak. At the same time, her upper torso, arms, neck and head were fully engaged in refined, even divine gestures and expressions. She astonished us. As we walked home, Stephen commented she would never get

A Second Look at Jesus

him. He would slip from sight like a garden snake racing through the high grass. I assented.

Now, our host had an opinion on this subject. He said spiritually advanced renunciates were relatively common. An enlightened householder, on the other hand, was at once more rare and more useful as a model for the rest of the population. He thought that maintaining a spiritual life along with a normal, worldly existence was harder to achieve, but it held the potential to do broader good.

After about six months in Madras, we were headed back to Maharishi's ashram in Rishikesh. It was the practice of all TM teachers to have several weeks of meditation retreat each year. Two retreats a year was considered minimal. We were long overdue. Along the way we stopped in to visit our counterparts in Bangalore.

At that time, India still had a large and active stable of steam locomotives. Stephen and I took one from Madras to Bangalore. This journey was a great adventure. We opened the windows wide. Coal soot mixed with the fresh air as we watched the rural Indian countryside roll on and on.

As our taxi arrived at the TM center in Bangalore, a stranger approached me. He had a somewhat odd, pinched quality in the region of his forehead. It was as though all of his attention was focused just above his eyebrows. He approached and said I was going to get married. I replied that he was wrong; I intended to be a brahmacharya (celibate student). He repeated I was definitely going to be married and he would give me the initials of my bride. Years later, after I married my wife, I told her this story. This is one of her favorite stories. My recollection of that event is a little fuzzy, but I believe that the first initial was an "A."

Chapter Ten

Holy men (and Women)

Hayah

The village of Rishikesh is the place where the Ganges River (properly pronounced Ganga) emerges from the foothills of the Himalayas and begins to enter the plains. The river flows east along the southern slopes of the Himalayas and eventually enters the Bay of Bengal at Calcutta. The glaciers of northwest India, near the border of ancient Tibet, are the source of the Ganges. This area is now controlled by China. More than 400 million people live in the Ganges River basin. This is the most densely populated land in the world. The Ganga is considered sacred and bathing in it was viewed as cleansing for the soul. I did some bathing, but it was little more than a quick dip as the water at Rishikesh was *very* cold.

Maharishi leased land a few miles upstream of the village and built an ashram there in the 1960's. Situated on the northern bank, it is only accessible by a small water taxi or a long walk and a suspended pedestrian bridge. The land itself is on a lofty ridge

A Second Look at Jesus

and is surrounded by the forests of a national wildlife preserve. The compound was surrounded by a chain link fence, was modern in design and constructed of concrete and masonry.

Nonetheless, plenty of wild life got through or over the fence. Large clans of monkeys roamed about. Sometimes they sounded like a herd of buffalo as they thundered across our roof. If an argument broke out their shrieking would make the mind search for cover. There were some large lizards. They were up to three or four feet long and liked to sun in the open. We were told they had a venomous bite. Peacocks would make their way to visit now and then. While they were a beauty to behold, they had a piercing call that simply could not be ignored. We were advised to always upend our shoes before we put them on so scorpions would not get a chance to sting us. Finally, there were the snakes. I saw only one snake, but it was a big one. It was at least six feet long and moving through the forest almost as fast as I could jog.

The community was led by Satyanand, one of the older monks who had been a disciple of Guru Dev alongside Maharishi. The first order of business when we arrived was several weeks of meditation retreat. We meditated all day and in the evening Satyanand would spend time with us answering questions and telling us stories. The meditation cells were creatively designed. They were constructed of concrete and sunken into the ground in two wings on the side of a large lecture hall. Each cell had walls lined with stones from the Ganga. There were no doors. Instead, each room was formed like a seashell with a spiraled entryway. We turned clockwise to enter and counter-clockwise to leave our cells. The result was a cool and deeply silent place to meditate.

From Satyanand we learned that Guru Dev summarized his spiritual program as Tap and Jap (both are pronounced with an "*a*" as in "about"). Tap stood for Tapas, which means austerity. In practical terms, austerity was moderate diet, moderate activity and refraining from excessive worldly ambition. Jap stood for Japa, which meant repetition of a name of God. A set of

Holy men (and Women)

strung beads (called a *mala*) was usually used to keep track of the repetitions.

Maharishi's teacher, Bramahnanda Saraswati, held the position of Shankaracharya of Jyotir Matha in northern India. The first Shankaracharya, born in the 8th century, was a reformer every bit as important to Vedic teaching as Martin Luther, Thomas Aquinas and John Calvin were to Christianity. Present day successors to Shankaracharya are likewise significant.

The position of Shankaracharya at the northern center in Jyotir Matha had been vacant for a long time when, in the 1940s, a search committee determined the best candidate to carry on was Guru Dev. The trouble was he took his oath of renunciation very seriously and was not interested in a new job. After following him and pleading for some time without success, the committee made a desperate move.

One day, during Guru Dev's morning meditation, they set up their religious paraphernalia and simply performed the inauguration ceremony associated with the post of Shankaracharya. When Guru Dev came out of meditation, he was presented with *fait accompli*. He graciously acquiesced to his new role.

By all accounts, he was an inspired choice. He encouraged everyone to do their duty and inspired them to renew their spiritual resolve. According to Satyanand, he also had the common touch so whomever he was speaking to would have the distinct impression that *he or she was* Guru Dev's favorite disciple. He was also free from religious bigotry. On one occasion, a Muslim Sufi came to him after his Pir (spiritual guide) had passed away. On the instructions of that Pir he was seeking to become a disciple of Guru Dev so as to complete his spiritual journey. Guru Dev emptied the room of other students so he and the young Sufi could get down to the business of examining and prescribing spiritual practices.

By contrast, Maharishi confessed his monkish temperament was an obstacle to easy social interaction, or an ability to touch the common person within the context of their worldly lives. He

A Second Look at Jesus

said the meditation practices he had done, the mantra he used, had the effect of burning all his worldly ties. The monk's path amounts to the cultivation of an extreme degree of self-effacement. The ideal for renunciates is to become alone with God.

Satyanand was open to virtually any question. For example, I remember once asking why the Indian people persisted in proliferating temples with various idols when they knew good and well that ultimately there was only one God. He replied with a playful look in his eye saying "We Indians like to play with dolls."

Periodically, TM meditators were taught a supplement or a refinement to their meditation practice. They were termed "advanced techniques." Maharishi liked to say they were like manure that was added to enrich the soil around a cultivated plant. At this time, I was due for my third technique and Satyanand imparted it just after my retreat.

I should point out we were asked by Maharishi to keep the mantra that we used in meditation private. He told us he did not want people to self-prescribe. Instead, he and those he appointed, would regulate such things.

After our retreat, we had time to explore the area a little more. Our favorite destination was a cave about fifteen minutes' walk further into the jungle. There, we found one of Maharishi's friends, Tat Wala Baba. I found his life story fascinating.

According to Satyanand, Baba had served in the British Army during World War 2 and was still serving during the partition of Pakistan from India. During this time, Hindu and Muslim refugees were slaughtered by their opposites with sickening regularity. At some point, Baba had experienced more cruelty than he could bear. He simply abandoned his weapon and his uniform and disappeared into the forests.

Now, twenty-five years later, he was an accomplished yogi with a magnificent soul. He was pleased to have us visit. We asked him whatever was in our hearts. He was an impressive sight. He was relatively tall and wore his matted hair coiled on his head. If uncoiled, his hair was so long it would drag on the ground behind

Holy men (and Women)

him. The only article of clothing he wore was a "tat," a loincloth. His soul was broad and subtle like the ocean on a calm day.

He had a few students. I heard one of them had been a German woman who was accepted and told to inhabit a certain cave. Later she rushed back to report, with some distress, that a King Cobra was already living there. She was sent back with instructions to make peace with the snake. He told her that he had an agreement with the snakes in the area that they would not strike humans so long as they were not molested. According to the story, this student did as she was told and everything turned out just fine.

One day, a recently graduated TM teacher came through and wanted to meet Baba. On that day, our translator was a Buddhist monk. The TM teacher proceeded to lecture Baba that the TM technique was the only way to accomplish a higher consciousness. Other methods were just a waste of time. The translator said this was insulting and he could not speak to Baba that way. Our "90 day wonder" insisted he translate *exactly* what he said. The translation was made. The answer, in Urdu, came back in due course including the intriguing expression "blub, blub, blub, blub." Then the translator said, "When a jar *full* of water is immersed in the Ganga it is silent. When an *empty* jar is immersed, it says blub, blub, blub, blub."

I was mostly interested in simply sitting in his presence. His being groomed and cleaned the nooks and crannies of my soul. He got to places I had been unable to reach myself, like having a friend or lover scrub your back or brush your hair. I once asked him if I would achieve enlightenment "in this lifetime."

He answered "Yes". I appreciated his encouragement.

Once every three years there is a gathering of holy men and women at one of four locations. This gathering is called the Kumba Mela and functions as something like a trade fair for the spiritually inclined. Here sadhus, yogis, and holy men and women of diverse descriptions emerge from all over India. Some of

A Second Look at Jesus

them had been hidden from public view for years so this gathering was a tremendous opportunity to meet and network.

We TM teachers had a modest presence and played videotapes Maharishi had sent over. When I was not needed, I was encouraged to walk around and learn what I could. Some teachers had a huge presence with numerous disciples, while others were solitary figures.

I was introduced to the successor to Guru Dev, the current Shankaracharya. His manner was very understated and modest. He also seemed deeply bored by all that was going on.

Once, a man stopped me as I walked by. He was a follower of Kabir, if I read his manner of dress correctly. He asked where my spiritual center was. I pointed to the crown of my head. That was where I was then experiencing the most intense sensations of unfolding and energy flow "No," he said, "it is here" as he placed his hand on my heart. Then we parted.

Kabir was an interesting character. He was born in the 15th century and was from a family that had recently converted to Islam. However, his meditation guide seemed to have been Hindu. He was both loved and controversial in his time because he wove elements of Islam, Hinduism and even Christianity into his teaching and poetry.

He also had audacity. For example, At one time he was unhappy to find he was becoming altogether too popular with the leading members of the local leisure class. He solved that problem by moving his home to a new location next to a slaughterhouse. The screams of dying animals kept the dilettantes away so they ceased to be a distraction for the serious disciples.

I wrote most of the poems found in this book. All of the others are from some delightful volumes creatively translated by Daniel Ladinsky. They include, <u>Love Poems from God, The Gift, and The Subject Tonight is Love</u>. These works contain poems from a broad spectrum of saintly authors of all faiths. Here is a sample of Kabir's work:

Holy men (and Women)

The Smart Dogs Ran Off
I sat with a priest who expounded on the doctrine of hell
I listened to him for hours,
then he asked me
what I thought of all that he had said.
And I replied,
That doctrine seems to be an inhuman cage;
No wonder all the smart dogs ran off.

Kabir[2]

The spiritual culture of India is at once profoundly diverse and yet harmonious and accommodating. One of the most helpful attributes of the spiritual consensus in the Indian culture is the certainty that God will prevail. This is not to say temptation, sin, and its consequences are not recognized. They are. What Hinduism does not recognize is somehow a superhuman bogey man will claim some souls for eternal torment. Instead, there is moral certainty that God will win out in the end. We are all destined to recover our identity within God. The only suggestion is that sooner is better than later. To that end, voluntary cooperation helps the process along.

This contrasts strongly with the theology developed in the western church. There, fear has played a major part of the teaching used to keep the faithful in line. In the end, this may prove not to have been helpful to individual believers. It has nonetheless been very helpful as a technique of social and individual control. It has also been a distraction from any rational cost/benefit analysis of the church over the years.

My time in India was ending. By this time, I was nearly out of money. I was also reasonably near to graduating from Antioch so I wired Maharishi and told him I wanted to leave India and complete my schooling. He wired back "If you want to come, come. If you want to stay, stay." I left for home. I made arrangements to meet Maharishi in London where he was scheduled to give a talk at Royal Albert Hall.

A Second Look at Jesus

I met Maharishi as he was exiting the hall. "What are you doing here?" he asked. Then he had me get into his waiting car. He told me to report and then he turned to greet his well-wishers as they came to the car window. I paused to wait until I had his attention again. He told me to keep talking. I reported the bare facts while he accepted flowers and greetings through the car window. Then, he told me to get out. I went home, feeling very much like a surplus part, slightly used.

Chapter Eleven

Klan Business

Hayah

When I got back to school, it was time for a serious talk with my guidance counselor. We assessed what credits I had and agreed I had most of the ingredients necessary for a BA in education. Over the rest of my time at Antioch, I applied myself to fulfilling the remaining criteria for graduation. For the next eighteen months, I attended school, taught meditation and got some practical experience teaching secondary school science. I graduated in 1976.

Then I was off to Syracuse, New York to lead a TM center. I was full of confidence. I taught a steady flow of new TM students. We paid our bills and we went on our periodic meditation retreats. At this time, Maharishi announced a supplementary meditation course intended to perfect our potential to harness our inner resources. The collective name for these abilities or powers was *Siddhis* (attainments or perfections). Of course, I was interested. All of us considered this course a very big deal. The trouble was, it was six months long and it cost of several thousand dollars. I had little money.

Undeterred, I looked in the yellow pages for charitable foundations. One of them was the Kahre-Richards Family Foundation

A Second Look at Jesus

in nearby Baldwinsville, New York. A few days later, its Director, Robert Pritchard, interviewed me. He seemed genuinely interested in what I had to say and invited me to come back several times over the next few months for meals and informal conversations.

Robert was a fascinating man. He was a concert pianist by trade. When he was a gifted youth, Robert had been become a protégé of the Richards family. They had built the mansion from which Robert later operated. By this time, Mr. Richards, a successful attorney, had passed away. His wife still lived, but she was frail. With the help of a staff, Robert was caring for her.

Robert had a health problem. He was coping with a rare genetic disease by the name of Porphyria. King George III had this same disease. This disease has to do with the absence of a particular enzyme necessary for the metabolism of certain amino acids. The result is the build-up of those unmetabolized amino acids, which have a toxic effect on the body as a whole, eventually driving the victims insane and bringing about an early death. Modern medicine had no cure although the symptoms could be managed. Robert knew he would eventually share the same fate as King George. In the meantime, he was able to function reasonably well.

In addition to administering the charitable fund set up by the Richards family, Robert mounted a determined and effective campaign to marginalize the Ku Klux Klan through an organization called the "Pan America Pan African Association." This work was mostly done through lawsuits, although sometimes intelligence gathering was needed. On a few occasions, "ritual confrontation" was used.

When I met Robert, he was in the middle of executing his plan to cripple the Klan. By this time, federal informers and prosecution for various crimes had considerably diminished the Klan. The public at large had also seen the malignant effect of the Klan on society. The Klan had been haemorrhaging members for years. The leadership of the Klan was currently attempting to redefine the Klan's role and rebrand it as a non-violent, white rights

Klan Business

organization. They offered themselves up as the white equivalent of the NAACP. What Robert did was show, by various means, that the new Klan did not materially differ from the old Klan.

The previous summer Robert had shown up for the annual Klan Klavern and cross burning at Stone Mountain, Georgia. Robert provoked them in two ways. First, he was black. Second, he chose to come dressed in his dapper best, an evening suit, spats, and a top hat. He also brought along a camera crew. In the recording I heard, the voice of a leader on the loudspeaker was telling the crowd "not to hurt that man." The plea was to no avail. Robert was beaten. This incident was recorded and publicized at the time. The resulting bad publicity played a part in the failure of the Klan's intended rebirth.

This was not out of character for Robert as he had led a colorful life. He told me a number of stories about himself. When younger and on tour, he had eloped with a Swedish princess. The royal family had promptly found them and quickly arranged to annul the marriage.

On another occasion, Robert went up against Papa Doc Duvalier. The dictator had imprisoned a poet friend of Robert's. In response, Robert borrowed a donkey, rode it straight into the presidential palace and then right into the dictator's office. Then he told the dictator, "You are a boor." Robert not only survived, but also became a valued advisor to that dictator.

Robert maintained a dynamic relationship with a circle of influential friends. From time to time, he would hold musical recitals at his home. Among those attending were ambassadors to the United Nations and various other notables in politics and the media.

At this time, Maharishi instituted a new program to honor local leaders who characterized qualities we valued. Although we were proud of the helpful effects that meditation had on our lives, Maharishi made it plain that many people were born with a very advanced state of consciousness. Not everyone is the same. There are plenty of wonderful people who maintain a truly splendid

A Second Look at Jesus

existence without the benefits of TM or any obvious spiritual practice. By honoring these people, I suppose that Maharishi hoped to gain allies who could help us to be more successful in propagating TM. I offered the "Highest Consciousness" award to Robert. He accepted this award and was honored along with a few other people in a public ceremony.

Robert was genuinely deserving of this recognition. He clearly had a formidable inner life. Although the details are vague, he told me he had long been practicing a form of Buddhist meditation from the Mongolian tradition. More conventionally, he was also a loyal Christian and a member of a local Episcopal Church.

Around this time, a regional TM leader visited our center and, in short order, I was removed from a leadership role in the Syracuse center. He said he had held a meeting with the other TM teachers and they were ready for a change. I was dismayed. I thought I was doing a good job.

Robert invited me to stay with him as a guest. I helped as best I could although I was far below the standard of commitment and professionalism of his permanent staff and interns. I only played a bit part in their activities. It was during this time I became involved with some of Robert's anti-Klan work.

In 1976, I drove along with some of Robert's other staff and interns to the annual Klan meeting at Stone Mountain, Georgia. We were there simply to observe and report. This was quite an experience. The racism we saw and heard expressed that night was exceedingly raw and threatening.

The Klan meeting that night was well attended. Thousands were there at the Stone Mountain State Park. Twenty percent of the attendees were dressed in immaculate robes and pointed cloth hoods. The Klansmen were mostly dressed in white, but some were in bright satin red, green, black, and purple. The opening of the meeting was a series of talks from Klansmen.

We were urged to play our part in restoring white Christian values and resisting the degrading influence of "nigger" culture. These men were dripping with malice and hate. The crowd

Klan Business

roared its approval. Then, to affirm the Christian values they claimed were the center of their values, torch-bearing Klansmen formed a large circle around a forty-foot cross wrapped in kerosene-soaked rags. The swirling fumes mixed with the venomous speech created a perfume of malice. The climax of the meeting was the lighting of the cross. The cross was "lighted," not "burned" to represent the fire of Christian virtue.

We were anonymous. We believed so long as we were not identified as "spies' we were in no danger. The only real anxiety came when our driver lost the car keys for some time.

One member of our group was a South American of German extraction. He was very pale and Aryan in his appearance. He was invited to a private planning session after the cross burning. Afterwards we drove in shifts straight back to Baldwinsville, New York to share the intelligence we had gathered.

A few months later, I attended a similar, but smaller cross burning in nearby Hamilton, NY. This was shocking to me as it was very near Colgate College. I had assumed racism was mostly a southern problem. I was wrong. The Klan phenomenon was widespread and had a long history.

The Klan had its start as a covert resistance force to combat the abuses associated with the federal occupation of the south after the Civil War. There were plenty of abuses to resist. Lincoln had intended to follow a path of reconciliation with the south. His successors did the opposite. Anyone who had served in any aspect of the Confederate military or government was forbidden to vote or serve in public office. With this, the black population instantly became a voting majority for the Republican Party. Corruption was rampant. Most politicians were for sale. White plantation owners simultaneously faced higher taxes to pay for rampant graft and the impossibility of raising crops without workers. Foreclosures were very common and northern opportunists called *carpetbaggers* bought such southern assets for a few pennies on the dollar. Southern collaborators who played a part in this process of pillage were called *scallywags*.

A Second Look at Jesus

In this context, the Klan resisted the politics of the day with intimidation and violence. At one time Confederate Cavalry General Nathan Bedford Forest was the nominal head of the Klan. He claimed there were 550,000 members and that 40,000 could be assembled on short notice. By 1868 the Klan was already in steep decline. It had lost much public favor as its violent measures were often used to settle petty local rivalries. By 1871, Forest called upon the Klan to disband as it had become "corrupted with criminals and sadists who were largely advancing private interests."

The modern Klan movement was clearly trying to harness the good will associated with Jesus to further their social agenda. Some under cover research has shown that protestant ministers were well represented in the Klan leadership. They usually served as a Klokard (lecturer) or a Kludd (chaplain). The fact that the methods of the Klan were absolutely abhorrent to the message of Jesus seems to have escaped each and every member of this organization.

Robert's foundation also mounted a number of lawsuits against the Klan in order to break them financially. I had very little to do with this part of his work although I would hear him discussing strategy from time to time.

During most of the time I spent with Robert, he received a steady stream of death threats. One night we heard a rifle shot. In response, he bought a couple of guard dogs and a pair of his staff stayed up through the night armed with shotguns. In his typical manner of doing everything with style, the guard dogs were elegant Irish Setters. I recall that the shotguns were profusely engraved Parkers or L.C. Smiths. These 20 gauge doubles were originally intended for gentlemen on a quail hunt. The dogs were only intended to bark and raise a fuss if an intruder came near. However, these shotguns would be entirely effective if necessary.

Robert had an open door policy. Anyone who had a genuine problem was helped. One day, a farmer contacted him with a request for help in negotiating with the US Department of

Klan Business

Agriculture concerning crop subsidies. Robert met with him several times and had a legal clerk on his staff work with him. Not long after the first meeting Robert called everyone into his room and told us this man was a spy for the Klan. He told us not to reveal this awareness to the man. We were to treat him with the utmost courtesy. Robert went on to resolve the problem concerning the crop subsidies. At the last meeting, the farmer told Robert: "You are the best nigger that I have ever met. I am going to tell them to leave you alone." That was pretty much the end of it. After a time, the threats tapered off and eventually the night time watches were suspended.

Interspersed with these events, Robert took the time to make me familiar with his views on life. In essence, he believed *holiness* is the result of being *whole*. This meant a person needed to be fully functional in all of his or her attributes. These qualities included an uncompromised connection with the creator, a sharp and lively intellect, a brave and loving heart, a strong and vigorous body, including a healthy sexuality. Robert believed that only when all of these qualities are awake and functioning can a relationship with our creator live up to its full potential. By this criterion, I still had some growing to do. Many of my potentials had atrophied from lack of use due to my previously monkish orientation.

Once, Maharishi talked with a small group of us on the topic of celibacy. He said that we each had accumulated personal energy or power and that "If we spent it, it got spent. If we saved it, it got saved." This attitude was found throughout all personal interactions within the TM movement. The first thing that we did when we met someone new was to ask how long he or she had been meditating. Such seniority was the baseline of all future interactions. A miserliness prevailed in the sharing of our spiritual gifts.

Maharishi did not touch. There was a vague sense that, for the most part, humanity and its mess were a malodorous stain on the pristine essence of God. This influence spread within his organization. People were mostly polite and friendly but, for

A Second Look at Jesus

every interaction, the dominant question was whether Maharishi would approve of what we did and how we did it. Personal interactions for their own merit were not common.

In contrast, Robert encouraged me to touch. He taught me to look for meaningfulness in every encounter and circumstance. I was encouraged to touch and be a blessing through the touch of my heart, my mind, and sometimes, my body. It was as though a gift of spiritual life, properly given and properly received in love was a sacrament of the first order. Therefore, such relationships were to be sought and cultivated. Regarding the "loss of energy", Robert assured me that, with a proper attunement, spiritual energy did not deplete upon sharing. It multiplied.

I found it interesting that Robert saw Jesus as a powerful and purposeful being. He pointed out that Jesus had said, "No one is taking my life. I am giving it freely." Jesus, under the guidance of God, was in charge of his agenda and he was going to spend his life in a way that would achieve exactly what was intended. He *chose* to play his part in the drama of his life just as it was divinely orchestrated. This macho view of Jesus was and is a provocative concept to me.

In spite of his refined manners, Robert lived by some very practical, down-home, maxims. For example, he liked to say, "Work your hoe where you are." His point was it would be a mistake to wait for an idea of the perfect circumstance to apply our talent or vocation. It was best to use all abilities whenever and wherever we could.

Robert advised me to commit to truthfulness. He said we do not make real progress in life until we learn to prefer an ugly stinking truth that may challenge our assumptions, to a sweet and perfumed lie that confirms our values.

In the course of many marathon discussions with Robert, I came up with another thought that I still ponder. I had no doubt I was effectively working my way back to my creator. The only unknown was how many companions could I bring with me? Company can make for a more joyous trip.

Klan Business

There is a realization that went along with this insight. I discovered that God realization is not just personal. The realization may start there, but this experience occurs in the context of the entire creation reaching back to its source. My unfolding was not isolated. It was part of a vast dance. One practical implication of this insight was the fact that I resided in the United States of America and within its culture. I could ignore this or not. I decided to pay some attention and act accordingly. Although I had long been a vegetarian, I began to eat whatever food was offered to me. I also began to embrace what is best in the culture of my birth. I saw that any other approach would have been unnecessarily narrow and distinctly unfriendly.

In addition, the United States is overwhelmingly a Christian and Jewish nation. All of our values were formed, or at least influenced, by that fact. What was I going to do about that truth? Ignore it? Also, there was an excellence both subtle and obvious about the way well-interpreted Judaism and Christianity uplifted humankind. I wanted more of that quality in my life.

Although Robert could be something of a snob, I remember that he took a homeless lady into his home for several weeks until she could get a fresh start. She came across his path and he simply did something to help. After that, he also sent some of us out to help at homeless shelters.

That fall Robert purchased the right to glean the remnant of a field of kale and beets that a local farmer was ready to plow under. All of us joined in with harvesting and preserving this produce. We gathered and processed enough beet greens and kale to last for a year or more.

Robert was not a fan of situational ethics. He said we must discover and follow consistent ethical principles. A life lived according to such principles is worth living. That is the only reliable way to orient our life decisions.

Robert would not tolerate idleness. When he found I was just wasting time hanging out with the other workers, he arranged for me to get some work at the local labor pool. He wanted me

A Second Look at Jesus

to recognize the nobility in being productive even if I was just defrosting meat lockers or sweeping floors.

Effectiveness was another discipline Robert recommended to me. He said it is a common problem among the spiritual seekers to become refined to such a point that their life on Earth was weak and ineffectual. The word he used to describe this condition was "effete." He said that we must guard against this.

Once, Robert told me something of his underlying intention when he prepared to perform before an audience. He said he was not an entertainer. Rather, he intended to "rip the beating heart from the chest" of every person present and show it to them. He did not intend to entertain them. He intended to offer them a life-changing experience.

Robert also took it upon himself to sensitize me to classical music. Such music was always playing in the background while we spent time together. At any moment, he might stop and say, "Pay attention." Then he would tell me what the composer was trying to convey and how he was doing it. Over time, I developed an appreciation for classical music, especially the work of J. S. Bach.

Gratitude was an important component in the values Robert tried to cultivate in me. He told me a healthy state of mind includes a constant sense of gratitude for the gift of life. It should be behind all of our thoughts, feelings and actions.

Robert actively composed music during my stay. He also was an enthusiastic promoter of a 19th century composer by the name of Louis Moreau Gottschalk. Robert sometimes offered private concerts. During these gala events, all of us on staff would pitch in to carry off the event successfully. We played the role of servants. He was the lord of the manor.

After a few months, another round of TM awards was offered. Robert asked to see the list of the new awardees. I was no longer the TM Center leader, but I was able to get the information Robert requested. He found to his displeasure that no person of color was included in this new group. He reached out to the local

Klan Business

TM Center to discuss this oversight. He put forward a few names of people whom he thought deserved consideration. He was rebuffed. After some time he made an announcement, he would publicly return his award at the next ceremony. The media began to respond to a press release Robert had made announcing this intent. They were more than ready for such a juicy and controversial story.

A few weeks later Robert was visited by two gentlemen in suits. A short while later I was called to meet them. They were from the FBI. They played a tape and asked me if I could identify the person who spoke. The voice I heard referred to Robert by name, mentioned that he knew what he was doing to embarrass the TM movement and ended with the statement, "I am going to kill that nigger." I had a serious problem. I knew exactly whose voice was on that tape. It belonged to an Indian man I had previously worked with in Switzerland. He was a TM teacher and lived not very far away. I told all this to the FBI.

Soon I was on the phone trying to reach Maharishi in Switzerland. Eventually I spoke with Jerry Jarvis, Maharishi's right hand man at that time. I asked and then I begged Jerry to help me defuse the situation. I have no idea what he actually said to Maharishi or what Maharishi said in response. However, several calls later, I had my answer. No apology or gracious reconciliation would be forthcoming.

I was dumbstruck. It seemed to me that this a very odd response to a very real situation. It appeared callous in the extreme. Personally, Jerry warned me: "Judge not **Lest You Be Judged**." I was devastated.

At that time, the entire web of my relationships and values centered with trust upon my teacher. This turn of events tore that fabric of these relationships wide open. How could my spiritual teacher be indifferent in such a situation? I had held him as a saint, an ideal person. He appeared far ahead of me in meditation practice. I aspired to be like him in every way, but now I wondered. Was I misguided? Were human kindness and individual

A Second Look at Jesus

spiritual insight compatible? One thing was clear; Maharishi had abandoned me. He not did make the effort to explain himself or guide me. I do not think he cared one bit about my distress or the affront to Robert.

I made a choice. I stayed with and supported Robert. I was wounded, but my path forward stretched ahead and I started to move slowly and painfully along that new path.

The end of this conflict was anti-climactic. Robert attended the next TM awards ceremony, but, surprisingly, did not make a scene. Instead, he quietly returned his award by mail. When I asked him about this later, Robert said all of the people at that TM award ceremony had nothing in their lives but TM. He said he would not take that from them. This entire episode left me exhausted and heart-broken. My outer life-path was in shambles.

In the aftermath of this experience, Robert counselled me. One of the things he said was that, while my spiritual experiences were genuine and valuable, I needed to "take a second look at Jesus" because I was "missing something important." Over the succeeding years, I have spent considerable time and effort doing exactly this.

As you may imagine, I have given considerable thought to understanding Maharishi's management style. In my opinion, he did not want a successor. He told us as much. He did not want anyone in his organization who would show too much initiative. Normally a leader trains his students to acquire the experience and wisdom necessary to carry on when that leader was gone. They are prepared to pick up where their teacher had left off and continue to build. That was not Maharishi's plan. Instead, he wanted the thousands of hours of videotapes he had made to carry on for him when he was gone. His successors were only to be caretakers. In this context, a genuine and creative successor would be a threat. Maharishi had a dread someone would tamper with and try to improve upon his work. Perhaps he had Christianity in mind as an example of tinkering by disciples. The

Klan Business

videotapes were considered a guarantee that his teachings would be preserved intact and without distortion. Only the future will show the wisdom of this approach.

Now might be as good a time as any to explain my understanding of illusion. It has to do with perception. Our senses gather information, but it is our mind that puts together the experience we call perception. What most don't know is that perception requires our active support. For example, movie film presents a series of still images that imply a sequence of action. The mind *perceives* movement by filling in the spaces between the series of images. This filling in process amounts to seeing something that is not there. This is illusion. Our mind only perceives a small fraction of the input the eyes offer. We literally see what we want to see. Our involvement in perception is our "buy in" to this world and accounts for our attachment to it.

This "buy in" is equally true for trusting a genuine friend or some convoluted Bible doctrine that has caught our fancy. This is the essence of faith, whether well placed or not.

The insight of regular, effective meditation brings a new dynamic. The screen of our mind begins to unfold and come more clearly into view. In due course, it becomes clear that the mind is not just personal, but is an extension of the divine mind. Under the influence of this larger context, the images projected upon our mind and our interaction with them become both more accurate and less engrossing.

Over time, we may come to see that not just our perception, but also the whole creation is created afresh each instant. The result of this perspective is we become freer in the midst of everyday life.

Therefore, I finally understood how unimportant I was to Maharishi. The evidence had been there all along. I had just ignored it. I was literally dis-illusioned, but I cannot be entirely ungrateful. I had received a rare opportunity to learn a truly effective method of meditation. I had seen up close what it takes to inspire and organize a large enterprise. I had been allowed to

A Second Look at Jesus

participate in and learn from a fascinating assignment in India. I also found that even admirable people are not perfect. We all have clay feet. Necessarily, personal responsibility reasserted itself within me and I turned away from the TM organization. For all this and more, I thank you, Maharishi.

A few months later, I got a phone call from John Deere, a member of Maharishi's entourage. His first words were, "Maharishi has heard that you have gone a little bit this way and that." For a moment I froze. John had spoken in code words, using a common phrase that Maharishi spoke when he was disparaging someone who had gone "off the reservation." In that moment I knew Maharishi would accept me back. All I had to do was humble myself; ignore the recent events surrounding Robert and the death threat, along with my sense of personal ethics. If John had said, "Let's talk this through and sort it out." I would have been happy to try, but that was not offered. The offer was limited and clear. The response needed to be equally clear. I was not willing to pay the price that Maharishi required. I paused and then said, "John, I simply don't want to talk to you."

A few months later, Robert suggested I spread my wings a little and see what else the world had to offer me. I still meditated every day. My inner life had sustained me in my crisis with Maharishi and had not been diminished in any way. The importance of this is that I was now sure that Maharishi did not own my relationship with God. God and I did.

I rented a room in a house near Syracuse University. I shared it with some foreign exchange students from Columbia and Brazil. Robert advocated a robust engagement with people and cultures outside my personal experience. These new friends were exotic and everything they did was robust. I remained somewhat shy, but engage I did. I learned to listen. I learned to converse. I learned to be a better friend. I learned to dance and I also learned a little about romance.

During this time, I met Diane. She was a refined, intelligent and straight-talking girl with an attractive cinnamon-brown

Klan Business

skin. I had a hard time keeping away from her. Whenever we were near, I kept my arm around her to draw her close.

This was when I had my first *personal* experience with racial bigotry. Sometimes when we were out, black men would try to get a private word with Diane. They wanted to know if I was "satisfying her." In fact, my relationship with Diane was quite chaste and sweet, but that was not the business of strangers.

I mourn the lack of a truly satisfying culmination of our dreams of interracial harmony and dynamism. It seems to me the path has been painfully clear for a very long time. If we can rise to the challenge of our humanity and perceive the "pearl of great worth" within each other, we will live in a transfigured world.

As summer advanced, I was ready to move on. I took a road trip, heading south. Along the way, I stopped at Antioch and visited with some freshman students who were living in my old dorm. They wanted to know my story and I gave them an abbreviated version. They seemed to appreciate what I had to say. By the time I finished telling my story, I felt very old, at age twenty-five. From there, I proceeded to New Orleans.

Chapter Twelve

Taking A Second Look at Jesus

Hayah

My southern migration was not a vacation. The first thing I found in New Orleans was a job. I started as a day laborer, unloading boxcars and cleaning cargo ship holds. A little later, I was hired to teach secondary school science at O. Perry Walker High School. I was astonished at the amount of money I was earning. Some of the other teachers complained about the pay, but I was more than satisfied. I loved that job and all went well enough until the first grading period arrived. I gave failing grades to the students who had refused to work. This caused major problems with the management. Apparently, there was a quota for failing grades and I had far surpassed it. From this point, my teaching career started to become more problematic. I knew I was more than competent. I had tested in the 86th percentile of all Louisiana teachers in my field. The teaching itself was a joy. I loved to explain how things worked. Discipline and motivation were a problem for me. I was accustomed to teaching

Taking A Second Look at Jesus

where the mind and soul of everyone present was raised to a very high pitch of receptivity. This was simply not the case in public schools. I tried to improvise, but to a great degree chaos won out. The disorderly and angry students spoiled the experience for others and I did not know how to stop them.

As a further learning experience, I decided to live in a poor, black neighborhood near the Mississippi River. Tulane University was about ten blocks directly inland from me. The Corps of Engineers had a facility on the river just behind my house. I was paying a very modest rent for a shotgun cottage at the end of Pitt Street. It was about the size and proportion of a boxcar. This type of house earned its name for its long and narrow shape. The name was based upon the concept that a single shotgun blast could enter the front door and exit the back door while making a clean sweep of any occupants. I was paying reduced rent in exchange for the labor of renovating the house. The construction was very primitive. The walls were nothing but a little framing and vertical planks. Narrow strips of wood were nailed over the gaps between those planks. The interior walls were horizontal boards. That was it. Fresh air was not a problem. Plenty of wind got through gaps in those boards.

After my experience with Robert, I had a clear case of prejudice *in favor* of black people. I was fascinated with them individually and collectively. I had discovered that their personal experience of insult and degradation had often stripped away much of the false pride that is so commonly an element of the human construct. What remained was the real thing; a nobility of the soul. With the corrosive effects of racial hostility bearing upon them, many either broke or developed an extraordinary strength and spiritual wisdom. The mindless mediocrity I often saw in the white culture was not so much in evidence within the black culture. It seemed that the highs were higher and lows were lower.

My black friends also had the advantage of a certain clarity and scepticism regarding the American dream. They knew from experience that life could have an ugly underside. As a result,

A Second Look at Jesus

they tended to be more awake to the real opportunities of value: friends, family, and spiritual life as they presented themselves.

Having black friends and lovers did much to help me become a more complete person. They drew somewhat different qualities from me as I tried to do my part in these relationships. Authenticity, spontaneity and careful attention to human feelings were called upon at all times. Meeting these expectations benefited me greatly.

One of the best discoveries I made in New Orleans was a wise old man who lived less than a block from my home. Walter was our neighborhood Bible scholar. He had gotten a hold of a Bible concordance. With its help Walter and would compose tracts that he would type out with two fingers on an ancient typewriter. He took great delight in bringing me into his modest home and sharing his latest work. Walter would offer me a glass of water; wait for me to read his essay and then say: "Okay, now feed me." He wanted to know what spiritual treasure *I* had found that week. What a fine concept this was.

Walter was remarkably free of concern about divisive doctrinal assertions. He just wanted to share insights that would be of practical and sustaining value. He respectfully left it to me to assemble the big picture as it applied to my view of life. Walter was, for me, a vastly more effective instrument of biblical teaching and inspiration than the bombastic, famous and wealthy ministers who constantly clamored for acclaim.

The concordance was and is a remarkable tool for Bible study. Long before Google or the Echelon surveillance system, it provided for key word searches. It used the words of the *King James* Version of the Bible as the keys. Perfected in the late 19th century by James Strong, it references each and every word in the Bible. They are placed in alphabetical order. Each occurrence of a word is quoted in the context of the relevant phrase and identified as to book, chapter, and verse. After this is, a reference number corresponds to the Greek or Hebrew word used in the original text. This could be used to locate a translation of that word in the

Taking A Second Look at Jesus

dictionaries found in the back of the volume. Overall, the concordance is an amazingly effective study tool.

What my friend would do was read the Bible until something special caught his attention. Then, using the concordance, he would look up the original meanings of the key words. Note here: there are sometimes several valid meanings for each word. Next Walter would reflect on the ways he had seen those values played out in his life and the lives of those he knew. Here the advantage of a long and observant life played an important part. Finally, he would write the description of what he knew, from both personal experience and guidance, would work best to build a better life. He did this every day and shared the product with his friends. What could be better? All that he asked was that I reciprocate in kind. He said; "OK, now feed me." At that time, I was unprepared, but I resolved to become the kind of man who feeds others.

In my own way, I was starting to respond to Robert's suggestion that I "give Jesus a second look." I spent some time traveling around town to visit various churches. Therefore, I had my first experience with Christian charismatic practices. I went to a large Assembly of God Church and, at one point in the service, most of the people opened up to an attunement of the Holy Spirit. The effect was spiritual pandemonium. The congregation was speaking in tongues, dancing, swaying, and falling on the ground. I can still perceive the animating force behind these phenomena.

What I experienced within, as people were acting out around me, was like being in a translucent cloud. The inner light associated with the charismatic experience is non-directional, diffuse and somewhat opalescent. It also has a distinctly sweet quality. It is intelligence and awareness without duality. There was no hint of a separation of subject and object. The experience I am describing was/is wonderfully nourishing and refreshing. The spiritual blessing is absorbed, as if by osmosis. What we were experiencing that day was like the spiritual nursery for the first sprouting of creation. This is the earliest act in which the unmanifest,

A Second Look at Jesus

which exists beyond time and space, becomes pregnant with all the possibilities of creation.

This is movingly described in the opening verses of the Gospel of John. Over all, it is a wonderful attunement to life. I am reminded of two references. One is the description of a certain stage in meditation as described by an anonymous 14th century English monk. He wrote a book of his experiences called The Cloud of Unknowing. The other that comes to mind is the many references Apostle Paul made to spiritual milk.

I will venture a guess that not many in the congregation were likely to see the validity of the path I had followed up to that point. Nonetheless, I, along with my eastern spiritual teachers, could easily see and appreciate the validity of finding God through Jesus. There is explanation in the famous Bhagavad Gita that spiritual liberation can be found by meditation on the being of a God-realized teacher. Here is how it is expressed there: Loving someone who loves God will bring both of you nearer to God. Loving God in someone who is intimate with God is even better. Jesus was much loved and respected by the *Yogis* I met. They consider him one of them. Some of these *Yogis* have looked into the Bible and these have found traces of harmony between their teachings and those of Jesus. For example, in Matthew 11:30 Jesus is quoted as saying: "For **my yoke is easy** to bear, and the burden I give you is light." The yogis note that that the word *Yoga* means yoke. Another favorite quote was from Matthew 6:33; "But **seek ye first the kingdom of God**, and his righteousness; and all these things shall be added unto you."

Christians, on the other hand, generally have little idea what they are missing by refusing fellowship with those outside their immediate religious family. In adopting this posture, they are getting themselves unnecessarily lodged in some very constrained and unspiritual positions. In fact, Christians are onto something wonderful. I just wish they would appreciate it more thoroughly and give the rest of humanity the credit it is due. It is perfectly

Taking A Second Look at Jesus

possible to learn spiritual lessons from others while remaining faithful to the path Jesus maps out.

Here is what I mean by appreciation. My time in meditation practice and training has enabled me to better personify an unblinking observation of life. This was made possible by a simple method of meditation I practiced. My Christian family did not bring this gift to my life. I am sure they would have if they could have. However, the fact of the matter is I benefited from the spiritual traditions of India and the Middle East. I am profoundly thankful for what I have learned and I do not mind admitting my debt of gratitude to my eastern teachers.

When I examined elements of my human nature, I was able to discover the most precious element in my life was seeping around the edge of a door, which **I was holding shut**! From there my path became so much clearer. I backed away from that door and the spirit of life flooded in. Freed from my habit of door holding, I found employment that is more interesting. I became an explorer. In this circumstance, true joy and genuine self-mastery became possible.

In contrast, it might be instructive to look briefly into the cultural phenomenon of Cargo Cults. The cultural anthropologist, Margaret Meade, and others have examined the reaction of the indigenous South Sea cultures to modern consumer goods and they found some interesting insights.

During World War II the US military logistical units had the job of delivering mountains of materiel to our fighting men throughout the Pacific. It was customary to enlist local people to assist in the unloading and carrying of those supplies to the combat units. Invariably, these local workers were paid with a portion of the supplies that they moved. In this way, they were introduced to the wonders of canned peaches, Spam, and Velveeta cheese. After the Japanese surrendered, no effort was made to repatriate most of the unused supplies. They were simply abandoned. This was, of course, a windfall for the indigenous people! Eventually, however all of these supplies were consumed too.

A Second Look at Jesus

What happened next is instructive. The cultural anthropologists documented a phenomenon that they term the "Cargo Cults." The local people had no idea about the culture, hard work, science, engineering and other qualities that made these consumer goods possible. All that they knew was that the goods arrived on ships or were dropped from airplanes. Accordingly, they set up altars with model planes and ships mostly fashioned out of empty tin cans and prayed to God to bring more supplies! Of course, this did no good, but in their minds, it *should* have worked. The practice persists to this day in some quarters in spite of a lack of results.

The lesson for us Christians is the devastating truth that at least some of what we are doing might *not* be very different from the people praying for canned peaches in New Guinea. Of course, the more successful churches have some of the more effective spiritual practices as part of the mix of their program. It seems to me the Christian reform movements of the past 2,000 years were all about trying to add back or reemphasize the elements that actually make a a difference to our spiritual life. Therefore, two question remain. Are we going to be satisfied with commemorating the ideas and accomplishments of Jesus and Paul? Are we really doing all that we can to fully develop our status as children of God?

The problem is both the effective and ineffective practices might seem to be indistinguishable. It reminds me of the old saying about the relationship between sales and advertising. Eighty-five percent of advertising is off-target and does no good whatsoever in causing sales to occur. The remaining fifteen percent of advertising is very successful and more than justifies the entire advertising budget. The problem is, most often no one is sure what parts of the advertising campaign are effective!

I do not believe this has always been the case. In the beginning, the written word for Christians, the *New Testament*, did not exist. We Jesus lovers were simply seeking to personify the full stature of God as Jesus had shown us. There are indications

Taking A Second Look at Jesus

we were sometimes doing a decent job of it too. This is the kind of Christian I wanted to be.

Some disparage non-Christian religions, but I do not think Jesus would approve of this practice. I am convinced that if Jesus, Moses and Isaiah could meet at the same time and place with Buddha, Mohammed and Krishna, they would not be disrespectful to each other. I believe, instead, they would love and appreciate each other. Further, they would have shared some interesting insights about how they each were able to work within their own time and culture to unlock the spiritual potential of the people who came to them.

Reflexive mistrust of unfamiliar spiritual traditions and cultures is not helpful. If we dismiss the practices and beliefs of others out of hand, we might miss something that could be helpful in our own life. Jesus was, after all, a master of spiritual potential. He said he expected us to accomplish all that he did and more. Should we not get on with that project, using any tools that are available and likely to prove effective?

Continuing with my exploration of Christianity, the next Sunday, I went to a very small, black Baptist Church where it was the practice for everyone to sing a hymn and then give a brief testimonial. I tried to honor their tradition. I did my best rendering of "Swing Low Sweet Chariot." Then I gave a vague reference to my spiritual birthday years before at Wheeler's Ranch. I was short on details since I did not want to give offense. A description of the sweat lodge and yoga on the tree stump would have been out of place. They were lovely people and I wanted to join in with them, not upset their program. Anyone who has not spent some time in traditional black churches is missing something important. A full-blooded affirmation of life with God is typically on display. You will find evidence of the moral courage of Martin Luther King. You will find the kind of life-friendly Biblical wisdom as espoused by T. D. Jakes. You will also find passionate, soaring spiritual artistry as displayed by Mahalia Jackson and Aretha Franklin. There is a revelation waiting in these churches that should not be missed.

A Second Look at Jesus

During this time, I ran an experiment. I wondered how stable my inner attunement was. Was it fragile and subject to rapid decay? Would it fall apart without constant tending and refreshment from daily meditation? I took a month off my usual meditation schedule.

To my surprise, not much changed. The cumulative effect of my spiritual practices had taken root. The change of my inner architecture was an enduring attribute of my life. I resumed my daily practice, knowing my status was not artificial and that future meditation was advancing me on a path of exciting new vistas.

One of the topics of interest was the role that translation plays in understanding scripture. Jesus almost certainly spoke and taught in Aramaic. By this time, Hebrew was no longer spoken in everyday use. Aramaic, similar to Hebrew, was adopted by the Jews during their time as captives in Babylon and was the lingua franca of the Middle Eastern culture at the time of Jesus. Greek and Latin were spoken in connection with the colonizing forces of those two empires and were unlikely to have been used for something as intimate and subtle as spiritual salvation.

Aramaic and Hebrew words are open to a number of equally valid understandings. Tradition, the intention of the speaker and the context of the surrounding words, all serve as guides to the meaning grasped. This language group lends itself well to reflection, poetry and word play with intentional double meanings and other significant content. Greek, on the other hand, is much more precise and definite in its meaning. Greek language lends itself more easily to distinctions and disputation.

Except for a few words, our *New Testament* scriptures are entirely written in Greek. What this means to me is the Christianity we know today amounts to the teachings of Jesus as understood by Greeks or as condensed for Greeks. In other words, the Greek language a filter that unavoidably removes some of the original intent and retains only selected meanings for our use. Jesus often referred to hidden meanings "for those who have ears to hear."

Taking A Second Look at Jesus

This would be very true in the Aramaic language. Aramaic and Hebrew are rich in poetic ambiguity. In Greek, much of the spectrum of those alternative meanings is no longer available to us. I concluded that my understanding the intended meanings of the teachings of Jesus would be advanced if I could learn Aramaic.

If the message of Jesus were primarily intellectual, then the Greek language would have been the perfect vehicle for his message. This clarity of distinction is the strength of Greek. If not, then we were in some trouble from our early days onward.

This should not be construed as a criticism of Greek philosophy and culture. The Greek experiment in creative thought has become an irreplaceable pillar of our civilization. It is full of powerful ideas that we simply should not do without. Likewise, the Eastern Orthodox Church shows a subtle and splendid appreciation Jesus and his teachings. I treasure its influence upon my spiritual life.

However, the message of Jesus holds the greatest potential if it is as authentic, and as accurately interpreted as we can manage. For this, at least a little understanding of Aramaic and its contemporary Mediterranean culture should be very helpful.

The church that operated out of Jerusalem, Damascus and Baghdad has always used Aramaic as their ecclesiastic language. Originally, this church followed James, the brother of Jesus, who led the Jesus movement from Jerusalem after the death of Jesus. These churches once used the early Aramaic language Gospels that were favored by the Jerusalem church: *Gospel of the Nazarenes, Gospel of the Hebrews and Gospel of the Ebonites*. These Bibles have since become lost to us. Instead, the Eastern Church made an effort (a possibly misguided effort) to harmonize their teachings with the "Western Churches" that operated out of Constantinople and Rome. At the same time, the "Eastern Church" adopted an Aramaic translation of the Gospel accounts of Matthew, Mark, Luke and John. This Aramaic text of the Bible came to be known as the *Peshitta* or "Pure Text." While doing this translation from Greek to Aramaic, I believe the Eastern Church

A Second Look at Jesus

intentionally incorporated the idiom and vocabulary of the earlier Aramaic language Gospels along with any Aramaic oral traditions they maintained into their rendering of the *Peshitta* text. This is the reason I value the *Peshitta* version of the gospels as a more precise and original source of guidance than the Greek does and Latin Bible manuscripts.

This branch of Christianity was administered mostly outside of the Roman Empire and, at its peak in the 13th century, had tens of millions of members throughout the Middle East, China, Mongolia and India. For a time Christians in this region benefited from the protection of Mongol leaders. Later, when the Mongols converted to Islam, protection turned to persecution. These numbers were much reduced by the persecutions of Timor Leng, known as Tamerlane and his successors. When the Mongols were overthrown in China, Christians were nearly exterminated as a "foreign religion."

Today the successor to this tradition is the Assyrian Church. It is very small, but they have kept much of their perspective intact. I believe they have much to teach us. This church is the Christian group presently suffering so much due to reactionary Islamic persecutions in Syria and Iraq.

What follows is the Lord's Prayer in Aramaic followed by a revealing translation by Dr. Klotz in his book <u>Prayers of the Cosmos</u> (HarperCollins, publisher)

Abwoon d'bwashmaya
Nethqadash schmakh
Tey tey malkuthakh
Nehwey tzevyanach aykannahd'bwashmaya aph b'arha.
Hawvlan lachma d'sunqanan yaomana.
Washboqlan khaubayn (wakhtahanyn)
Aykana daph shbwoqlan l'khayyabayn.
Wela tahlan l'nesyuna
Ela patzan min bisha.
Metol dilakhie malkutha wahayla wateshbukhta l'alam almin.

Taking A Second Look at Jesus

Ameyn

Starting with the Aramaic text, a truer translation to English might be:

Oh Birther of the cosmos

Focus your light within us-make it useful
Create your reign of unity now-

Your one desire then acts with ours,
as in all light, so in all forms.

Grant what we need each day in bread and insight.

Loose the cords of mistakes binding us,
as we release the strands we hold
of others' guilt.

Don't let surface things deceive us.
But free us from what holds us back.

From you is born all ruling will,
the power and life to do,
the song that beautifies all,
from age to age it renews.

Truly, power to these statements-
may they be the ground from which all
my actions grow:
Amen.[3]

Is this not food for thought?
With the idea of immersing myself in the Aramaic culture, I hired an international employment agency, based in New Orleans,

A Second Look at Jesus

to see if I could get a teaching job in one of those small towns in Syria and Iraq where there is still a sizable Aramaic speaking population. I was disappointed that nothing practical was found.

I investigated a little further and learned that the usual pathway to learning Aramaic was through Biblical Hebrew. Accordingly, I enrolled for a beginning course in Hebrew at Harvard Divinity School that next summer. While there, I also intended to look up Diane, who had moved to Boston. We had been corresponding and I wanted to find out where our relationship might go if given a chance.

Before I left, I had to consider a suggestion that Diane had made: If I was going to make a sincere approach to Christianity, I should consider relinquishing my attachment to the other spiritual paths I had followed. After some reflection, I brought the trunk that contained nearly all of my books, papers, notes, correspondence and mementos relating to my time in India and with Maharishi into the back yard. I took out two pictures and an address book. Then I burned every remaining scrap. I resolved to be as whole-hearted and as open as possible for whatever lay ahead.

Chapter Thirteen

Seeking Jesus the Jew

Hayah

For nearly three months, in the summer of 1978, I resided at Harvard Divinity School. While there, I had Hebrew for breakfast, Hebrew for lunch, Hebrew for dinner and then a little more Hebrew for a bedtime snack. The hard-working teaching assistants kept shovelling and I kept chewing. Eventually, we could read verses from the *Old Testament* with some proficiency. Meaning was more elusive. Slow and laborious dictionary work was needed as our vocabulary was limited and our grasp of grammar was tentative. Nonetheless, we got a good start in Hebrew in a remarkably short time.

One of the things I most wanted to learn was the correct pronunciation of the name of God used by the Hebrews. I wanted to use it for meditation. I was surprised and disappointed to learn that this was considered more or less impossible.

Originally, Hebrew was written only with consonants. The reader had to provide the vowels from his memory. It was not

A Second Look at Jesus

until well after the time of Jesus that notations were added between the consonants to indicate vowels. The problem is, by this time, it was customary to avoid saying the name of God aloud to avoid profaning it. This is called the "Ineffable (inexpressible) Name" doctrine. This teaching apparently came from a mistranslation in 257 BC of Leviticus 24:16 into the Greek language Septuagint Bible. The Greek translation says: "And he that **names the name of the Lord**, let him die." In the original Hebrew, it says; "Anyone who **blasphemes the name** of the LORD is to be put to death." There is a world of difference between these two sentences.

For generations, the temple priests had taught that ordinary people were unworthy to call upon that name. Instead, only a small, elite among the Temple priests claimed to be worthy to carry on the direct knowledge and use of this word. Under their rule, the use of *YHWH* came to be authorized only once a year and under very restricted circumstances. This sacred word was only supposed to be pronounced aloud by the high priest and then, only during the yearly celebration of Yom Kippur, the Day of Atonement. At the climax of that ceremony the high priest, far removed from the people and standing alone in the most holy and remote portion of the temple, would pronounce it once. In fact, he was never heard as musical instruments were also reaching at a crescendo at that same moment.

My teacher told me that after the second defeat by the Romans in 135 CE and the subsequent exile of the Jews, a consensus was reached that God was angry and it may even be dangerous to attract the direct attention of their creator. Even thinking of that sacred and powerful name would just invite wrath. Instead, synonyms such as Lord (*Adoni*) were substituted for *YHWH*. Thus, within a few generations, the direct use of *YHWH* and even the knowledge of how to pronounce it disappeared.

By contrast, it seems that during the times of Moses and in the early days of Israel, all Israel carried *YHWH* on their breath.

Seeking Jesus the Jew

I will sacrifice some delicacy for clarity by saying that this doctrine associated with the unworthiness of ordinary people to pronounce the name of God is perverse. It is the creed of slaves. This teaching of excessive restrictions on this name of God has had the effect of reducing the strength and clarity of the individual spiritual life of the ordinary people. In this diminished state of personal experience, the people of Israel would be less confident within themselves and more inclined to be dependent upon the priestly class for some sort of relationship with God. This magnified the importance of priestly and temple-related activities. It also raised the importance of the city of Jerusalem and it's King as a focus of power and authority. Spiritual experience based upon calling upon the sacred name of God was no longer available for anyone to have an immediate effect and from any location. I believe that this turn of events has proven disastrous in every way. The marginalization of religion has been a direct result of this emasculation.

The Christian Bible has evidence in John 17:26 that Jesus took another path. He said; "And I have declared unto them *thy name*, and will declare *it*: that the love wherewith thou hast loved me may be in them, and I in them." This quote clearly shows that Jesus, acting contrary to the trend of his time, not only knew how to pronounce this name of God and used the name himself. Further, Jesus taught the name of God to his disciples. What happened since then? That question is hard to answer with clarity and precision. Regardless, it appears that today, no one, Jew or Christian is entirely certain what the correct pronunciation is for that name of God. I consider this a loss of great magnitude.

Although actual meditation on this name of God has been discouraged among the Jewish faith for a very long time, I suggest that God and we might be better served if we use this name and others like it again. I am not proposing profane use or casual use. However, in the context of teaching with a sacred intent, as we have here, I believe its use should be both permitted and recommended.

A Second Look at Jesus

One reason I have suggested the use of *Hayah* as a vehicle of discovery prayer is, unlike *YHWH*, its pronunciation has never been in question. Another reason to incorporate *Hayah* into our lives is that its effect is wonderfully benign and nourishing. It is about perfect as a beginning practice. In addition, for serious spiritual exploration simpler is better. The traditional name of God is an important and profound sacred word but it is somewhat long and complex for efficiency in spiritual transformation, especially in the early days of practice.

Concerning the mystery of the pronunciation of the word *YHWH*, I should report there has recently been a resurgent interest in recovering the original word[4]. As an experienced consumer of sacred words, I can also report that many of the proposed pronunciations of *YHWH* do not function very well as a spiritual tool. Frankly, some of the proposed versions have the resonant qualities of a brick. Others show promise. I have been following this study for some time and have tried to use both academic plausibility and spiritual discernment to arrive at a worthwhile and trustworthy result.

I am now reasonably confident that *Yahuweh* is a good and useful recreation of the traditional Hebrew name of God. I pronounce it Ya Hoo WaeeH. The first syllable is pronounced like the first syllable of "*Yu*mmy." The second syllable is pronounced like the word "*who*." The final syllable is pronounced like the word "*way*." If this is not an exact recreation, it is at least a very good start.

My pronunciation is not in full conformity with the consensus opinion of scholars. Many agree that the first vowel should be an "*a*" as I do. A minority prefer an *e* sound as found in *e*ffort. In general, scholars believe that the "*u*" vowel should be nearly or completely silent. Some think the final "*e*" sound should be pronounced like the beginning vowel of the word *e*ffort. I am sure that they have evidence to support their opinions. All that I can say is that their versions of YHWH do not sing, as they should to justify all the fuss this sacred word has raised over the years.

Seeking Jesus the Jew

I have tried in prayer every pronunciation scholars have proposed and I have found the pronunciation *Yahuweh* to meet and exceed my expectations. It is a luxury vehicle for spiritual access. Its effect upon me also reflects well the character of God as described in the Old Testament.

Anyone who engages on a path intended to lead to intimacy with the creator is likely to hear the *Old Testament* claim that "No man can see the face of God and Live" (Exodus 33:20). This outcome is commonly offered up as if it is something bad, something to be feared. Nothing could be further from the truth. We all die of something. Annihilation by God is highly desirable. There is nothing more sad than a long, uneventful, and superficial life. Nothing is more desirable than a profoundly appreciated death. Death is our moment of truth.

In fact, physical death is not a likely outcome of a successful spiritual quest. What *does* happen is our identity, our identification with our limitations, is shattered. Then, in the aftermath, we carry on with a hybrid existence. We find ourselves at once always and everywhere while simultaneously fond of a good beverage and quality conversation.

My time at Harvard was not entirely taken up with lofty spiritual matters. We students were invited to listen to guest lecturers and attend receptions. The well-moneyed assurance of that place was a lesson unto itself. Everyone and everything was first class in every way. I am thankful for the opportunity to learn Hebrew and see a well-executed business in the thought industry.

I was unable to afford further academic study after my summer course, so my pursuit of the Aramaic knowledge was put on hold. After summer school, I got a job as a mechanic at the Ford dealership and focused on other things for some time.

I discovered, with considerable regret, that Diane had lost all romantic interest in me. She wanted me to visit her thriving Apostolic Faith Church. That was all. The church was located in near-by Somerville and had some interesting things going on within. They were Pentecostal, scripturally conservative, and

A Second Look at Jesus

quite disciplined. Their minister kept a firm hand on everything. The members of his church were young, having been mostly recruited while attending college. The congregation was also racially integrated although the white members were in a clear minority.

The racial aspect is interesting because, according to their rendering of church history, the modern charismatic movement was initiated from an unexpected spiritual event led by a black preacher at a mission church on Azusa Street in Los Angeles in 1906. That first "charismatic" congregation was racially mixed, and the original Pentecostal movement was remarkably free of racial prejudice.

Race only became a problem later, when the movement tried to spread. At this time, racial prejudice was rampant among the public and mixing of the races was even criminalized to a great degree through a system of laws designed to prevent interracial exchanges and enforce social taboos. These were called "Jim Crow" laws. On the theory that racism was a spiritual disease that could only be cured by the Holy Spirit, getting racists into these meetings was of great importance to the early Pentecostals.

This was seen as a "Catch 22" situation that called for a tactical adjustment. On a friendly and voluntary basis, the white Pentecostals split into the Assembly of God Church and the black Pentecostals became the Apostolic Faith Church. Today, the racism that caused this split has receded, but the churches remain separate. Fortunately, interracial harmony among all Pentecostals endures to this day.

These folks believed in full-immersion baptism. The feeling and attunement of that experience is wonderfully expressed by the old Negro spiritual hymn "Wade in the Water." Unlike the practice of mystics who fully intend to be "swept away" by current, these prospective converts keep contact with the river bottom as they approach the baptizer. Even when the one baptized is swept off his feet and immersed, the baptizer is standing and firmly in control. This spirituality is intended to enrich, but not

Seeking Jesus the Jew

upset life too much. The mind and intellect keep a firm grip most of the time. I am not disparaging this more staid approach to God. I am simply trying to be accurate. In truth, I found this form of worship to be quite beautiful and full of significance.

A key point of doctrine and practice for the church I attended was they were not Trinitarians. They viewed the trinity of the Father, Son and Holy Spirit as a useful concept, but not a viable approach to personal experience. Instead, they taught converts to call on the name of Jesus. They taught us the person of Jesus has the access point for all aspects of the trinity. We were taught to *tarry* (wait) in prayer in the *upper room* of the church, calling on the name of Jesus in imitation of the apostles who did something similar after the departure of Jesus. I tried it. It worked.

The Holy Spirit found me and I had an encounter with the risen Christ. At the same time, something broke loose within me and I experienced that gift of *glossolalia* or speaking in tongues. I still treasure and draw upon this experience today.

At this church, I also took notice of a practice now common among many Christians who refer to the entire Bible as "The Word of God." This use or possible misuse of that expression can be construed as true in one following sense. The ancient Hebrew writing practice used no punctuation or separation between words. Therefore, THEWHOLEBIBLEWOULDHAVELOOKEDLIKETHIS, or, more correctly, SHTKLDKLVHDLWLBBLHWHT, since vowels were not written and reading is done from right to left. In this sense, the entire Bible literally is one word. I agree this would let someone honestly refer to the Bible as The Word of God, but I do not consider this the original, primary or most useful meaning of that expression.

Today, the expression "The Word of God," is also commonly taken to mean that God speaks truthfully and is faithful in keeping the promises found within the Bible. I would reply that truth can be found in the Bible, but uninspired and uninformed reading can also yield untruth. Those promises found in the Bible are fulfilled for those who are in genuine communion with God. In such a state, we are then inclined to pray for only those blessings in harmony with God's larger perspective. For others, this is orientation less true. Dilettantes and the ego-driven are on their own. The Deity is not bound by human social, literary or legal expectations. Rather, it is our job to discover the blessings that the *creator has in mind* for us and accept them.

My church believed that the Bible was "The Inerrant Word of God." We were told what to believe and then we were expected to reorder our inner life to conform as necessary. This amounted to reverse engineering from result to cause. This approach was the exact opposite of what had worked so well for me during the previous seven years. An intent to be open to the Holy Spirit helped, but overall, I did not find indoctrination to be a very effective approach to God. I expect that I would have had even less success if I had not previously practiced meditation for several years. Sometimes the Spirit suggested that my leaders did not know what they were talking about. That was problematic.

I enjoyed sharing with that church community and found a rich experience there. However, the extended doctrine that came as part of the complete package began to trouble me. First, there was the firm belief that unless someone bought into their doctrine in every particular, that person's destiny was in peril. I doubted this. It seemed to me that their beliefs included a mixture of truths and misunderstandings. For some time I was happy to simply focus on their virtues and the other benefits of associating with this good church. Eventually, however, it became clear their assertion of certainty extended into the belief that only we *true believers* had access to the saving power of God. I knew this was not true. Our pastor was even in the habit of slandering non-Christian spiritual paths from time to time. I would not have objected to informed, respectful, and thoughtful criticisms. I would have found them helpful. What I heard instead was a flippant dismissal of other spiritual paths. It just seemed like a cheap shot and I found it offensive.

Seeking Jesus the Jew

Eventually, I found I could not be a party to this injustice any longer. That day I went forward on an altar call. When the minister asked me, what I wanted him to pray about, I told him. I said that, in my experience, the Holy Spirit was at work in all religions, not just Christianity. That did the trick. He pointed to the door and said, "Get out." I did.

I understand that my perspective made my pastor queasy. I wish that he had kept me around for a while so that we could have spoken together. I was not saying that all spiritual paths are the same. There are differences. I believe that the truth embodied by Jesus will benefit every living being if they were exposed to him. Still, there is no excuse for arrogance and bad manners. Respect of those who differ from us pays great dividends. If we want to communicate effectively with someone, the first step is to discover what they love and the very best they have to offer. That will get the conversation going on the right note.

If given the opportunity I would also have gone on to explain something like this: the spirit found through a number of religious teachers was somewhat flavored by them. Just as when choosing between tea, lemon water, limewater, or sugar water, the truly important content, refreshing water, remains the same. Only the flavor and certain nutritional values vary.

I was in that church to learn about their declared topic: Jesus. The preacher's comments about the worthlessness of other teachings were not only wrong, but also out of order. I wish he had stuck to presenting Jesus and simply done a good job of that. I aspire to a humble and friendly relationship with all I do not yet know. I am bothered when those in authority act as though they know where God is not.

In contrast to the closed Christian system taught at that church, I believe in an open system in which Jesus is understood, not only for his spiritual qualities, but also in the context of his humanity and his environment. Jesus offers me a path to intimacy with God. Jesus is, for me, irreplaceable. He is a food that provides an important, nourishment in my spiritual life. He also

A Second Look at Jesus

demonstrates for me an ideal scope of action that should follow the establishment of a genuine relationship with God.

I see Jesus, as a superlative example of the inherent human potential for intimacy with God. He is unique in the *degree* of that intimacy and with his *faithful expression* of YHWH. He put himself "on the line" to a remarkable degree. He is not just a philosopher or a spiritual guide. He is a force to be reckoned with. He *proved* that he cares about our torment.

Nonetheless, other teachers from other spiritual traditions can be acknowledged for their insights and accomplishments without diminishing Jesus. Nothing about the life and witness of Jesus invalidates the life and witness of others who have made a sincere attempt to embrace God.

The view of my preacher was that Jesus represented a unique, one-time fix by God to correct humankind's alienation from our creator. Therefore, nothing outside of the mission of Jesus was of any useful spiritual value. For him, the opportunity offered by Jesus was a closed system in which perfect compliance with his church's interpretation of Biblical criteria spelled the difference between living in liberation with Christ and a certain consignment to hell.

That church was run something like a Jesus Club, in which no rule was too arcane or irrational to justify expulsion for noncompliance. Alternatively, perhaps, it would be better to call it a Jesus franchise since brand identification and money was involved too. In my minister's view, his doctrinal formulation reflected the only true understanding of the character of God. I listened carefully to that man. I was not convinced. The fact that he was very emphatic did not make him more convincing. Samuel Clemens, popularly known as Mark Twain, contributed a useful thought that seems to apply here. He said; "It ain't what you don't know that gets you into trouble. It's what you know for sure that just ain't so."

The other variable in religion is the human material that the teacher has to work. What key insights will reach into the culture,

Seeking Jesus the Jew

mind, heart and soul of the people of Israel, India, Arabia, Persia or China to free them and renew their relationship with God? This topic might interest an enlightened teacher such as Jesus. I believe Jesus *taught as he did* because the challenges that existed in the lives of the people he addressed *were as they were*. My reading of the Bible also informs me that Jesus was also willing to step outside of his immediate culture to touch the lives of non-Jews if he encountered them.

Here is a Biblical example. Mark 7:24-27: "Jesus" left that place and went to the vicinity of Tyre. He entered a house and did not want anyone to know it; yet he could not keep his presence secret. In fact, as soon as she heard about him, a woman whose little daughter was possessed by an impure spirit came and fell at his feet. The woman was a Greek, born in Syrian Phoenicia. She begged Jesus to drive the demon out of her daughter. 'First let the children eat all they want,' he told her, 'for it is not right to take the children's bread and toss it to the dogs.' 'Lord,' she replied, 'even the dogs under the table eat the children's crumbs.' Then he told her, 'for such a reply, you may go; the demon has left your daughter.'"

Until
I think that we are frightened every
Moment in our lives
Until we
Know
Him.

Rumi[5]

I have something to offer to my Charismatic friends. Many of us use the name of Jesus as a sacred word. This use is similar to how sacred words are used in Eastern meditation practices. This can be the basis of a different kind of prayer: Discovery Prayer. I know from experience that correct pronunciation of such sacred

A Second Look at Jesus

words is important. The problem is the modern, English pronunciation of the word Jesus is a serious distortion of the earlier name. Jesus is a Westernized rendering of what may be more accurately rendered as the Hebrew name *Yahushua*. It should be pronounced; *Yahu-shoo-wa*. It means God (*Yahu*) saves (*shua*). Later, the *hu* was dropped and this personal name became *Yashua*. Some sources suggest it may have be pronounced *Yēšū*, but that is a topic for another time. In our time, this name is pronounced Joshua or, among modern Christians, Jesus. Clearly, pronunciations of some names has been extremely fluid over the past 4,000 years. Some effort is needed to recover earlier forms. I will revisit the question of the name of Jesus later in this book.

I am not trying to find fault. I am only trying to be helpful. So far, we Christians have coped with our technical weaknesses with the power of sincerity. We assume God knows whom we are calling for. I am suggesting that care in this pronunciation can yield benefits for *us*. The weakness, the maladroit approach is in *us*, not God. A carefully pronounced sacred word helps to prepare *us* to open more comprehensively to Reality. It is *our* responsibility to do what *we* can to improve *our* ability to commune with God. Perhaps, I have wondered, should we Christians try calling on the name *Yahushua* or, if our theology permits, simply *Yahu*.

I am approaching this question of sacred words from the perspective function. Sacred words are tools like any others. When used correctly and with enough repetition, sacred words function by enlivening central aspects of our personality. They operate by reorienting our subjective posture at the junction between our capacity for language and our identity. They prepare us to interface more deeply with our creator. I have been using sacred words in this manner for more than 40 years. I have personally experienced the effect of many vowel and consonant sounds upon the human instrument. I have also read many literary descriptions of the effects of ancient, sacred words.

Consider a hand plane. It is designed to shave wood to make it flatter and smoother. To function it must have a sharp blade

Seeking Jesus the Jew

that projects at a correct distance and angle past a flat working surface. The upper portion of such a tool should also be easily grasped. The result of all these attributes is a functional tool. If these attributes are missing then it is not properly designed, assembled or adjusted. Any carpenter would know this. In other words, sacred is as sacred does. Like any other tool, sacred words must function well to justify that title.

From the human point of view, a sacred word is a spiritual catalyst and facilitates spiritual transformation. We all have some idea what we think should happen in our spiritual lives. We all have an idea what we would *like* to happen. A sacred word, properly used, helps to open the way for what *needs* to happen and *can* happen within us.

I have found the growth we *need* is usually not exactly what we expect. A sacred word facilitates spiritual growth without imposing the opinions of the world upon the process. A sacred word is an expression of the language of the soul. When this vocabulary, even one word, is well articulated, it leads to the music of the soul: the playful interplay of light and matter, wave and particle. This experience is worth having. Much good will come from incorporating such an opening into our lives.

From the spiritual point of view, a sacred word is a direct and efficient tool for the Holy Spirit's use in its ongoing work of perfecting the human vessel. This is a way to gently penetrate past the endless blah, blah, blah of our opinions and embrace the eternal reality. It provides for us a glimpse of what *is* and provides a "hand hold" for God to guide us into what *we can* be.

Chapter Fourteen

Love in My Life

Hayah
Over the next year and a half, I held various jobs, lived here and there in the Boston area. Along the way, I learned a few things about Buddhism, Taoism and Tai Chi. I also had some brief lessons in homelessness, business, assault and battery, and armed robbery.

I tried to sell vacuum cleaners door to door. I was a miserable failure at this job. My trainer discounted the only one I sold so severely that I made no profit whatsoever. My target area was in Roxbury, a poor, rough part of town. One evening, a group of teenagers mugged me as I left an appointment.

I was just outside the front yard gate when I saw a cluster of teenagers approaching from my left. They were about six in number. I was encumbered with three large, cardboard boxes that contained my sample vacuum and its attachments. They laughed and joked amongst each other as they approached. Then they flowed around me and one of them announced that they had a gun and I should not move. They roughly rifled through my pockets, extracted my wallet, stripped out the cash and move on down the street. The entire event was over in about 30 seconds.

Love in My Life

That month I could not pay my rent. At that time, I was living with a group that taught the finer points of the Macrobiotic diet and the Taoist philosophy that it was based upon. A married couple ran the place and the wife dispatched her husband to tell me to be gone the next morning. In preparation, I cooked a large batch of brown rice the night before my exile and put it in a plastic bag.

It was the middle of a cold Boston winter. That next night I slept in the back of my van. When I woke the next morning, I discovered that my breakfast had frozen solid and closely resembled a small boulder. I owned a warm sleeping bag, but this was still a difficult time.

One day, I called a member of my former church and he took me in for a night, but told me I should make other plans for the next day. I pulled out of my slump by finding regular work at a labor pool. I was paid only minimum wage, but that was more than enough to rent a room at a local flophouse. I bought a used pot and a hot plate, and soon I was running a financial surplus again!

Spending time homeless and out of money teaches some essential lessons that cannot be properly learned any other way. It is refreshing to spring back after failure; finding a new way to engage the world.

With the rediscovery of some prosperity, I became more interested in meeting new friends. One of the better places I found to meet people was a dance event, "Dance Free," held Wednesday nights at the Unitarian Church at Harvard Square in Cambridge. They played several hours of good, danceable music. The atmosphere was wholesome and socially relaxed. We all danced for the love of it. Some professional dancers were there too, just for fun. If we saw someone interesting, a formal invitation to dance together was optional. We could also simply move rhythmically across the floor and see if we could attract a response. One day, in the fall of 1979, I hit pay dirt.

I spotted a pretty girl, about my age, with an easy smile and a head full of bushy brown curls. She was a little shy but there was a grounded, feline grace in her movements. We danced,

A Second Look at Jesus

spoke and danced some more. Her name was Alice and she had to leave soon. There were two children at home with a sitter and she needed to get back.

The next week Alice was there again. We danced and danced. A few days later, I visited her at her work. A few days after that, Alice and I had dinner at her home. Alice was different from the girls I had met earlier in my life. In the first place, she was a mature woman, an adult, with an unwavering love for her children and a fierce work ethic. She loved fun, but she also made sure that she managed her family with lively warmth and a gentle discipline. She was also unambiguous. I was given every sign that I was welcomed to share my life with her. In a remarkably short time, it was clear to me that this is what I wanted too.

I joined Alice and her family on January 1, 1980. I felt as though I was coming home. Alice's boys, Oliver (6 years old) and Sam (1 year old) began to warm to me. I worked to earn their trust and affection. I was a little stiff and unsure of myself. Alice was the warm sun of love and had a practical grace that melted all sense of awkwardness and separation between all of us. This was more than love. It was finding the home of love.

Alice was trying to finalize a divorce and my arrival triggered some difficult times with her ex-husband. I did what I could to support her. She spent some time crying after most of the phone calls she received from him. I tried to get accustomed to the idea that I would be playing a supporting role in this matter; supporting Alice and trying to not make things worse.

Alice had led a more traditional life than I had. My family had moved eight times before I was fourteen years of age. She was the third child of four and had grown up entirely in Rye, New York. Her father had a seat on the New York Stock Exchange and took an hour train ride to and from the city each day. He liked to joke that he paid for the children's college education with the winnings from backgammon games on that commute.

Love in My Life

The Everett family belonged to the Episcopal Church in Rye. Today, Alice playfully refers to it as the "church of etiquette" for the light spiritual burden it placed upon her.

Alice's family traces their ancestry to England through Richard Everett, who arrived as an indentured servant (under a seven-year labor contract) to Massachusetts Governor John Winthrop in 1632. Richard was mostly employed as a surveyor in the central part of that state. After his term of service, he was given a tract of land and he sent for his wife to join him.

The social life of Alice's family revolved around the American Yacht Club (established 1883). Alice's summers were taken up with sailing small boats like the Blue Jay and the Lightning in practice and competition. Hers was a good, wholesome environment in which to grow.

Alice interrupted her college education early to marry a local boy. When I met her, Alice was living in a Jamaica Plains' apartment building owned by her cousins, Sue and John. They were her protectors. I later found out that they had counselled Alice not to do anything rash regarding me. I admit I appeared to be a risk.

Alice held a responsible job. She was the manager of an inspiring silk-screen fabric store. The fabric, European-designed and printed in bold, colorful scenes was often stretched and framed in the manner of paintings. Sometimes parts of the picture were quilted with muslin on the backside of the print and certain features of the picture were stuffed with a filler to lend a two dimensional effect for emphasis. This technique was called "trapunto."

Alice possessed the virtue of a fully developed work ethic. Her mornings began at about seven A.M., getting the kids organized for their day. She took a train to Boston and opened her store by ten A.M. She left the store around five P.M. and came back to prepare dinner for the children. She lavished attention on them until their bedtime and then worked doing trapunto and other sewing work until eleven or twelve P.M.

A Second Look at Jesus

After all, of this, she still found the wherewithal to be a lively and passionate companion for me. She was and is an amazing being. Her selfless conduct and purity of intent far exceeded anything I had known. I am in awe of her.

Chapter Fifteen

The Islam Few People Know

Hayah

One Saturday afternoon, in March of 1980, Alice arrived back home quite out of breath. She had run all the way home to tell me about a lecture on women's spirituality she had just attended. She was on fire with enthusiasm. The teachers, women of some stature, had told her about some of the spiritually great women they knew. The particular spiritual orientations of Mother Theresa, Rabia, Theresa of Avila, Mira Bai, Hildegard Von Bingen, and Julia of Norwich were conveyed with verve and delicacy. What these teachers honored and appreciated was the special spiritual contribution that women embody: the ability to make the abstract real and functional. Alice wanted me to know all about her great discovery. I was interested. I suspected that the Sufi leader of the organization that sponsored the event might be the same person who had impressed Maharishi years before.

Together we followed up by attending a few meditation meetings at the local Sufi center. A month later, we participated in a

A Second Look at Jesus

weekend meditation retreat that was led by Pir Vilayat, the head of the Sufi Order of the West. Pir was a fascinating and inspiring man.

His approach was surprisingly broad in the scope, yet he was clear, focused and very thorough in his presentation. Pir spoke with a refined British accent. He had been educated at the Sorbonne, Oxford, and the Ecole Normale De Musique De Paris. His education showed. He was erudite. His eyes were bright and his carriage was both animated and dignified. He knew so *much* and it was *useful* spiritual knowledge. Every spiritual concept came with a practice designed to help us experience and master the quality in question.

At the end of the retreat, Pir initiated Alice and me into the Sufi Order. Everything about Pir and his teaching was light, open and liberating. I was confident he would not misuse his relationship as my teacher. As long as I knew him, Pir was painstakingly scrupulous and ethical.

Pir's background is revealing. His father, Hazrat Inayat Khan was a descendent of the 17th century ruler of Mysore, Raja Tipoo Sultan. Inayat Kahn was trained as a classical Indian musician. Then, at a mature age, he had turned to Sufism. The Sufis provide a mystical outlet for Muslims and others who desire to progress beyond standard religious pieties.

It will be worth our while to gain some perspective on Mohammed and his teachings. His story is clearly laid out in collections of eyewitness testimonies known within Islamic tradition as *Hadith*. We learn in these testimonies that Mohammed was always spiritually inclined as a young man. While still a youth, he married an older and wealthy widow, Khadija, whom he came to love dearly. With her support, he spent protracted periods of time meditating in caves around his home city of Mecca. He likely had a meditation guide to help him get started.

We cannot be sure who that might have been, but I have a candidate. A group rejected Idol worship before Mohammed. They were known by the name of Hanefites. It is known that

The Islam Few People Know

Mohammed spent time talking with them shared their beliefs and their aspiration to know the one true God of Abraham. Chief among the Hanefites[6] that Mohammed knew was a man from the same Quaresh clan as Mohammed. His name was Zeid ibn Amr. He had been expelled from Mecca by the idolaters and lived on mount Hira. This is the same mountain where Mohammed prayed in a cave. It is very reasonable to suggest that Zeid guided Mohammed.

How did Mohammed seek God? Before Islam and the popular emergence of Allah as the approved name of God another word existed for God. It was *al' ilah,* which means "the God" or "The unknown God." This same word is present today in the standard Islamic declaration of faith. That sentence says: *lā ilāha illā-llāhu.* This means: "There is no God except God." I consider that it is likely that Mohammed called upon God by using the name of *ilah*. This Arabic name of God was not associated with any idols. I speculate that the Arabic word *"ila"* might have derived from the ancient Hebrew word for God *"el."* El is the name of God that Abraham would likely have used.

One day, Mohammed had an overwhelming vision. In it the Angel Gabriel compelled Mohammed to speak the truth concerning the unity of God. Mohamed was greatly alarmed by this experience. In distress, he turned to his wife. She heard him out and said he should trust his vision. Then she brought Mohammed to see her uncle, Waraqah, who was a devout Ebionite Christian and, according to some sources, Mecca's Christian priest or preacher. After Waraqah had heard Mohammed tell his story, he also counselled him to trust his vision. These two, Khadija and Waraqah, are considered the first converts to Islam, which means *submission*. That is, submission to the will of God.

Waraqah bin Nafal was an interesting person. He was born a pagan and left Mecca to study *"the way of Abraham."* He learned to read and write Hebrew. He later converted to Christianity. Waraqah would have been in a strong position to teach and guide Mohammed on spiritual matters, for at least the fifteen years

A Second Look at Jesus

after Mohammed married Khadija at age twenty-five, until he received his first revelation at age forty. Significantly, Mohammed and Khadija turned to Waraqah *first* in their time of spiritual crisis.

When Mohammed was nine years old, another uncle, Abu Talib, had brought him to meet a famous Christian mystic by the name of Bahira in Bastra, Syria. There, Bahira prophesied that Mohammed would be a prophet to the Arabs. Surely, this too influenced young Mohammed.

Like Waraqah, Mohammed's wife, Khadija, was quite likely a Christian in the broad sense of knowing about Jesus and believing that he was an inspired representative of God. She was certainly not a pagan. For this reason, it is also likely that she and Mohammed were, at the very least, under the influence of Christian teaching if not confessing Christians themselves. Mohammed may even have been married Khadija in a Christian ceremony.

It is a widely attested fact that Mohammed consistently showed great respect and reverence for Jesus, Mary, Kadija, Zeid, and his uncle Waraqah. When viewed from this perspective, perhaps Islam could best be understood, at least in part, as an attempt at a Jewish/Christian reform movement that did *not* seek to deify Jesus and *did* seek to reemphasize the sovereignty of God alone. In this, Mohammed would have been in reasonable harmony with the Old Testament teachings and the actual words of Jesus at least as expressed in the Gospel of Mark. For both Mohammed and the Jerusalem/Syrian Church, Jesus was a God-ordained vessel of the Holy Spirit. Yet, only God is God. The Holy Spirit expressed the Divinity of God through Jesus. That was all.

Mohammed's teaching that God is one unified being also cast the pagan practice of idol worship in a bad light. Eventually, Mohammed was successful enough in his preaching that the guardians of the various pagan temples around town began to lose a distressingly large fraction of their prestige and livelihood. There were threats and then violent action against Mohammed

The Islam Few People Know

and his followers. Eventually it became clear that he and his followers would likely not survive if they stayed in Mecca.

Apart from his rivals, Mohammed was widely considered a good, wise and fair man. When he was fifty-two, he was invited to live near the town of Medina as a judge and peacemaker. Going there, he and his followers found a haven. They, along with the Medina confederation, thrived. As his influence grew, his old enemies and some new ones tried again and again to strike him down. In the early days, most of Mohammed's visions had to do with the nature of God and God's guidance for us to enjoy a better life. From the time of these attacks onward, Mohammed turned increasingly to military defense and his visions became more concerned with community cohesion, guidance for survival, and victory than the nature of God. Eventually, Mohammed prevailed in his struggle and, at age sixty, returned to Mecca. He died not long thereafter.

Upon his death, Mohammed's followers struggled to determine who would lead Islam into the future. One faction, made up of Mohammed's oldest followers, advocated for continuing, as they had before, with the use of military power to make way for the spread of Islam. To a certain extent, within this faction, the spirituality of Islam was been appropriated and harnessed as an animating force within a geopolitical ambition.

Mohammed's nephew, Ali, led the other faction. I am told that Ali was much as his uncle Mohammed had been in his youth; a spiritual dreamer and idealist. If Ali and his sons had prevailed, they would likely have led Islam into a more introverted, spiritual orientation. While they did fight, Ali and his sons, especially Hussein apparently did so more sparingly and with greater chivalry. Then, in an act of treachery, his political opponents assassinated Ali's younger son Hussein and extinguished this tendency toward a more spiritual form of Islam.

With their rival gone, the militarists consolidated control of Islam and established a system of strict compliance to their interpretation of the traditions of Mohammed and a succession

A Second Look at Jesus

(*salaf*) of leaders to enforce that authority. They have never relinquished this perspective or their belief that they alone are qualified to speak for Islam. Those Muslims who deplore this turn of events became what we know today as Shiites, while the winning faction are known as Sunnis.

The Sufis I know personally tend to be as innocuous and as apolitical as possible. It is as though, within the community of Islam, the *Salafi* branch of Islam has tried to take custody of the pride and power aspect of their culture while Sufis have laid claim to the spirit, insight and love. Neither has much interest in the possession of the other.

The vast majority of Muslims are drawn with varying degrees to both camps. Like any of us, Muslims love their children and want a good life with love, honor, friendship and a reasonable degree of prosperity. In our dealings with the Islamic world, we might want to keep this in mind. Therefore, a sincere combination of respect, admiration, and co-fraternity, where appropriate, may ultimately resolve our problems with the Islamic world.

None of this is possible, however, without a proper understanding of how their society works. The slanderous diatribes offered by some so-called Christians will lead to nothing but trouble. There are important differences between the teachings of Mohammed and Jesus, but getting our understanding right will take some time, some sincere effort, and some good will.

If we all visited a Mosque from time to time and observed what is taught there, this might yield some useful understanding. I have found that Islamic Imams are generally doing their best to lead people to know and respect God. Most of the virtues they promote are not very different from those honored in Christian churches and Jewish temples. There will be some differences too. All the information you gain is likely to be useful.

The Mogul Muslims who conquered India in the 16th century tended to be open minded in their religion. Along with their leader, Babur, they were mostly from central Asia. Like most believers in that region, Sufi influence was strong among them. For

The Islam Few People Know

example, the third Mughal Emperor, Akbar, devoted a great deal of time in his court to sharing insights with the foremost spiritual teachers of his time. All spiritual paths were represented in Akbar's court, including Christianity. This ecumenical spirit and practice nurtured Pir's father, Hazrat Inayat Kahn.

While respecting and drawing from this rich tradition, Pir Vilayat advised his students not to take the step of converting to Islam. He said, if we did, we would have to "toe the line" of present day Islam. What is the problem with "toeing" the Islamic line? Once you join Islam, there are some in that community who think they are entitled to control you with minute precision.

If Christians want to understand Islam, they might begin by considering how Christianity would be different if Jesus had decided to resist his oppressors rather than offering himself as a willing sacrifice. What if he had prevailed in such a resistance? That will give you a good start on understanding the Islamic perspective. If you want to get more up to date, imagine that the Klan or the neo-Nazi party was operating as a well-funded, worldwide organization intent upon enforcement of a strident, literalist version of Christianity on the entire world. The equivalent is happening today with the militant, hateful version of Islam.

Fascism has powerfully influenced modern-day Arabic politics. Consider the following history. In December, 1941, Amin Al Husseini, the chief Imam (Grand Mufti) of Jerusalem, met with Adolf Hitler. He went on to assist in the recruitment of more than 20,000 Muslims into SS Divisions. This same Imam called for the extermination of Israel upon its birth in 1948.

The Ba'ath party that dominated Iraq under Saddam Hussein and guides Syria today under Assad, idolized Hitler and sheltered many Nazis after WW2. The Ba'ath party has always been little but an Arab version of Fascism. Their fanatical desire to exterminate the Jewish people is likewise shared with their Nazi progenitors. This ideology has gained and maintained broad and deep sympathy across the Middle East. All of this is tragically far

A Second Look at Jesus

removed from the great respect and delicacy that Mohammed displayed in his dealings with Christians and Jews.

Paired with this fascination with Fascism, Islam has its own version of heresy that is enforced with the active threat of a death penalty. The Islamic version of heresy is a prohibition against "innovation." *The Kor*an says that Mohammed was "the seal of the prophets." That means *his* words, as presently recorded and interpreted, are the *final word* from God. My problem here is I know very well that God has not spoken the final word to humanity. The *Salafi* may as well try to prevent the world's rain from falling. Therefore, in the interest of peace and spiritual freedom, I keep a respectful distance from traditional Islam. At the same time, I accept with gratitude whatever inspiration I can gain from Mohammed and those who safeguard the essence of his inspiration.

Most Sufis consider themselves diligent and correct Muslims. They view their Sufi practices as a way to enrich and hasten their journey to intimacy with Allah. However, a problem emerges when the successful use of Sufi practices begins to produce an intimacy with God. Progressively, intimacy begins to give way to identification with God and then recognition of union with God. Because of this process, these mystics tend to say some shocking things. Naturally, those who are not passing through this succession of experiences are likely to take offense. This is a subtle and dangerous time for the mystic. Such subjects as intimacy with God are more profoundly and *safely* expressed in metaphor and poetry than prose. For this reason, there is a vast trove of Sufi poetry which I recommend reading. Here are some samples:

Manic Screaming
We should make all spiritual talk
Simple today:
God is trying to sell you something,
But you don't want to buy.
That is what your suffering is:

The Islam Few People Know

Your fantastic haggling,
Your manic screaming about the price!

Hafiz[7]

A Divine Invitation
You have been invited to meet
The Friend.
No one can resist a Divine Invitation
That narrows all of our choices down to just two:
We can come to God
Dressed for dancing
Or
Be carried on a stretcher
To God's Ward

Hafiz[8]

Hazrat Inayat Khan thrived on the teachings he was given. In 1910, shortly before passing, his teacher Abu Hashim Madani, dispatched Inayat Kahn to the west to bring the spiritual teachings of the east. Inayat Khan, known to his students as Murshid (guide) toured the United States with considerable success. He offered musical performances and spiritual lectures that were well attended all across America and Europe. Along the way, he met and eventually married an American woman, Ora Ray Baker.

From there, Murshid toured Europe. This was a critical time in Europe and he had exchanges with some fascinating characters such as Tolstoy. He and his growing family eventually settled in France near Paris. His oldest son, Vilayat, was born in London in 1916. Inayat Khan died in 1927.

Vilayat Kahn was my spiritual guide for more than twenty-five years. He received a classical education in France and England.

A Second Look at Jesus

Although spiritually sensitive, he was not effete and not a pacifist. When the Nazis began to prevail in 1940, Vilayat and his sister, Noor, retreated to England to join the fight. Once there, Vilayat joined the Royal Navy. I am told he originally joined the flying service, but was kicked out for flying, low and inverted, over the base one time too many. Noor worked as a French translator and later joined the SOE (Special Operations Executive).

By the time, I met Pir Vilayat he was one of several teachers who were teaching in the name of his father. It is fair to say that his approach was traditionally spiritual with a strong intellectual component. Pir was diligent and thorough in uniting the spiritual teachings of his father with the leading thinkers of his time. In his personal spiritual journey, he learned and practiced meditation with the leading lights of his day. He explored Hinduism, Buddhism, Christianity, Judaism and other paths to God.

He was also an avid consumer of western intellectual thought through the writings of Teilhard de Chardin, Carl Jung, Fritjov Capra, David Bohm, Martin Buber, Emmanuel Swedenborg, Itzhak Bentov, Dietrich Bonhoeffer and others. These ideas, the culmination of millennia of classical Western thought, found themselves side by side with Eastern concepts and practices of spiritual enlightenment and liberation.

Pir was also an enthusiastic amateur musician who played the cello. He often used music to help guide us to a particular attunement. Sacred music was an important part of our training and sensitization. Pir was partial to Bach, although he searched worldwide for music that would convey the flavor of the spiritual attunements he was trying to introduce to us.

For example, he introduced us to the transcendentally beautiful **Miserere**, by Italian composer Gregorio Allegri (1582-1652). He told us an interesting story about this music composed as a commission from the Pope at that time. The music remained a papal secret thereafter. It was only performed for the Pope, and invited guests, once a year, at the Sistine Chapel. One year, the Pope invited the young Mozart to attend. That was a fortunate

The Islam Few People Know

mistake. Mozart had perfect musical memory. He went home and promptly wrote the entire work down. That is how we came to have it in the public domain today. I suggest you take a minute to hear the wonder of the *Miserere* yourself on YouTube.

Pir told a story about the very special opportunity he once had to receive a cello lesson with the great master Pablo Casals. He came in to the room where Pir was seated with his cello and began the lesson with a simple instruction: "Move me." Is that not what every person wants when they meet someone new? Would it not be a fine thing if we could satisfy this unspoken desire?

In all of this, there was a remarkable lack of intellectual pride. Knowledge with Pir was just a tool. Sophisticated, technical descriptions were combined with the simplest, homey expressions. Spiritually, he was a man of genuine experience, not just an intellectual. He was a mystic. He was also scrupulously truthful. If he had not personally experienced a particular truth, he would admit he did not know the answer. He once shocked some peers at a conference when he said that he was "groping for the truth," concerning the question before them. One of the other luminaries commented, "Pirs do not grope!"

Pir disagreed and so do I. Spiritual growth occurs at the margins, the borders of our being, the zone where the unknown begins to be known. This is like feeling our way through unfamiliar terrain in the early dawn. If we are not willing to leave the noonday sun, we will consign ourselves to a life dedicated to reviewing the apparent and adding little to human knowledge or experience.

Pir taught that we are spiritually formed and tested primarily in our heart. Certainly he was. Late in the war, his sister was the last radio operator working for the SOE, Special Operations Executive, out of Paris. In the summer of 1944, a French woman betrayed Noor for 100,000 francs. After capture, Noor was tortured and finally killed at Dachau late in the war. She was posthumously awarded the Croix de Guerre. There is a statue in her honor dedicated in 2013 in Gordon Square, London. There are

A Second Look at Jesus

several books about Noor's life and a movie is in the works. After the war, Noor's betrayer was located. Pir struggled throughout his life to forgive that woman who had betrayed his sister to the Nazis.

Later, Pir met with a woman who became the love of his life. She died in a motorcycle accident with Pir Vilayat driving. Pir knew from personal experience the part a broken heart plays in spiritual awakening.

Pir remained a daring and resourceful adventurer his entire life. He had a fascination with flight. He owned and flew hunting hawks and even took up hang gliding while in his seventies.

That summer of 1980, Alice and I had an opportunity to get a more thorough grounding in the Sufi path. We attended a week-long Sufi Meditation Camp at the Sufi Order's facility near New Lebanon, New York. They called it the Abode of the Message. In the 19th century, this land had been part of a Shaker community. Some of the original buildings were still in use by us. We camped and learned on a forested hill adjacent to the original 18th century dirt road that linked Albany to Boston.

The Shakers were a rather large and well-known Christian reform movement. Branching from the Quakers, they emphasized simplicity, celibacy, and ecstatic worship in prayer and dance. They believed the shaking they experienced in their worship was a symptom of the gift of God's purification. Converts and large-scale adoptions of abandoned children replenished their numbers. At their peak, there were about 6,000 Shakers. Today only three remain.

The Sufi summer camps lasted a week and were held under a large, round canvas shelter deep in the forest. There were about a hundred of us. Some cabins were available, but most of us camped in small tents among the trees. Alice and I were together in those tents, learning the ways of Spirit and growing in Love and nurture of each other.

Merging Tributaries

Chapter Sixteen

A Graduate School for Mystics

Hayah

Pir began to teach us his accumulated wisdom and insights from his long life. The dimension that made this teaching so meaningful was each lesson in philosophy was preceded or followed by an effective and relevant form of meditation. With that assist, we experienced, to varying degrees, what Pir Vilayat was describing. Those teachings were very broad as they applied easily to the various faith traditions being examined. He used plain language descriptions wherever possible, although key terms were spoken in their original language. He was also careful to give ample credit to his sources so we could follow up on our own.

In broad outline, it might be useful to think of the approach to spiritual growth in four phases: *in, up, down* and *out*. *In* refers to a disentangling with the objective world and a reorientation toward the subjective aspect of our lives. *Up* refers to the progressive experience of more subtle and refined aspects of our being that eventually lead back to our source in God. *Down* refers to

A Second Look at Jesus

a purposeful return to our limited, human circumstances, while bringing the renewed vitality we have discovered in our union with God. *Out* refers to the enlightened and compassionate action made possible with a growing quotient of Divine content in our lives. What follows is a brief exposition of the essential teachings of various world religions that illustrate their unique approaches.

The first concept Pir offered is that meditation is a process of remembering our original relationship with our Creator. Pir told a story to illustrate this point. At the dawn of creation, when humanity was still "in the loins of Adam," the Creator asked us if we would honor the sovereignty of God. We all answered, "YES!" This affirmation initiated the process of our birth, securing both our freedom and our limitation.

The traditional form of Sufi meditation corresponding to this perspective is called dhkr (remembrance) and goes as follows: while sitting, we moved our heads and shoulders in counter-clockwise circle while repeating (in Arabic), "There is no god." Next we bowed down and focused on the solar plexus while saying "except." Then we would slowly bring our head upright as we said "God." The gist of the meaning was this world around us is not God. Only God is God. This is negation of the lesser reality in order to affirm (and perceive) the greater reality. This was more or less the Islamic equivalent of the vow of renunciation entered into by Hindus who are taking the Sanyasin oath.

Sanyasi means *without fire*. There are two meanings. The first is that while seeking God, the seeker will not make a fire to warm himself or prepare food. Rather, if food or shelter is not offered as a gift, he will simply go without. Dependence upon charity is intended. The point is the Sanyasin are supposed to be focused on mastering their inner lives, not making their outer lives more comfortable. One is supposed to trust God to provide as necessary. These seekers of God have also pledged to give up the fire of anger and desire that come with attachment to this world.

A Graduate School for Mystics

At this stage, the Buddhist approach is similar to that of Hindus. A process of discernment helps the student to observe and then disidentify with the limitations of their human existence.

Among Christians, the same idea is contained in the understanding that our impulses toward greed, anger and selfishness inevitably steer us toward sin, which causes alienation from God. Sin and its precursors must be renounced so that God can be found. In the west, we Christians call this *Via Negativa* (path of negation) and amounts to eliminating from our lives everything that is a distraction from God. Then, what remains, is God. Thomas Aquinas was an advocate of this approach.

In my view, the clearest Christian call to inner growth was the Great Commandment. According to Jesus, the first and greatest commandment in the *Old Testament* should be summed up as "Love the Lord, our God with all our heart, all of our mind, and all of our strength." How are we to go about that? Most people have little idea about what their minds are. The heart is even more of a mystery. Yes, people experience some thoughts, impulses, and feelings, but what of the mind apart from thoughts or the heart without personal emotion? Strength? What is true strength? To answer these questions we need to rediscover the full extent of our minds, hearts and strength. I view this as a clear mandate from Christ for spiritual exploration and inner mastery.

Initially, this is accomplished by disentangling and clearing oneself of extraneous attachments. Next, we need to become empty vessels so we have the capacity to accept a full measure of God's blessing. Halfway measures will produce halfway results. Having been cleared, our souls need to become supple and capable of stretching so they can accommodate a growing and intensifying experience of God. I believe this is what Jesus had in mind for us when he said, "Be yea perfect even as your Father in heaven is perfect."

A Second Look at Jesus

Jesus went on to say the next commandment was like the first: "Love your neighbor as yourself." I believe these two are connected because, in the process of making your life a satisfactory response to the first part of the Great Commandment, we are going to lose ourselves in God. Thereafter, you will see your neighbor as God sees him. You will also get a glimpse of yourself as God sees you.

In Judaism, Egypt is considered a place of captivity, but also a place of material safety and sensual pleasure. Escape and a resolute opposition to a return to the familiar comfort of captivity were the indispensable preconditions to a later encounter with *YHWH* in the wilderness. This clean break with the past is required before a new beginning.

A second spiritual test came later. When Moses went up Mount Sinai to have a direct encounter with *YHWH*, the people of Israel were waiting below. What the people of Israel experienced, even from a distance, was so awesome they were afraid. They begged Moses to spare them such close encounters. Instead, they asked Moses to provide them with a system of rules allowing them to live in alignment with God's intention without exposure to such daunting experiences. This nuanced solution has allowed the benefit of a life in relative harmony with *YHWH* without the destruction and tumult that result from a direct encounter.

Let me say this tracks closely with my experience. A close encounter with God *is* a daunting experience. Of course, among the people of Israel, not a few recovered their nerve and rededicated themselves to a life in the closest possible proximity with *YHWH* while allowing for acceptable human function. These people were called prophets. This embrace of direct intercourse is what Moses wanted for his people. In Numbers 11:29 he is quoted as saying: "I wish that all the Lord's People were prophets and that the Lord would put His Spirit upon them." There were once schools to teach the basics and an organization to support and encourage them as they progressed. Today we only

A Graduate School for Mystics

know about the famous prophets who made it into the *Bible*, but at one time, the movement appears to have been very broad and deep. I am convinced that many thousands became prophets with varying degrees of success. (Chronicles 18, 1 Samuel 10: 1-11, 1 Kings 18).

Now, having resolved to begin the return path to God, we need to find a way to *ascend* to the presence of God. This is the *up* portion of the *in, up, down and out* sequence described earlier. This is not a task we can accomplish by our will. The reason is, by our numerous mistakes in the past, we may have become spiritually weak and alienated. This has compromised our ability to do much more than change our orientation or intention. Moving in the new direction is another matter. While before, we may have been resolutely plodding toward oblivion, perhaps now, we are at least facing in roughly the right direction.

Now, in our weakness, we can and must accept God's first wish for us: that we stop resisting Him. Until now, we have been perverting the grace of God. We have strengthened our individual identity in such a way that it obscures the comprehensive reality of our Creator. Perversely, we have used the Creator's own power to do this! We need to stop this misuse of God's gift of life, which nearly exhausts us and is doomed to fail!

From this point onward, we should simply trust in our Creator's, or nature's, ability to revive and reorganize our lives. Cleaning house comes first. Then, starting as we are, we need to allow the power of the Creator to open the way and lift us out of our constraints. The various spiritual paths all use variations on this same theme.

Sufis see human life as part of a continuum with the poles of so-called inert matter at one extreme and unlimited divine potential at the other. The God-realized human being is in the exact middle of this range. He or she is a clearinghouse. The creation joins him or her in reaching back to its source in the Creator and the Creator reaches through him or her to touch the nitty-gritty

A Second Look at Jesus

of creation. Spiritual practices are intended to restore us to this natural and complete mode of function.

The Jewish mystics of King David's time came up with an elegant expression for a concept that was expressed something like this:

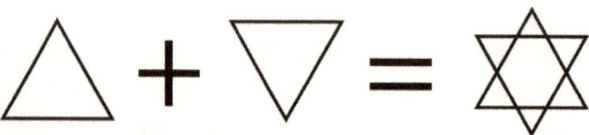

One of the interpretations of this symbol is that the equilateral triangle with the broad base represents humanity reaching up from a base of material creation to a point of ultimate focus upon the essence of God. In a similar manner the triangle with the apex pointing downward represents complimentary "outreach" from unbounded potential "in heaven" to fully penetrate the material world and infuse it with divine potential. When superimposed these two triangles represent the potential of embodying the drama of this dynamic within the human form. This profound reality can be carried and expressed from within the heart, the center of the human being.

On the Sufi path, once committed to a return to God, the seeker proceeds by experiencing the divine qualities that constitute our birthright. These qualities are often enumerated as the "99 names of God." They are, in fact, the human apprehension of the qualities of the divine manifestation. Their appreciation lends context and interrelation to the unfathomable depth of the divine mystery. As appropriate, for the particular make-up of the seeker, a meditation guide prescribes one or more of these qualities as suitable objects of meditation.

Sufi meditation guides make a particular effort to respect the unique makeup of each person who comes to them. Each of us is a unique combination of divine qualities; some are more prominently manifested, others are recessive. This singular formulation

A Graduate School for Mystics

of each unique personality distinguishes us from one another while still drawing from a unified source in God.

An attempt is made by meditation guides to individually intuit the divine quality or qualities nearest to emergence within our lives. Then, the guides prescribe appropriate spiritual practices to facilitate our ability to place an effective claim upon that particular divine inheritance. The idea is to support our unique evolutionary path rather than impose the same template on all people.

One of these names, for example, is *Alim*. In practice, it is usually intoned or sung with focus and intensity. An emphasis is on the second vowel. It is pronounced *ale-e-e-e-e-m*. We intone it with an attempt to create a very clear, piercing and resonant effect. For this type of meditation our body functions much like a musical instrument. We aim to resonate.

This is where emptiness pays off. Even a fine guitar will not resonate much if it is full of junk. I suggest you pause and repeat this word a few times. Sample the effect. Are you surprised to know this divine name is usually interpreted to mean "insight"?

In order to give a rounder view of Mystic Islam, here are some other *names of God* commonly used in the Sufi tradition. *Rahim* is compassion. *Azim* is glory, *Hayy* is vitality or life, and *Hu* is imminence of or intimacy with God. *Ahad* is the unity of God. Often practices are prescribed in complimentary pairs such as *ya wali/ya alim* (mastery/insight) or *or ya hayy/ya haqq (life/ truth)*. The aim of these practices is ecstasy. When I was taught these sacred words, I was told to precede them with the word *Ya* which, in Arabic, is an evocative form of address. When combined with a sacred name like *Hu* to form *Ya Hu* it means "O Divine Intimacy."

Christians have their own opportunities. For example, we can call upon the name of Jesus or Ya-hu-shua.

As you do this practice, it will be more effective if you can get into the feeling, the emotion of Jesus. He personified the attributes of his name. If we can intuit his personality we can more fully incorporate his qualities into our lives. His attunement to

A Second Look at Jesus

his Creator has a unique quality. Try to find it. The creator remembers. The special virtue of Jesus was/is his extreme intimacy with God and the fidelity of his life to God's will. We should all seek to attain that standard. There is no good reason to be satisfied with less. I suggest that, if you trust Jesus, you will not be disappointed.

The meditation practice I was given during my term with the Tibetan Buddhists was utterly simple and very effective. I was instructed to simply be aware of my breath. This deserves some further comment.

In Aramaic and Hebrew, the word for Holy Spirit is *Ruah*. In Arabic, it is *Ru, which* means: wind, breath and spirit. In Arabic, Aramaic and Hebrew this word is a feminine noun. In Greek, the same word is translated into *Pneuma* and is without gender. In Latin, it is translated as *Espiritu* and has a masculine gender. This evolution demonstrates another example of how elements of meaning can be lost in translation.

After doing this breathing practice for some time, I noticed an interesting effect. In addition to bringing air into and out to the lungs, there is an energy, component, a vitality associated with each breath. That energy is drawn into us, passing through and reinvigorating our vital individuality as we inhale. As I breathe in, there is a sense of a gathering in and rising. At the peak of the inhalation, my attention is drawn back to the dawn of my own creation. As I exhale, all of those qualities of this primal vitality flow *down and out* into the world. This is a projection of our Source into this world until it ends in concrete expression. This cycle, in and out, is tidal in nature.

A Tryst with Ruah
Fragments of my tattered clothing are scattered here and there.
Ruah was fierce last night.
She helps me to locate my pathetic shirt and pants.
My underwear is holey,
Patches and new tears abound.

A Graduate School for Mystics

*Some of the ancient fabric is so worn that it is
little more than a good intention.
I present a scandalous sight.*

*My luminous flesh is on display where modesty
is in serious jeopardy.
Another day of humiliation is coming up.
Strangers gawk. Friends whisper among themselves.
They think that I am a wastrel.
They are right.
Its Ruah's doing.
I ask for a change of attire, but she says, "Nothing doing."
Then she winks and whispers,
"I like my special friends to look that way."*

*I Sigh, try to brush off the stardust
and do something about the wrinkles in time.
Then I wonder.
What kind of relationship have I gotten myself into?*

John

Taken as a whole, each breath, beginning with an inhalation, is a complete cycle of emergence at birth, ending at death. The inhalation that follows is resurrection and a reunion with our eternal identity. When we pay attention, each breath is a recapitulation of the entire life cycle and is an opportunity for us to be a vehicle to bless and reinvigorate the entire creation. In the process, we, as vehicles for this blessing, are uplifted too.

Another nice effect about this practice is that breathing is mandatory and constant in life. All that is necessary to harness this enhanced benefit is to pay attention to what is going on anyway. It is likely Jesus was conveying such a blessing when he *breathed on* his disciples in John 20:22: "With that he breathed on them and said: 'Receive the Holy Spirit.'"

A Second Look at Jesus

It seems to me that the traditional church has missed a major opportunity here to highlight this most essential of all Christian phenomena as a sacrament. What can be more important than receiving the Holy Spirit? Certainly less well attested sacraments like Extreme Unction and Confirmation are widely observed. Why should the receipt of the Holy Spirit be relegated to an adjunct status in support of other sacraments? I can see no valid reason.

The matter of receiving the Holy Spirit is further clarified by the description of the Pentecost experience of the disciples of Jesus. In Acts 2:1-21 we read; "When the day of Pentecost came, they were all together in one place. Suddenly a sound like the blowing of a violent wind came from heaven and filled the whole house where they were sitting. They saw what seemed to be tongues of fire that separated and came to rest on each of them. All of them were filled with the Holy Spirit and began to speak in other tongues as the Spirit enabled them."

"Now there were staying in Jerusalem God-fearing Jews from every nation under heaven. When they heard this sound, a crowd came together in bewilderment, because each one heard their own language being spoken. Utterly amazed, they asked: 'Aren't all these who are speaking Galileans? Then how is it that each of us hears them in our native language? Parthians, Medes and Elamites; residents of Mesopotamia, Judea and Cappadocia, Pontus and Asia, Phrygia and Pamphylia, Egypt and the parts of Libya near Cyrene; visitors from Rome (both Jews and converts to Judaism); Cretans and Arabs—we hear them declaring the wonders of God in our own tongues! Amazed and perplexed, they asked one another, 'What does this mean? Some, however, made fun of them and said, 'They have had too much wine." Then Peter stood up with the Eleven, raised his voice and addressed the crowd: 'Fellow Jews and all of you who live in Jerusalem, let me explain this to you; listen carefully to what I say. These people are not drunk, as you suppose. It is only nine in the morning! No, this is what the prophet Joel spoke:

A Graduate School for Mystics

'In the last days, God says,
   I will pour out my Spirit on all people.
Your sons and daughters will prophesy,
   your young men will see visions,
   your old men will dream dreams.
Even on my servants, both men and women,
   I will pour out my Spirit in those days,
   and they will prophesy.
I will show wonders in the heavens above
   and signs on the earth below,
   blood and fire and billows of smoke.
The sun will be turned to darkness
   and the moon to blood
   before the coming of the great and glorious day of the Lord.
***And everyone who calls
on the name of the Lord will be saved.***"

Here we see the continued application of the teaching of Jesus concerning the use of the Name of God in John 17:26 and the fulfillment of the blessing of Jesus by God in John 20:22. Now, on Pentecost, it was time for action!

From the pinnacle experience of our encounter with God, we are in a position to do some profound good. This is the realm of Divine intimacy. This is where blessings come from. The next portion of our sequence of orientations is the *downward* focus. The various religions all express this a little differently.

The Hindu (Vedic) ideal is to remain absorbed in the transcendental reality of God and, from that lofty and impartial perspective, perform virtuous action. It is being awake beyond life and yet engaging within the life of limitations. The clearest expression of this state of being is found in these words from Krishna in the Bhagavad Gita: "Established in union, (with God) perform action." By doing this, a God-realized person demonstrates the supreme accomplishment in life and is able to inspire any who encounter him or her to do likewise. As he or she moves through

A Second Look at Jesus

life, he or she cuts a swath through creation, cleaving it from top to bottom and revealing its riches and subtle mysteries for the observant.

The Sufi ideal is a little different. As we reorient ourselves to engage our daily life, we recognize ourselves as a vehicle for bringing the divine qualities of our Creator into the world through our lives. We can aspire to be like a cornucopia, a useful vessel for effectively delivering a share of God's blessing to the world. In doing this, we rediscover the limitations of human existence. The way that Pir Vilayat expressed this is that God is human perfection and human life is Divine limitation.

The Buddhist view is similar to the Hindu ideal, except that a conscious choice is made whether to withdraw from the world or not. The *down and out* portions of our sequence are considered optional. An "enlightened" person can choose to fully embrace final liberation when he or she finds it, or to compassionately defer full liberation *until all creatures achieve such an enlightenment*. The compassionate option is encouraged in Buddhist teaching. This is considered the path to the perfect liberation.

The Christian approach, upon reengaging daily responsibilities, is found in the second half of the Great Commandment given by Jesus. After "loving God with all of our mind, all our heart and all our strength", we are told to "love our neighbor as our self." From the earnest attempt to "be perfect even as our Father in heaven is perfect," we discover that human limitations *crucify* the unlimited stature of God. We are instructed to, nonetheless, take up that cross and do as Jesus did with love for our brothers and sisters. Perhaps Jesus saw this historic encounter with Pilate and the cross as a necessary reenactment of this central fact of the human limitation. Death is inherent in life. Perhaps, what Jesus did, is simply embrace this reality without reservations and demonstrate for us exactly what does and does not die.

From this perspective, the *out* portion of our spiritual endeavor is to simply live out our inner realization. In order to function effectively it is necessary that we not perpetuate the error of

A Graduate School for Mystics

self-aggrandizement. At one point, Jesus was addressed as "good teacher." He put a swift stop to this kind of talk. He said, "No man is good, only God." It would be best if we would come to see and conduct ourselves likewise. I love the poignant beauty of his personal humility while expressing of the nature of God.

Before we go on, I want to tell you that I do *not* recommend superficial Syncretism as a practical spiritual system. Even though its proponents are well-intended and aim to emphasize the harmony of spiritual truths, Syncretism distorts what it touches. In an attempt to remove the points of contention between religions, authenticity is lost. Truly, it is good and useful to emphasize the points of harmony among the various religions; however, it is a mistake to downplay or conceal their unique and sometimes odd characteristics. When the unique and perhaps inconvenient characteristics of a spiritual path are ignored, we will miss vital clues left by our predecessors for our upliftment and edification. Often the oddities point to vital insights. To function as intended each spiritual path must be allowed the fullest and most faithful expression.

A harmonized spirituality that results from simplistic syncretism can become a collection of bland platitudes. An attempt at syncretism will also put too much faith on the one who is trying to do the summary. Can one person responsibly claim to do justice to thousands of years of human aspiration and spiritual discovery? Does a person who aims to summarize spiritual teachings possess an original aptitude for the profound insights of the originators of our world religions? I do not think that is likely. Do you?

While I recommend focusing on a single, or at most, just a few spiritual practices for daily use, I also advocate for a broad knowledge of what is available in the spiritual market. I am unqualified to speak with real authority on the details of every spiritual path, but I will share what I have experienced and have good reason to trust. There are plenty of other qualified people

A Second Look at Jesus

available. I recommend that you use them to round out your understanding as necessary.

When considered together, Judaism, Islam and Christianity differ from Hinduism, Buddhism, and Taoism in one important respect. They are commonly presented as *revealed* religions. In practical terms, this means an emphasis is placed upon the reports and insights of their prophets, leaders, while the methods, and techniques they used to prepare for those insights are deemphasized or unreported altogether. Nonetheless, I am confident spiritual practices played a part in clearing the way before the revelations occurred.

This is how I have seen life unfold. Advancement comes when both preparation *and* opportunity meet to create a moment of transformation. With God, opportunity is constant. The preparation is usually the missing element. Triggering a spiritual event is like building a fire. First, a proper mix of kindling materials is placed together. Only then is a spark effective. Without preparation, nothing much happens.

This habit of not reporting the beginning steps our great prophets depended upon for their spiritual evolution does a disservice to spiritual aspirants today. History is important. Context is important. The intimate details of how they worked their way past their limitations to find God are important. Without this information, we are left with the impression that God chose His representatives and prophets for a leading role arbitrarily or out of predestination alone.

I think the prophets began their careers as competent spiritual vessels. Their capacity then allowed them to appreciate, accommodate and act upon the spiritual challenge of the revelation they experienced. Continued practice and service to the Divine allowed them to grow further as they matured and become increasingly effective representatives of Truth.

As free individuals, it is our job to make our own way toward a balanced and fulfilled life. It does not matter what religious environment we find ourselves. We are individually responsible. It is

A Graduate School for Mystics

our life, after all. If the religion of our birth is not doing the job for us, then it is our responsibility to research our options and make changes and adjustments as necessary.

Chapter Seventeen

Preparing to Launch

Hayah

Back in Boston, I was earning my livelihood as a carpenter. I enjoyed the opportunity to engage in practical action.

For the first six months after I met Alice, I helped a crew to convert a large apartment complex into condominiums. After that, I joined with a Sufi friend to do independent carpentry projects.

I also found a hobby. I had discovered a wooden sailboat, which had overstayed its welcome in someone's driveway. I recall I paid no more than $100 for everything. It was a 24' sloop with a retractable, steel keel. Next, I found a sympathetic neighbor with some extra space and soon I was spending much of my spare time scraping and sanding the hull or tinkering with its quirky inboard engine. International Harvester originally designed this four-cylinder engine for a small tractor. In its nautical form, it was marketed as the Atomic Four. The boat was basically sound. I painted the outer hull a dark green and the interior white. A few months later, Alice and I were sailing Boston Harbor.

Preparing to Launch

Nautical locomotion was a revelation. When it worked, the engine made a satisfying sound. It was a low-key thumpa thumpa thump. Then, when I turned the engine off, the magic began. The wind leaned into the sails and the sea parted with a murmur and a sigh. This vessel, I named it *Alice*, became a dynamic womb that carried my new family into a new life of gentle purposefulness. In it, we listened to the sermon of the ocean for hours. We learned to work together, sharing the work, the exhilaration and the challenges. However, there were problems.

There was a mysterious leak. We were never able to locate its source with any certainty. We suspected it came from the centerboard casing because the leak intensified whenever we put stress on that part of the boat by sailing into a stiff wind. At an unspoken moment, Alice would move into action with the bilge pump. A grey, plastic affair which looked like a magnum-sized bicycle pump. The lifting stroke did the work. If things really got out of hand, I would luff the sails and pitch in with a bucket. The children, securely trussed up in miniature life preservers, came to see this as a normal part of the sailing adventure.

The goal was to keep the carburetor and starter on the engine free from the rising tide of bilge water. On one occasion, a combination of problems from rising water, weak battery and other sources seemed to have us checkmated. The starter was wet and out of commission. I took a long strap from our stores, wrapped it around the heavy iron flywheel and started the engine with a single pull, to the amazement of all. The wonder intensified when the flywheel spun faster and kicked up a rooster tail of bilge water that flew twenty feet in the air. Then, I detached the cooling water intake from the seawater fitting and used the engine's water pump to help clear the bilge. In twenty minutes, our boat was dry, the sails were stowed and we were moving purposefully toward our berth on the Neponset River. That $100 was the best investment I ever made.

This narrative may make our sailing excursions seem more dangerous than they actually were. Sailing with more restraint

A Second Look at Jesus

slowed the leak to a trickle whenever we wanted to regain more control of the situation. There were also other watercraft around us. They would have rendered assistance whenever we asked for it. The challenges did focus our minds, however. As a result, every trip was a genuine adventure.

We usually had a few fishing lines out and we often brought home dinner. Alice's sons, Jolly and Sam, knew, beyond a doubt, where dinner came from and what it took to provide for them. For a while, I even toyed with the idea of suspending my carpentry career and making *Alice* the only sail-powered, commercial fishing vessel along the Massachusetts coast. With all of this quixotic activity, Alice either joined in or practiced a benign, loving tolerance. We worked and shared. Everything that needed to be done was done. Along the way, I did my best to help Alice and her sons live a joyous life.

I was also digesting some things that Pir Vilayat had said near the end of the summer camp. It was occasionally his practice to offer an encounter known as *Darshan*. This Sanskrit word means sight or vision. This is an opportunity for the student and the teacher to *see* each other as they truly are. To make this phenomenon work, both the one giving and the one receiving *Darshan* allow their defences to come down and observe what is really transpiring. When successful, the teacher is a bridge between the student and the teacher's experience of God. The teacher also perceives a view of God emerging through the student.

After our *Darshan*, Pir invited me to walk with him. He said some encouraging things about my progress and then told me I was exactly the kind of person who should be a Sufi teacher. As we walked, he asked me about my background. When I told him about my time with Maharishi, Pir commented that the TM training tended to make all of us (TM students) alike ("of a type"). In contrast, he would be offering a "graduate level course" in spiritual development.

This might appear to be an insult, but it was not. Maharishi's method is streamlined in the extreme. It is easy to teach and

Preparing to Launch

practice and it produces a rapid, strong result. However, these virtues come at a cost. The quality of a single mantra has a defining effect upon the practitioner. The Sufi approach is more nuanced and takes more time to unfold. Teaching and learning is more involved and sometimes, complex. Each individual practice is balanced and tempered with the others. As a result, the practices tend to guide and provide context rather than define.

Pir Vilayat's kind and respectful manner showed me he took our relationship seriously. This was the opening of a new chapter in my spiritual life. I really appreciated the lack of hype and posturing that characterized this new path. Pir's manner made it clear that, although he had some things to teach me, we were all in this together.

A few years before I met him, Pir Vilayat had abolished nearly all titles of rank and seniority within his organization. Although we still addressed him as Pir, he preferred we think of him as Coach. The former leaders were "demoted" to Representatives. Teachers in training, like me, were known as Coordinators. Those who had previously held various senior titles were now to just be known as Senior Teachers.

The changing of titles illustrated a fundamental concept that Pir was trying to implement. His father, Inayat Kahn, had always said it was best if we recognized both a democracy among egos and the aristocracy of the soul. Ego trips among people were best avoided while the sovereignty of God was embraced.

Pir had also made a decision to stop tolerating the use of drugs among his students. Previously, many people had entered the Sufi Order from a culture that had included some use of marijuana. Pir had reached the conclusion that often he was wasting his time with some of his students because drugs were holding them back. In spite of widespread hurt feelings and a sizable exodus, Pir stood by his decision.

Apart from my daily meditation practice and the reading of some books by Pir and his father, I took on something else. I took a series of increasingly long meditation retreats. I was pleasantly

A Second Look at Jesus

surprised. Each retreat was individually crafted to fit me and the time available. Later that winter, I started training to become a retreat guide myself.

The next year I sold my sailboat for a good profit and bought a more capable craft. It was a double-ended sloop built in Yugoslavia. Like its predecessor, it was a wood boat. This one had a fixed keel, so that leaks, if any, would be coming from a different source. It was a few feet longer, proportionally wider and was much sturdier. I found a friend who was willing to rent me some space in their driveway and began work on the new *Alice*.

Chapter Eighteen

A Friendly Southern Invasion

Hayah

That spring, in 1982, Alice's divorce was finalized and we decided to put some distance between herself and her *ex*. I found a one-year wooden boat-building program at a community college in North Carolina. Alice found a business partner there, to join her in running a printed fabric store.

In July, Alice and I launched our boat and turned south. The boys were with Alice's mother in rural Vermont. We made good time passing through the Cape Cod Canal and proceeded toward the protected waters between Long Island and the mainland.

We had some trouble near Providence, Rhode Island. The night before our arrival, we went through an intense rainsquall that drenched us, along with nearly all of our belongings. At dawn, we discovered we had wandered into a gigantic fish trap that stretched for miles along the Rhode Island coast. The trap was designed as a funnel of nets to capture large quantities of

A Second Look at Jesus

fish. To escape, we had to heel (lean) the boat severely to slide sideways over the net cable that was buoyed taut at the surface of the ocean.

Next, we made for Newport harbor and approached the dock of a splendid, full-service marina that offered hot showers, washing machines and dryers. Unfortunately, as we came near, the dockhand motioned us away. Apparently, they were not interested in customers as scruffy as we were. Instead, we anchored off a public beach. We loaded all of our wet laundry into our sail bags, rowed to shore, and caught a cab. I will always remember the firm, aristocratic clarity of the dockworker's gesture that sent us on our way. It reminded me of the act of brushing a bug off of a pant leg.

A few days later, we had some serious concerns about our passage through Hell's Gate, where Long Island Sound opens up into New York Harbor. We had been warned that even some powerful craft had gotten into trouble there. The problem is the immense volume of water in Long Island Sound pushes and pulls through that relatively narrow opening near Manhattan, sometimes creating a ferocious tidal current. Combined with this is the powerful tidal influence of the New York/Hudson area that can be somewhat out of sync with the Long Island Sound. The resulting current can be fierce.

Alice and I did some careful calculations and set out intending to arrive at Hell's Gate just as the rising tide stopped pushing a flow into New York Harbor. This strategy worked like a charm. We were pushed south, through Hell's Gate with the last of the rising Long Island tide, and then were sucked past Manhattan on the falling Hudson tide. We never even started our engine and this was a good thing because it did not have much help to give.

Months before, I had bought a used engine, another Atomic Four. I was assured it was a completely rebuilt unit with a fresh coat of red paint. I finished installing it just a couple weeks before we launched. The moment I tested my installation I knew we would need to make alternative plans. The engine had a knock as

A Friendly Southern Invasion

bold as an irate neighbor did. I knew right away that the engine would be contributing nothing but ballast. As a substitute, I put an outboard bracket directly on our large "barn door" rudder. Then I purchased a pair of used Sears and Roebuck five horsepower "Game Fisher" engines. I used them alternately, all the way to my destination. As one failed, I would use the other while doing repairs on the first. I had to climb halfway out of the boat every time to start those engines. I steered the whole rudder/engine assembly with a tiller. Our speed under power was very modest. We also had to avoid the pitching motion accompanying a head-on encounter with any sizable waves, as sometimes, we completely submerged our little engine **while it was running**. The need for repairs was frequent, but those engines did their job, serving us all the way to my new home.

 The night before we entered Norfolk, Virginia, Alice demonstrated an important principle in sailing. She had offered to sail through the late night watch to help us get to Norfolk the next morning. As she started her shift, we came along a buoy and noted the number on its side so that we could be certain of our position using our chart. I gratefully went below to get some sleep. Near dawn, Alice cheerfully woke me to say we were coming near another a buoy. She was rightfully proud of her solitary effort.

 In the middle ages, most ships could not sail very "close" to the wind. The big, square sails were at their best sailing down wind. With careful angling and bracing of the sails, it might be possible to sail within 70 degrees of the direction of the wind. No more. When the Arab pirates adopted and perfected the triangular *lateen* sail system, they were able to sail within 55 degrees of the direction of the wind. At the time, Christians considered this skill the "work of the Devil." Using this system, the Arab pirates preyed most effectively upon Christian trading ships. Today, our best sailboats sail within about 30 degrees of the wind direction.

 Our boat *Alice* had a relatively wide or beamy hull and a shallow keel that limited our ability to *point* upwind to an unimpressive

A Second Look at Jesus

45-50 degrees. To reach our intended destination, Alice and I sometimes had to sail a zigzag course, tacking (turning) to the left and then the right of the oncoming wind. Little by little, we got where we were going, but the rate of progress to windward was painfully slow.

What was happening through the night was just as Alice was preparing to tack, the wind would shift so the wind was in a less advantageous direction than before. Nonetheless, she did the best she could and displayed her usual tenacious perseverance. We approached a buoy at dawn with hope; we were shocked to see that it was **the very same buoy we had passed the night before**.

This was condensed a bundle of lessons. We learned about the limits of sail technology. We also learned skilled effort can come to nothing if nature is against you. We also learned about perseverance. We had to struggle just to avoid losing ground!

Later the same day, we entered Norfolk harbor and began a passage through the Inland Waterway. We were going to motor south from here until we passed the treacherous Cape Hatteras, which projects far out, from the North Carolina coast. Its dangerous combination of winds, currents and shallow waters is reputed to have doomed more than a thousand sailing vessels over the years. We were not up to *that* challenge with the equipment at hand. We took the inland route.

The Inland Waterway was developed in the latter part of the 19th century and perfected during the 20th. With it, shipping would avoid menaces such as bad weather and German submarines. The waterway ran in a dredged channel mostly between the coastal barrier islands and the mainland from Florida to New York. The portion we were about to enter ran through some real estate with the daunting name of the Great Dismal Swamp and then down the Alligator River. The "iron breeze," provided by our little Sears motors, moved us along at three to four miles per hour. The scenery was mostly about what you would expect, given the route's name.

A Friendly Southern Invasion

Near the end of the first day, we were shocked to run aground in the middle of the channel. The minimum depth in most of the waterway was supposed to be ten to twelve feet. Our boat only drew three feet! I jumped into the water and pushed us free.

Later that night, as we were creeping along in nearly total darkness, we heard a distant throbbing. As it came closer, we saw an extraordinarily bright light sweeping left and right like a menacing Cyclops. As this apparition came closer, the resonant rumble of the engine took on a visceral growl that churned in my solar plexus. The scene and the emotion behind it closely resembled reality depicted in The War of the Worlds. We headed for the weeds on the right side of the canal and tied up to some trees. Soon, an immense barge, pushed by a mountainous tug, emerged from the dark mist and swept by not ten feet from the place where we cowered among the weeds. Now I know how a roach or mouse feels when confronted by the human colossus and their machines. It was a dredge. Perhaps it was on its way to clear the channel blockage we had discovered earlier. At the time, however, rational thought was hard to come by. Fear had made a visit.

A few days later, we rented some dock space for the boat at Belhaven, NC. It had taken a month for us to get this far, but we needed to pause and to return to Boston. It was time to collect our children from their Grandmother, pack the large delivery van I had purchased and move the household to our new home.

My parents, who then lived in central North Carolina, picked us up and brought us to the airport for the trip back to Boston. After listening to the whole story, my mother opined, since we had made a trip like this and were still cheerful with each other; our relationship might just work out.

A week later, we were headed south in our rough-looking step van. The back was full of our furniture. I had numerous spare tires strapped to the top. There were only two seats up front. The rest of the family sat on a sofa just behind the driver's seat. As I recall, we had four or five flat tires on that trip. The other

A Second Look at Jesus

notable event was the escape of our cat. She hated the noise and commotion of the moving van. When we stopped for a break in Maryland, she darted out and away. That cat never looked back.

We rented a duplex that had originally served as expedient housing during WW2. During that time, the population doubled and most of these 25,000 new residents worked in the shipyard. In all, they built 243 Liberty ships and other cargo vessels from late 1941 through the spring of 1946.

A few weeks later, my boat-building instructor and I spent two days bringing our sailboat the rest of the way home. I had a beautiful experience the night before we arrived home. I was standing watch alone, as I motored along the inland waterway, under nothing but faint moon and starlight. Dawn was still a few hours off and I stood in the cockpit to get a better view ahead as it was hard to detect my position in the channel. Every now and then, I would come close to striking a dock, projecting from the mainland on my right, as it loomed, without warning, from the darkness.

I extended all my senses to their limits in order to keep myself safely centered in the channel. As a result, some of my deeper sensitivities were mobilized too. I became intimately aware of the fertile vitality that played upon the brooding landscape. My whole being scanned the unknown ahead. It was like lightly passing my fingers over the alert, receptive body of my lover. Now and then, I touched something sensitive and there was an immediate, surging response. When this happened, an intimate, diaphanous vitality blazed up and touched me back in a display that enlivened me more and more as time and miles passed by.

Suddenly, I heard a boisterous commotion behind me. There was a confusion of splashing, gasping, and snorting that initially made me wonder if I had encountered one of the herds of wild horses that populated some of the undeveloped barrier islands on my left. The tumult came closer and closer as I reached for my flashlight and turned. In that harsh light I was surprised to see a pod of breaching dolphins, nearly at arm's reach, rising and

A Friendly Southern Invasion

diving rhythmically as they expelled and took in air. Suddenly, they were gone as they dove, passed beneath my vessel and preceded me on my journey to my promising, new home.

Once settled we sold *Alice* to a taxi driver for $3,000. Then we bought a small, old house in truly terrible condition with that same $3,000. Our house had water damage from a leaking roof and termite damage rising from the ground. The two threats met somewhere in the middle to their mutual benefit. The structure was in deep distress. We tried to take advantage of government loans to facilitate its renovation, but the officials just shook their heads. They judged it hopeless.

Alice had a good credit rating and I had experience in home renovation. With these strengths, we went on a tour of the various banks in town. We collected a large number of no's. One banker told us Alice's credit rating did not count because it was acquired north of the Mason-Dixon Line. Another joker actually put our application in the trash while we were still talking with him. Eventually, we found only one bank officer who was willing to loan us money. He doled out $15,000 in small increments, inspecting for progress as we proceeded. I was going to school full time during the day and working nights and weekends on the house. We bought our house in the fall of 1982 and moved in less than one year later.

Our new home was only about 600 square feet. Andrew Pierce (1853-1931) and his wife Mary (1862-1935) had originally built it in 1884. Andrew was a ship caulker and was part of the rising middle class of skilled black craftsmen who held the balance of political power during the reconstruction period following the Civil War.

Our home still had the original lapped siding and double hung windows. The structural framing was consistent with the manner of 19th century ship and house building methods. Large beams, posts and corner braces were mortised into each other. Major joints were held together with pegs known as trunnels (literally "tree nails"). Termites had attacked my

A Second Look at Jesus

framing from foundation to rafters, but the resin-saturated yellow pine "fat wood" had stopped them cold wherever it occurred.

Originally, there were four small rooms off a central corridor. Experts call this configuration a "4X4 square." I removed two corridor walls to create two small bedrooms and a "U-shaped" common area. The rooms all had twelve-foot ceilings, which made some rooms taller than they were wide! There were four fireplaces; one for each room. Later, a kitchen had been added to the back. The simple, one story design was vaguely Italianate and it rested upon an unusually high crawl-space foundation. It was a little rough and a little odd, but it was ours. It also came with a dark history.

In the winter of 1898, the Democrats of Wilmington, North Carolina staged an armed insurrection against the corrupt, but legally elected Republican led government of Wilmington and New Hanover County. The Democratic Party represented the pre-war, white ruling class and their allies. This included many unrepentant Confederates, prosperous merchants, and poor, semi-employed whites. The Republican majority was mostly made up of former slaves such as the Pierces.

I possess a copy of a petition dated 1898 that contains the names of many of the Democratic conspirators that carried out the armed revolt later that year.. I also have a copy of a booklet, dated 1898, on the "Constitution and Bylaws" of a shadowy group that called itself the "White Government Union." William McKoy led this group. This same William McKoy was also the chair of the Democratic Party in 1898. The names on the petition were thoroughly cross-referenced by my friend, Kent Chatfield, for profession and membership in various organizations such as the Wilmington Light Infantry Regiment and the Democratic Party.

In the later years of the 19th century, there were increasing efforts by the leading White Democrats to re-establish themselves in economic dominance. Beginning just before, and increasingly in the years following the Wilmington coup of 1898,

A Friendly Southern Invasion

Andrew and Mary Pierce lost properties to foreclosure, including the home I later bought in 1982. They were not alone. Many black citizens were either killed or exiled in 1898. Most of those who remained were progressively marginalized in the business community. Black entrepreneurs were often forced to return to the status of employees of white business owners rather than independent business owners themselves. In 1889, Andrew was listed in the city directory as a ship's carpenter. In 1900, he was listed as a caulker. In the 1912 directory, Andrew Pierce's profession was listed as "selling soft drinks." In 1914 and 1916, he was listed simply as a laborer. Thereafter, he disappears from the city directory.

Kent has also documented the methods used to appropriate the property of targeted black owners. He claims that following the coup there were many coercive and fraudulent transactions by the conspiracy leaders. According to Kent, this activity resulted in a vast haul of illicit wealth for them. Further details concerning this story will be the subject of a documentary film called "Wilmington on Fire" which is intended to premier in 2014.

Another old friend, now deceased, told me a story about those days he heard as a youth. He listened to an old man at a pool hall who described his experience as a sniper operating from the top floor of a certain building in downtown Wilmington. From there he used a Sharps rifle of the type designed for shooting Buffalo at long range. This old man reported ranging north along Front street toward Market street and "stacking up n-----s like cord wood" as they fled Wilmington trying to reach the Cape Fear River and escape to safety.

Now and then, I am dismayed by the course of modern, black political thought. At these times, I find it useful to remember that my personal history is *very* different from that experienced by black folk not so very long ago. Much of that history tends to wound and inhibit souls. True stories, ugly stories like these are passed down within black families from generation to generation.

A Second Look at Jesus

How then can I judge if this history obscures our country's original promise for many of its citizens? How much good and sincere behavior today is needed to overcome past history like that of Wilmington in 1898? This is not my question to answer. Without trust, nothing happens. There is nothing more intimate and personal than the decision of whom to trust and when to trust. Although trust is earned, the balance of trust is beyond persuasion. It is an individual gift. It is based upon the intuitive power of the soul and it must be respected. Still, I wish we would all simply focus on joyous pursuit to our full potential as members of one human family. That would be a better lesson to draw from the past.

Chapter Nineteen

Working the Ground

Hayah

When Alice and I had lived in Boston, we were consumers of cultures and services we valued highly. We attended weekly meditation classes at the local Sufi center. There was also a steady stream of top-level speakers at Boston-area institutions on interesting topics. We took part in meaningful political and social causes. We generally knew much less than the people speaking did. Once we settled in Wilmington, we discovered that nearly all this cultural environment was absent. These circumstances conspired to make us leaders instead of followers as we had been in Boston. If we wanted to have a community of people who shared our interest in meditation, art or politics we needed to organize it ourselves.

Soon, we found a group of people who shared our enthusiasm for spiritual matters. I specialized in leading the meditation. Alice focused on leading spiritual dance. These dances, properly called Dances of Universal Peace, were usually circle dances and

A Second Look at Jesus

were done with an attunement and words that made a spiritual point.

Politically, we brought with us a dedication to the work of a group called Amnesty International, which was a favorite of Pir Vilayat. Amnesty is dedicated to taking up the cause of political prisoners who are victims of torture, secret confinement, and other forms of political abuse in the legal system. We did not mention the political actions that had led up to their arrests and we did not criticize their captors for taking measures to direct and control their country. Our sole focus was to ask if the circumstances surrounding the confinement of our adopted prisoners were legal, ethical, and humane.

When we wrote letters to the prison wardens or government ministers, we always tried to be polite. We just asked for information about the circumstances of the prisoner. Often if the international community was watching, there was a moderating effect on the conduct of the governments in question.

Our method was to act on an alert from Amnesty with a single letter from each member of our group. Several groups like ours were assigned to write letters as the needs arose. If the circumstances of the prisoner changed, we were notified. The other way Amnesty functioned was by assigning a single letter-writing group to a single prisoner whom they continued to champion until he or she was either released or died. This was morally satisfying work.

Alice and I met some interesting characters. There was an old man known as Elijah, who had lost a leg and was confined to a wheel chair. He sometimes got very drunk and rolled down the middle of our street loudly singing in the middle of the night.

Over a period of a few years, we had become acquainted with Rickey Nelson ------. He and his girlfriend lived next door to us. Rickey was generally an amiable and easy-going person. I asked him about his name once and he said his mother had named him after the famous singer. I found this interesting since Ricky Nelson the singer was very white and my neighbor was very

Working the Ground

black. I thought it was a neat cultural crossover that his mother had a crush on a white "heart-throb" singer.

Another person who interested me was Crazy Wolf. He was a full-blooded Apache Indian. He was in a relationship with a German woman, with whom he eventually had two children. All of them, Wolf, his wife, and the children had strikingly good looks.

I later found out, there is a strong cult of appreciation for American Indian culture in Germany. Like-minded people would gather into tribes and establish Indian camps over the weekend. Everything was done with careful attention to authenticity. The East German government sponsored numerous Wild West movies where the heroes were the Indians and the evil Yankee cavalry was booed.

A more profound beacon in my life is a relationship I formed with a kindly couple who bought one of the condominiums I built. Alfred and Anita Schnog have always personified a quality described in the Old Testament as *heseth*, best translated as *loving kindness*. Everyone who encounters this loving couple is treated with the most wonderful and heart-felt respect and kindness. They are not patsies. In fact, they are astute business people. Nonetheless, every encounter with them begins with a sincere examination of how they can help you.

Alfred's personal story is remarkable. His father was a broker in steel alloy metals. He arranged for a job at the Dutch branch of his company after the Nazis appropriated the parent company in Germany. In the fall of 1938, he and his family were in a hotel, preparing to cross over to Holland the next day. That night happened to be Kristallnacht or "the night of the broken glass." On this night the Nazi Brown Shirts broke the windows of Jewish shops and burned Temples all across Germany. Alfred's parents showed him this event from the safety of the hotel and told him to remember what he saw.

The next day the rules had clearly changed. At the border, the Nazi official told Alfred's family they could proceed, but the boys

A Second Look at Jesus

would be taken to a children's camp for *safekeeping*. The parents could collect them upon their return. Alfred's mother sprang into action. She took out a small, sharp fruit knife that she kept in her purse and held it close to the throat of Alfred's brother. In a loud voice and in full view of the nearby Dutch border officials, she said if she could not bring her children with her she would sooner end their lives. After a suspenseful pause, the Nazi stamped their passports and said, "Take your brats and get out." Alfred's mother carried that knife in her purse to the end of her days.

Many Jews did not or could not take the decisive action necessary to escape Germany. They believed God alone would protect them if they were righteous. They also believed even the Nazis would not be so foolish as to waste them as productive and loyal members of their society. They were wrong. We can all be surprised by the initiative of evil. Sometimes it is simply beyond our imagination.

Like my father, I have always appreciated the value of earthy friends and their brand of wisdom and humor. Whenever I started to get too high fallutin', one of these friends might start to call me "the professor." If I really needed some stronger attitude adjustment, one of my redneck friends might say, "What? You think your s**t don't stink?"

I am going to be circumspect about the next person I describe. I *may* have known a doctor who came from a wealthy Georgian family. He had been through a divorce and, frankly, he was lonely. He was also unsure if the local women he was dating were unduly influenced by his family wealth. After consulting with each other, Alice and I decided to introduce him to one of our friends, a recently divorced woman, who was a professor of Philosophy at our local university. This woman had a deep love of and commitment to the rights of animals. If my memory serves me well, they came over to our house for a meal of homemade vegetarian lasagne and whole wheat bread. Every one talked freely and pleasantly until the meal was nearly over. Then our surgeon friend told a story.

Working the Ground

My friend's large plantation derived a substantial income from the harvesting of pecans from thousands of trees. The previous year he had planted several hundred small pecan saplings. One day, his neighbor's goats got free. This was not the first time and he had warned this neighbor to take care this not happen again. Those goats ate every pecan sapling, nipping them neatly at ground level. My friend took out his rifle (I believe it was a Beretta AR70.) and dropped every goat where it stood. My animal-loving friend excused herself and left immediately. I suppose that my wealthy southern friend was just acting expeditiously to see if the relationship had a chance of going somewhere. He knew himself. Sometimes, my friends were simply too divergent to get along with each other. I appreciated them, but they could not tolerate each other very well.

In spite of this spectacular failure at matchmaking, Alice tried again a few months later. In this case, the woman was the daughter of a member of our Peace Works organization. He, too, was a physician and they were both Quakers. To the surprise of all, a marriage and a pregnancy followed!

Our surgeon friend also had a taste for Southern, home-grown justice. At this time, he had a large family practice. As is common in the rural south, he would treat patients whether they could pay immediately or not. Often he would accept payment in eggs, vegetables, or services rendered.

One of his patients was a married woman who was consistently showing up with bruises and other signs of abuse by her husband. She would not press charges against this slime and the situation really started to bother my friend. Eventually, he reached out to a couple of especially rough southern boys. Those boys took the offending husband for a ride down a remote dirt road and delivered an epic ass whooping. They then explained if he ever laid a hand on his wife again, they would be seeing him and would show him what they were *really* capable of. That problem was solved; she was never struck again.

Beginning in 1985 Alice and I became involved with a Central America advocacy group called Witness for Peace. They were

A Second Look at Jesus

acting in opposition to the government policy of offering training and aid to counter revolutionary commandos (Contras) who were attacking Nicaraguan communities from bases in Honduras.

That U.S. government policy was designed to reverse or, at least, contain a popular revolution that had recently overthrown a nasty Dictator, Anistazio Somoza. He and his father before him had created a country that brought tremendous wealth to an elite few. These elite ran large plantations that exported crops of fruit and rope fibers for cash. The mostly landless majority of peasants were given minimal participation in the wealth they helped to produce. Harsh methods were used to preserve this status quo. President Roosevelt had summarized American policy with Nicaragua in 1939 by saying, in a cabinet meeting, "He (Somoza's father) may be a son of a bitch, but he is *our* son of a bitch."

When a popular revolutionary group known as the Sandinistas succeeded in seizing power in 1979, they confiscated many of the large estates of the dictator's close friends and allies. These large holdings were then split up so the peasant majority could each hold title to a small tract and farm their own land. The Sandinistas had won their revolt with aid from Cuba and Russia and they embraced many of the Socialist and Communist ideals that Cuba and Russia espoused. For these reasons, the Reagan Administration targeted them for attack.

Our role in all of this was twofold. At home, we and those we recruited promoted the idea that the American people should not consider the current Nicaraguan government to be our enemies. We also decided to join a number of Americans who were present in the border areas that the Contras frequented. In theory, the Contras would need to avoid the negative public relations associated with killing Americans. We intended to become a human shield of sorts.

The local paper was quite unsympathetic to our cause. They would print some of our letters to the editor, but, after an initial article, they never used any of our material in their own news or

Working the Ground

opinion pieces. The editor in chief felt it was not his job to cater to local people who "suffered from delusions of grandeur." I remember thinking at the time he was suffering from delusions of obscurity. He also thought we were insufficiently mature to know we were dupes for the Nicaraguan Communists. He might have had half a point there, although we did try to be critical of all claims made by the Nicaraguan government too.

Later, we arranged for a newspaper interview with some missionaries who had worked in El Salvador for more than twenty years. These people really did understand what was going on. The newspaper editor declined to run that story too! The excuse given was that these people were *too* experienced and his reporter would be unable to discern if *he* was being deceived. We were never able to make much progress with that newspaper. Instead, we organized demonstrations and purchased billboard space with local donations to make our point.

That year, my local newspaper taught me something of the hidden power of editing. During my more political years, I adopted a regular practice of writing letters to the editor. They tended to conflict with the newspaper's editorial policy. I soon discovered a pattern in my treatment by them. They edited my letters. They consistently removed the sentence or the paragraph that contained the point I was trying to make. The writing that remained was lame and useless. At one point, I got angry and sent in a complaint letter about this bad treatment. However, on this occasion, I sent the letter in a heated rush and neglected to ask Alice for the editing services she usually provided. The newspaper printed 100% of my letter with every error of spelling, grammar, syntax, and continuity fully intact.

Alice and I took a trip to Nicaragua in the spring of 1984. We, along with about two dozen others, landed in Managua and soon we were headed up to Estali, near the border with Honduras. Our Nicaraguan guide told us, in the event our bus was attacked and disabled, we should take one of two actions. If the Contras used

A Second Look at Jesus

machine guns, we should take cover in the ditch. If they used mortars, we should run. These instructions perked my ears up.

The politicians were about what we expected. They tried to stir up the people to perform virtuous social actions with grandiose speeches. The big revelation for us was the common people. In the border area, it seemed that nearly *everyone* was carrying a Russian AK-47. They did not seem to take much joy in these lethal tools. One of them made this point as he carried his rifle draped upon his shoulders. He told me his rifle was his cross to bear until the attacks stopped.

These were not godless Communists. They were Christian Communists who were evangelized to recognize that Jesus was on the side of the poor. They took seriously the social organization of mutual sharing among the earliest Christians, as depicted in the Book of Acts. They knew their *Bible* and acted upon it as they thought right.

They partook of a movement called Liberation Theology. In this reading of the scripture, God was partial to the poor and powerless. The expectation was the yield of the land should be shared equitably. The greedy were condemned roundly for failure to share their wealth. These revolutionary Christians could marshal a great deal of biblical material to support this point of view. Close attention revealed that Jesus and the later prophets gave considerable attention to this topic.

This was in stark contrast with the teaching of the institutional church in Central America. The church taught the common folk to respect and obey the rulers as God had appointed them, to administer in His Name. Many, many priests who taught Liberation Theology were branded as Communists. These priests often disappeared in the middle of the night along with revolutionary organizers and fighters.

My Alice was especially impressed by the humble and loving service the Christian nuns demonstrated in serving the everyday needs of the Nicaraguan people. Likewise, former nuns mostly organized the American side of this peace movement.

Working the Ground

The example of these Godly women reminded Alice of what Christianity could be. She had them in mind when she later decided to rejoin the Christian church.

Eventually a political compromise was reached. An election was scheduled. The attacks tapered off. The Sandinistas lost their political mandate in that next election and then regained it later. Few missed the former days of the "string man" Somoza.

Chapter Twenty

Harmlessness

Hayah

One day, my son, Sam came home very agitated. We calmed him and coaxed the truth out of him. He had witnessed a terrifying scene. At the peak of an argument, a neighbor had pinned his girlfriend to a wall, held a knife against her eye and threatened to kill her. We were floored. As the shock wore off, we tried a number of corrective measures. We made some inquiries and discovered the neighbor was on full Social Security disability and his only obligation was to take his meds regularly. Regrettably, he did not *like* his meds and was *not* regular in taking them. In the end, I was unable to affect a lasting social solution. That neighbor was going to stay *where* he was and *as* he was.

One thing I *did* do was re-examine my commitment to pacifism. I was not especially afraid to die. My spiritual practices had given me a good view of what came next and I felt ready for that chapter when the time came. However, I was not prepared to make the same value judgment for my family. I generally avoid force with every art of charm, persuasion, and guile. However, I decided then and there that I would not rule it out. I do not believe our world is ready for purely non-violent passivity.

Harmlessness

Instead, while force must never be allowed to become the default method to solve our problems, counter-force has a place in the protection of my family, my friends and my country. In my opinion, a weapon should be available to those who are faced with an imminent and grave threat. Waiting until the crisis arrives before changing your mind is just poor planning. Some preparation is necessary. Otherwise, it seems a community of sheep begets a community of wolves. Do we really want a world where only ambitious politicians and criminals control weapons? I do not. Predators thrive on prey. I aspire to be neither.

After a little research, I found a copy of an M1 carbine offered for sale in a local tabloid. I was short of money, but I worked out an agreement with the seller to do some repair to his sports car in exchange for the gun.

The M1 carbine was designed during WW2 as a light and compact semiautomatic weapon for situations not requiring the range and power of the standard-issue Garand rifle. The carbine was a good weapon for close protection. I had not done any shooting since my high school years, so I took the time necessary to become proficient again.

A few years later, that same neighbor threatened to kill me over a trivial matter. Nothing came of the threat. The only result of my interaction with my neighbor was I ceased to be a pacifist.

I continued to be active in anti-war politics. Eventually, I became the leader of the local peace organization. We held a minority opinion in our conservative, southern town. We were, nonetheless, able to exert a certain amount of influence. A friendly radio talk show host gave us open access to his audience. Our congressman, Charlie Rose heard us out, but made us promise not to let anyone know he was sympathetic.

My thinking on war and justice came to a head a few years later, when Saddam Hussein invaded Kuwait. I was shocked to find a majority of the members of my *peace* group were against any attempt to reverse the invasion. I was against aggression,

A Second Look at Jesus

but they were apparently against the use of force for any reason whatsoever.

This western understanding of pacifism superficially resembles a Hindu concept known as *ahimsa*, which means "harmlessness." Within its *Vedic* culture, *ahimsa* is considered an aid to spiritual growth because during meditation we come across abilities and potentialities that can easily be harnessed for personal advantage. If taken too far a person can make quite a nuisance of himself with self-aggrandizement and other follies. In the process, such a person can do quite a lot of harm to himself and others. In anticipation of that harm, such a person might best be isolated from further insight and unable to access their deeper parts until their intent changes. The unseen spiritual government makes the necessary arrangements. Spiritual progress is slowed or even reversed. Dullards or the confused are not much of a threat to others.

On the other hand, a person who can practice self-restraint and use his abilities in a strictly harmless manner and for the benefit of others will not *need* much external restraint. Doors are opened and a spiritual bounty pours in. This is the desired effect of the discipline of *ahimsa*.

This is not, however, the same as pacifism. There are times and circumstances when standing idly by will allow harm to others. This is moral slackness and allows the perpetrator of violent acts to gather sin. Pir's father lived in France during WW1. During that time of national crisis, he observed if the French army adopted pacifism, the Germans would be in Paris the next day. More harm would result, not less.

Simply offering oneself, as fodder to any random bully is likely to make things worse, not better. This just encourages the wrong element. I have come to view weapon ownership as a necessary measure while we try to bring about the spiritual and cultural conditions to make such tools obsolete. In the meantime, the model I hold is that of a healthy immune system. I have chosen to assume some of the abilities of a white blood cell. I move

Harmlessness

gently in society. However, if you are within my sphere of observation, I am prepared and willing to protect you.

While minimizing harm, we retain responsibility for keeping our society balanced and moving in a generally positive direction. The point is that harmlessness in our complex world requires enlightened intent, wisdom, and skill. True harmlessness is a Godly virtue; we can only approximate it. It remains necessary that we try to do maximum good and minimum harm in each decision we make. This is true in our relationships, our government, our interaction with the natural world, and with the spiritual realm.

I aspire to strength, mastery and the ability to control my life, yet without vulnerability there is no spirituality, no growth, no evolution and no life. Determining a healthy balance in this aspect of my existence is a dilemma I am challenged to face daily.

The leading spokesperson for the pacifist view in our peace organization was a man who had formerly been a Catholic monk. He and his wife (a former nun) were good-hearted people although somewhat naive. However, he had been deeply disappointed in his spiritual life. When I had tried to talk about meditation with him, he dismissed it as "Tinkerbell stuff." I mourned for him. In the end, I had to withdraw from the Peace Movement since we had scant basis for understanding each other.

Chapter Twenty-One

Child Takeover

Hayah

I deeply enjoyed my boat building school. Wooden boat building is both a practical, and a poetic endeavor. I kept my tools sharp. Every day I learned more about forming, bending and fastening wood. The art was in the bending. The boat ribs and bulkheads defined the hull shapes. Bending planks around them created a symphony of tensions that produced sensuous, curved forms. The water did not object to their nuanced passage.

On a whim, I developed a nautical theology. I saw that my life, when seen as a whole, might resemble a sturdy, but plain sailboat. Organized religion, tradition and history make up the weighted keel. While it is mostly dead weight, it is very helpful for keeping me upright and on track. The hull is made up of my life choices. Consistency builds a watertight hull and cabin, and results in a reduced need for bailing! The decision to do more than drift requires having a spiritual life and that requires a mast and rigging. The sails are my spiritual practices. I change them from time to time, as weather requires. The water is this world and the wind is the spiritual realm. The art and science of life is adjusting the trim of the sails and guiding the whole vessel in an advantageous relationship with the wind and water.

Child Takeover

After graduating from the boat building program, there was most likely no job in that field which would provide for my family. Instead, I acquired and renovated two more houses on Queen Street. I rented the houses and was poised to do the same thing for years. Then I made a change in my work strategy. I became qualified as a General Contractor. I went to the extra trouble and expense of getting a commercial license to do both residential and commercial work. Thereafter, I derived most of my income in this line of work.

I had the good fortune to get some simple and effective advice at the very beginning of my contracting career. An older, experienced man advised me that if I got firm prices from reliable specialists for each aspect of the job, I could know my costs within a very small margin of error. Then, if I could keep my overhead low and add a reasonable mark-up, I would be able to earn a living. I found this formula reliable, as long as I followed it and the economy was not too perverse.

This line of work was also good for my soul. It required that I develop the ability to build teams of good quality people, communicate clearly and see jobs through to a timely and good quality conclusion. The work helped to root me in the *here and now* and prevented me from getting lost in the *always and everywhere* I was discovering through meditation.

Alice had a similar effect in the more personal and intimate realm we shared. Her love and desire for me brought out tender qualities that complimented and completed the rest of my being. In the end, she may prove my greatest teacher.

Alice told me her experience of meditation differed from mine. While I talked about energy and the experience of being very high and broad, Alice said, for her, meditation was like entering a deep and silent cave. *Vive la difference!*

A Second Look at Jesus

Hayah

My Daughters
Two living poems,
Sacred sprouts, from the Garden of Life
Delivered to the temple of Love
With passion and tenderness,
Entrusted
To my beloved friend and partner
This fine autumn night.

John

After many years of frequent and passionate practice, Alice and I decided to try our hand at making a baby. A few months later, Alice and I conceived fraternal twins who were born in May of 1986. I was overwhelmed by the wonder and challenge of being a father. I was there at their birth. Alice experienced a prolonged delivery and performed like a champion. I caught both of my daughters as they emerged. Their tender perfection charmed me beyond words. Shanti came first. She was 5 lbs. 12 oz. Emma followed an hour later and weighed 6 lbs. 3 oz.

After a few days, Emma developed jaundice and she needed numerous transfusions of fresh blood to dilute the toxins her liver was slow to eliminate. I will always remember her grasping my little finger with her tiny hand as her blood was drained and replaced. She was so tender and vulnerable.

By this time, we had moved to a new house down the street. The girls had their own small room adjoining our bedroom that served as nursery. Alice chose to nurse the children. Due to this and the general demands of mothering twins, she was exhausted much of the time. I helped and she persevered. I was and am so proud of her.

As usual for our enterprises, childrearing was an occasion for improvisation. This was before the present era of specialized twin gear. Instead, we purchased a pair of lightweight, folding strollers

Child Takeover

and I simply attached each to the other with three 2x4 blocks and drywall screws, which worked like a charm. I made bunk beds out of yellow pine. Shanti, the more daring child, claimed the top bunk. Emma would kick from below when she was provoked.

Alice and I joked our children were more like opposites than twins. Where Shanti would sparkle and flash, Emma would radiate and glow. Shanti had the habit of politely sticking her tongue out in greeting to all strangers. Emma favored hugs. If Emma was crying, we could be reasonably sure Shanti had provoked the tears. Emma would then follow up with an appropriate counterstroke. Both girls were gifted artists. Shanti was left-handed and, we discovered, dyslexic like her mother, uncle and her grandfather.

Alice and I each named one of the girls. I chose the name for Shanti because her bright sparkling soul reminded me of the resonant Sanskrit name for peace. In India, the pundits always ended their chanting of Vedic Hymns with "Aum Shanti, Shanti, Shanti." This peace is not the peace of final resolution at death. Rather, it is the harmonious peace of abundant, sparkling potential at the dawn of creation.

Alice chose the name Emma that is Germanic and means whole or universal one. This fit her gentle, soulful nature well.

I tried to be a good father. I hope all of my children will overlook some of my shortcomings and focus primarily on my intent. I wanted them to thrive. I believe they are all successful in their chosen paths today and I take delight in them.

I Was Wrong
The other day, as I wandered among my luminous
inner spaces I detected a stale, malodorous whiff
It seemed to come from a deep aching pain
A little to the left of center
It ran from crown to toe, cramping all points in between
Looking closer I came upon a closet with captives so
tightly bound that breathing was nearly impossible

A Second Look at Jesus

*Drawing them out I applied loving breaths day and
night until they stirred and began to tell their story
They were a collection of subtle, tender tendencies of
little earthly use or harm to anyone
They had gotten in the way of my ambitions
I had not thought myself to be such a brute
I was wrong*

John

The 10,000 Idiots
*It is always a danger to aspirants on the Path
When they begin
To believe and act
As if the ten thousand idiots
Who so long ruled
And lived Inside
Have all packed their bags
And skipped town
Or died.*

Hafiz[9]

The Sad Game
*Blame
It keeps stealing all of your wealth
Giving it to an imbecile with
No financial skills.
Dear one
Wise
Up*

Hafiz[10]

Chapter Twenty-Two

Ripening Crops

Hayah

The Beginning
In the beginning I wanted enlightenment
and cosmic consciousness, too.

I had just the sketchiest idea of what that meant.
It just seemed a neat concept.

Now, forty years on,
theory has been traded for fact.
Now and then, my soul purges itself.

Like a binge drinker,
I vomit out the hypocrisy of this world.

Then, from the depths of my being, comes an irresistible in-breath,
The last gasp of a drowning man.

My entire human form becomes an irresistible straw,
drawing in the essence, the nectar of life
from its unfathomable source.

A Second Look at Jesus

*With this authoritative power, transformers
have come alive all along my spine.*

*Their humming, radiant, oscillation
forms a sonorous background,
As the remaining days and nights come and go,
and a galaxy of new possibilities present themselves.*

John

Alice and I kept up with our meditation and study. We meditated for about thirty minutes morning and evening. We read widely and taught classes. Once a year we attended the weeklong meditation camp with Pir Vilayat in New Lebanon, New York. I also completed my training to become a retreat guide.

In 2004 my trusted spiritual guide, Pir Vilayat, died. His son, Pir Zia has taken over responsibility for the Sufi Order established by his father and grandfather. He has taken his own course. Among other initiatives, Pir Zia appears to be working toward reintegrating the Sufi Order of the West into the traditional mainstream of Sufi teaching and practice.

During this entire time span of 1981 through today, Alice and I have experienced steady spiritual growth. The roots of our lives went deeper, the branches reached wider. The practical result for me is that fear played a progressively smaller role in my life. I thrived by mixing elements in my life that normally are segregated in our society. I was an avid gun owner, even as I was also an ardent lover of peace. I was a passionate husband and caring father who loved solitude. I had many friends; young, old, Democrat, Republican, rich, poor, black, white etc.

Ripening Crops

New Product at the Kiosk
I have been selling the contents of my soul.
Business is brisk.
I am locally famous for my referral service.
My server hums and glows as I introduce The One to the many.
Truthfully, it is getting a little old.
I have discovered a new product.
It is the original spring, pristine and still.
Broad shores beckon, offering any number a private access.
Living Water in unlimited quantities is ready to flow.
The problem is the price.
If I try to give it away, the customers may suspect a con.
It really does appear too good to be true.
Perhaps I should give a free coupon with the lunch special.
Then people might try it.
They will discover its true value soon enough.

John

My inner life had become an area beyond strain or concern and just kept rolling along. The more difficult challenge was translating from that cornucopia into something practical and effective in everyday life. I became downward and upward reaching in equal measure. Marriage, parenthood, livelihood were tremendously important to my life. I loved the beauty and challenge of the relationships. The loving complexity of my family kept me from losing touch with earthly concerns.

Burnt Sacrifice on Oleander Drive
My truck and I were doing some minor
damage to a speed law.
The intersection of Oleander and Independence
was coming up fast and the light was still green.
I pressed harder.

A Second Look at Jesus

Suddenly, my soul collided with a spiritual fact;
I saw the Earth and all it contained reaching up
and through an ancient priest with a sacred fire.
The sacrifice of all creation was transformed
into a sacred essence
that rose up
and
dissipated into the infinite sky.
While this brother of Melchizedek reconciled for us,
my truck passed on down the road
I don't think that anyone noticed, but me.

John

Now and then, Alice and I would take solitary meditation retreats. In particular, I remember one that went on for several weeks, in the winter of 1998. I was in the New Hampshire countryside. Every day my guide, Aziza, brought me a fresh menu of meditation practices. These were interspersed with music tapes and walks in crystalline, wintery nature.

The high point of that time was an entirely unexpected encounter with something entirely new to me. In the higher, angelic realms (upon which our earthly existence depends), we have a purer and more splendid stature. At a certain degree of refinement, we can apprehend ourselves as vast spheres that spin with an indescribable joy and majesty. When I came upon this vision, I was deeply moved. The event that came next devastated me.

These spheres do not exist in isolation. Now and then, we would intersect with others of our kind. As we interpenetrated, a music of cosmic scale, an unsurpassable splendor resulted and was felt throughout my being. It began like a cascade of crystalline chimes and progressed to deep bass tones before ascending again. I found that the spheres flexed and yielded to each other, in a nearly organic manner, accommodating with

Ripening Crops

pure joy their impact and interpenetration. This communion of souls we seek in vain to express with words.

I did not know what to make of this encounter. The next year I described it to my meditation guide, Azimat. She brightened up and said; "Yes, yes, *that* is the music of the spheres."

With all due respect, to Gene Rodenberry, outer space is *not* the final frontier. Inner space far excels the outer in scope.

The following poem is *not* suitable for literalists with no sense of humor. They should pass it by.

Omnivore

We were born to be consumed
We resist this truth to our detriment
Our Creator has lavished infinite care and resources
so that we may be ripe and savory,
according to our nature,
in various combinations of sweet, salty, pungent and sour.
Then, with an inconceivable range of appetite
He delights in consuming all.
Truly, some of us seem somewhat gamey or putrid.
Others appear mostly roughage.
Nonetheless, a little extra roasting or munching
makes everything go down just fine.
Our essences are released and, in a joyous reunion, the whole
story of our experience provides endless joy for all.
There is one variation on this process,
an early release program,
so to speak.
Sometimes, knowing what is in store,
and desiring to enjoy the great climax now,
we can voluntarily submit ourselves to
cooking and tenderizing
while we live.

A Second Look at Jesus

*If skilfully done, we become tasty morsels
so enticing the diner accepts them
here and now.*

*As we serve up portions of our selves the Great
Gourmand obligingly gulps them down
Our heart
Our mind
Our soul
Our strength.*

*Eventually only a shell remains, filled with the
transcendental perfume
of divine satisfaction.*

Surely, such a death is preferable to any other.

John

Alice went back to college after the twins were old enough to enter kindergarten. She got a bachelor's degree in interior design. Then she went on to open a successful business designing and selling kitchens. She gives wonderful service to her customers. They are lucky to have her.

Just as Alice was thriving in her new career, I was enjoying my own. I was also honored to serve on the local board of Habitat for Humanity. It was a good way to use my professional abilities to help people to achieve more mastery in their lives.

Intention
Thank you, Lord, for accepting the toxic, blinding brew that we have concocted and exchanging it for your own sweet shining nature. Surely, life as your servant is preferable to lordship over the sad, pathetic kingdoms that we have cobbled together. Our relationship, so implausible and yet real, is your

Ripening Crops

*eternal gift. Thank you again and again for your gift of
life and the grace of time, so that we can come around
to your point of view.
With your own love*

John

In the mid-1990s, I added electoral politics to my interests. I started life under the political influence of the Democratic Party. My parents were staunch believers. In my grandfather's home, Franklin Roosevelt was revered. In the late 1950's my father became the Democratic Party Chairman for Marathon County, Wisconsin. I remember helping him run for Congress in central Wisconsin in 1962. At age eleven, I shook hundreds of hands at various county fairs and distributed thousands of pieces of literature. He also flew Congressman David Obey, Governor Nelson, and others around the state in a single engine Cessna.

My parents were proud, committed liberals. I recently looked at a piece of my father's 1962 campaign literature. He advocated for minimum wages and college loans. Among his qualifications, he listed experience as a small businessman, father, and membership in an anti-Communist discussion group.

My father read constantly and broadly. I remember he had a particular respect for conservative William F. Buckley. Often, he would urge me to sit and listen to Buckley's television show <u>Firing Line.</u> Buckley challenged all of my father's political views, but he was brilliant. My father wanted me to experience that excellence of thought.

Over time, I saw virtues and vice in both liberal and conservative persuasions. In the end, I have become most satisfied with the political view of the Libertarian Party. It seemed then and still seems now that their twin focus on freedom and responsibility come closest to a viable and adaptable political philosophy. Libertarians also have the virtue of having a worldview that closely resembles the one present among our founders when our

A Second Look at Jesus

nation was formed. For me, the Libertarian approach has been a Rosetta Stone to help me untangle the history of our country and the competing claims in present day politics.

The following is a line of analysis that has become meaningful to me. From the time of Moses to King Saul, the people of Israel had very little government. For the most part, they simply tried to live up to their spiritual and ethical laws as defined in their scripture. If a dispute arose among them because the application of those laws was unclear, they would seek out a mutually respected mediator, a judge, to clarify the correct application of the religious law. If there was a great crisis, such as an invasion from a neighboring power, the most respected judge was selected to lead the nation as a whole until the crisis had passed. Then, everything would revert to local resolution of local disputes.

At that time in Jewish history, during the 12th century BC, there were frequent emergencies. The people conceived a desire to appoint a permanent judge, a King who would establish a permanent national army and deal with menacing neighbors. The leading prophet at that time, Samuel, warned the people that God did not approve of this enterprise. In first Samuel 8:10-18 he said: *"So Samuel told all the words of the Lord to the people who were asking for a king from him. He said, 'These will be the ways of the king who will reign over you: he will take your sons and appoint them to his chariots and to be his horsemen and to run before his chariots. And he will appoint for himself commanders of thousands and commanders of fifties, and some to plow his ground and to reap his harvest, and to make his implements of war and the equipment of his chariots. He will take your daughters to be perfumers and cooks and bakers. He will take the best of your fields and vineyards and olive orchards and give them to his servants. He will take the tenth of your grain and of your vineyards and give it to his officers and to his servants. He will take your male servants and female servants and the best of your young men and your donkeys, and put them to his work. He will take the tenth of your flocks, and you shall be his slaves. And in that day,*

Ripening Crops

you will cry out because of your king, whom you have chosen for yourselves, but the Lord will not answer you in that day.' " Having heard all of this, the people insisted upon having a king and Saul was chosen to rule Israel.

European kings considered themselves to be like Saul, appointed by God and answerable only to God. In essence, they owned the country along with all the assets and all the people. They delegated some of their power to local royalty who represented them, but the system was entirely a top-down affair. This system could work reasonably well if the king was wise and virtuous. However, more often than not, the kings were no more wise or virtuous than average. Sometimes, they were much less.

In the middle of the 17th century, Charles I of England was widely considered an especially foolish, lazy and self-centered King. Parliament, which had been chosen to advise him, chose instead to gather an army and establish its own control over the country. Even after his capture, the King adamantly refused to share power. He eventually lost his head on the chopping block. Later, the son of King Charles was invited to come back to England to rule, but with a much-reduced scope of authority. The elected parliament would now control all public revenue and set the nation's policy. The king would only be allowed to rule within the guidelines established by Parliament. This lesson of English history was front and center in the minds of America's Founding Fathers.

In the run-up to the American Revolutionary War, King George III and his friends in Parliament began to impose their will upon the American Colonies in a way that was inconsistent with the limits of power established by Parliament a century before. Colonials resisted this attempt to reverse the gains in liberty that had been won at the time of the English Civil War in 1651 and then reaffirmed by the Glorious Revolution of 1688.

This hard-won *status quo* was considered the most enlightened government system in the world and was the British constitution guaranteed that arrangement. From that perspective, King

A Second Look at Jesus

George III was true rebel and he was trying to destroy our rights as Englishmen. We colonists knew the true situation and we prepared to say no to our King in a manner that he could not fail to understand. The details of that argument offer an enduring lesson for those who understand history.

Another event needs to be mentioned. The ability of government to control the population through religion began to unravel in the colonies. Previously the Pope and then later, the King of England claimed the power to speak for God's Church and make religious judgments in the name of God. During the later Colonial period, especially in the frontier areas, people were not much connected to established religion or they were practicing a specialized form of Christianity such as the Anabaptists, Quakers, Huguenots, and Mennonites.

In the 1730's and 1740's, many "unchurched" Colonials reengaged religion in a new and more exciting fashion than ever before. Great Christian orators, such as Jonathan Edwards and George Whitefield, deemphasized the importance of church doctrine. Instead, they put a greater focus on the individual and his or her spiritual experience. The people responded with enthusiasm and in vast numbers. George Whitefield, for example, possessed such a dramatic flair and a powerful voice that he was able to preach outdoors to crowds numbering in the thousands.

The political effect of this religious activity was that large numbers of Americans became accustomed to listening, reading, and thinking for themselves in important matters such as religious association. Those associations were also more democratic in nature than in the established church. Churches grew from the *ground up* rather than from the *top down*. Often individual churches hired and fired their ministers. If a church ceased to please or satisfy, a member could simply attend another church that seemed better in his estimation.

A new political concept began to form because of all of this political and religious ferment. People began to conceive of themselves as "sovereign individuals." Instead of looking to the King

Ripening Crops

or his Bishops for authority, people began to act upon their experience of God personally touching them. They considered the King's mandate to rule in no way superior to their own authority from God to live according to the virtuous examples of Jesus and the prophets. The range of their authority may not have extended beyond themselves and their affairs, but it was not inferior in quality to the King's authority. Now, between sovereign individuals, democracy made sense. For religious sceptics the same concepts were framed in terms of Providence and Natural Law. This kind of thinking may seem conventional today, but in the latter part of the 18th century, it was entirely fresh and powerful.

Thomas Jefferson and many others among the founders were believers with reservations as to the literal truth of the Bible. They were influenced by biblical critiques and analyses by authors such as Joseph Priestly, David Hume, and Edward Gibbon. To them, it seemed clear that Jesus operated from a basis of authentic connection with the Creator with great knowledge, wisdom and mastery. However, many considered the followers of Jesus to be governed more by superstition and personal prejudice than by the virtue of Jesus. These sceptical perspectives formed a point of reference for the Age of Enlightenment and the ideals that formed the U.S. Constitution. As a result, religion was placed in a separate but highly valued symbiotic relationship to government.

American Founding Fathers took the teachings of the *Bible* seriously, but many were not literalists. Many were minimally Christian Deists. They were deeply moved by the ethical philosophy of Jesus. They believed in God, but they were sceptical about the miracles and some parts of Christian doctrine. Thomas Jefferson, for example, produced a slimmer *New Testament Bible* with portions he trusted cut out and glued in a blank journal book. The portions he was sceptical about were put aside.

Patrick Henry reported in 1775, an itinerant preacher (likely a Baptist) was actually whipped to death in Culpepper, Virginia, for preaching without a license. At that time in Virginia, the

A Second Look at Jesus

Church of England held a monopoly on religion. Although he was a traditional Christian himself, Patrick Henry joined with a majority of founders to insulate their new country from religious factionalism and the divisive passions that arose from it. At the same time, the founders honored the virtue that came from a widespread interest in and dedication to the teachings of Jesus.

Libertarians are more or less up to speed on all of these concepts. Libertarian philosophy offers two guidelines for human behavior that elegantly sum up their worldview:

First, we should not initiate force. Defense is permitted, but we are not entitled to solve our other problems with force. Choices free of coercion are usually better, since we choose based upon our intelligence and make personal commitment to the path chosen.

Second, we should not practice fraud. Truth, or its absence, are central to every interaction. With accurate information, we can make decisions that are more informed. Any informed choice should be respected so long as we do not harm others. It is between the parties in the agreement and God. If we do not like the outcome, we can make a better agreement next time.

With these two principles in force, the rest of the Bill of Rights and the spirit that directed the design of our Constitution become sensible. So long as people are free to make mistakes and all of us are able to learn from them, humankind as a whole *will* progress. Only deception and coercion have kept us ignorant and confused. This approach to political thought makes sense to me. Inspired by political philosophy that reflected my experience and values, I became more politically daring.

Politics could be fun too. I remember reacting to a local example of government waste. In the late 1990's a large public housing development was torn down along one of our busiest roads. That housing was structurally sound and at most, needed renovation. Nonetheless, down it came. Then, for a number of years, the land remained vacant. I decided the situation was ripe for a comment.

I had a stack of scrap plywood I had acquired in connection with my contracting business. My political friend, Paul and I primed

Ripening Crops

it in white and painted our message on one of them **YOUR TAX DOLLARS AT WORK**. We attached it to an existing chain link fence in front of the large vacant lot on Dawson St. Thousands of cars drove past our sign every day. In a few days, the sign disappeared. We replaced it. This one went down more promptly than the first. We replaced it again with advanced adhesives and special high security fastenings that could not be removed with normal tools. We kept this up for a month with increasing ingenuity on our part. The Housing Authority responded with escalating diligence and efficiency. I suspect they developed some kind of quick reaction force. I suspect they had to remove many of those signs in little pieces.

Our local newspaper, *The Star News* was located just a short distance down the same road, but they took no notice. The paper was politically disinclined to find any of this newsworthy or interesting in Libertarian philosophy. It was a drama for the observant alone. I eventually ran out of free plywood and rested from my efforts.

Within a relatively short interval, the vacant land was filled with a large, new housing complex. It was actually rather attractive. Years later, I made a passing reference to these signs to the housing director and he reacted as if he had seen a ghost. He asked, "Did you have something to do with that?" I smiled.

I am deeply thankful for the opportunity of living in the United States of America. The confluence of personal freedom, tolerance, and a relatively nonintrusive government has provided a very good home for the kind of well-rounded growth I aspire to. I thank God and my brave and wise ancestors for this wonderful country.

When I became politically active, I ran for state and local offices four times over a six-year span. I never won any of those races, but I earned the respect of my peers for the way I ran. As a result, the local office holders have always made themselves available to hear my perspective.

A Second Look at Jesus

I also learned plenty about human interaction. Running for office is like doing serial job interviews with thousands of individual employers. Brevity and clarity are mandatory as a proper attitude. A politician is supposed to be a public servant. If taken seriously, this resolve cultivates a nobility of character.

Around this time, I began to better appreciate the character of our veterans. I found them to be remarkably free from the frothy consumer mentality that our popular culture cultivates. This may be partly the result of their recognition of mortality and an abiding gratitude for the gift of their survival.

It has been said that humanity can be usefully divided up into those people who run away from trouble and those who run toward it. Without getting into the ethics implied here, I came to value the superior friendships that can be developed with people who face challenges. I also came to prefer the simpler, more objective problems associated with facing threats. People self-select for threat orientation. While soldiers, police, and firefighters are rich in this front-facing perspective, I have found that the brave can be discovered anywhere. I am constantly on the lookout.

I learned to fly in 1998. Aviation was a severe challenge and I loved it. Safe flying requires acute situational awareness, coordination, technical-analytical skills, and the ability to perform well under stress. Nothing could be a further stretch from the calming and intuitive experience of meditation.

Eventually, I became an instrument-rated pilot. Nothing I had ever done was more difficult. Normal flight primarily involves looking out of the cockpit to determine direction and elevation. Supplementing this is the sensation of the airplane moving under you. You literally feel changes where you sit. This is where the expression "flying by the seat of your pants" comes from. The view out of the windshield, the instruments, and the sensation of the aircraft moving, combine to give an accurate assessment.

In instrument flight, all of these subtle indicators are unavailable or are deceptive. If you are in the clouds, it feels as though you are inside a washing machine. Everything around you is a

Ripening Crops

translucent grey or white. At the same time, the aircraft is constantly jostling around in response to the complex air currents. On average, an untrained pilot who enters clouds loses control of his aircraft after two to three minutes. Death usually follows shortly thereafter.

Instrument pilots need to unlearn much of their earlier training and ignore all normal sensory input. Instead, the information observed on the instruments such as the artificial horizon, compass, airspeed indicator, and altimeter must be the sole sensory input considered. Successful instrument flight requires using all of the information from half a dozen instruments correctly, interpreting them moment to moment while making numerous, small corrections with the controls to keep the aircraft upright and on course. Talking to air controllers, changing channels on the radio, and changing navigation settings, all need to be done effectively while still keeping the aircraft stable. This is a tremendous challenge. One of my most satisfying accomplishments was entering clouds within moments of take-off and not seeing terra firma again for another several hours, just before landing at my destination.

In all, I have nearly 1,000 logged flight hours. Those hours include many family trips that have bound us closer together. They also have provided thrilling insights that could not be obtained otherwise. Passing around or through mountainous clouds at 160 mph is a mind-expanding thrill. We have all seen rainbows. When seen from the air they are not arcs, but perfect circles of multi-colored light. I am thankful for the experiences that my instructors and modern technology have brought me.

I would be less than truthful to say my flying career was one triumph after another. About ten years ago, I mistakenly landed at a very small, private airport near the larger one at which I had intended to land. As soon as I was on the ground, I realized my mistake. I had my family with me and I was embarrassed by my error. My judgment was impaired by my pride and further mistakes followed.

A Second Look at Jesus

Taking off usually requires more runway than landing. Getting off the runway is obtainable in a few hundred feet because the "ground effect" of the ground supporting air under the wings. Accelerating another thirty or forty miles per hour is then necessary before moving through the air fast enough to climb away.

In this instance, the short runway had tall trees on one end (bad) and a pond on the other end followed by a cornfield (not so bad). I was airborne halfway down the runway as I should have been, but I was going too slowly to climb away by the time I got to the down-sloping hill and pond at the end of the runway. The plane followed the contour of the earth as it sloped down toward the pond. I flew over the pond, but my landing gear struck the soft dirt of the cornfield. The landing gear was plucked off the wing and we all came to a rapid stop among the cornstalks. My head was banged up. Everyone else was untouched except by the shock of the experience.

What I *should* have done was lighten the airplane. I should also have safeguarded my family by offloading them. I would also have been wise to remove some fuel from my nearly full tanks. Waiting until the air was cooler (and denser) near dusk would have been a good idea too. I am sure that if I had swallowed my pride and stopped to think rationally, I would have taken off safely. Instead, my bad judgment could have been deadly.

There was another important lesson coming my way. The owners of that airport took us in and treated us with abundant kindness. They provided every kind of practical help. I have no idea that their religious views were, but that family personified Christian love for us.

The insurance company was great too. They actually paid me more than I had invested in the airplane. They kindly encouraged me to learn from my mistake and keep flying. I was later able to buy a more powerful version of the same airplane (a Cherokee 180). This more powerful 235 horsepower model would certainly have gotten my family safely out of that situation. There are so

Ripening Crops

many good people around and it is an uplifting surprise to see how they rally in a genuine crisis.

Similarly, during this time, I spent some time and treasure upgrading my firearm gear and training. I became a student and later, an instructor with a rifleman training organization called the Revolutionary War Veterans Association (RWVA). The traditional methods they used, such as acquiring a natural point of aim, taking a repertory pause, and following through are mostly neglected today, except by the Marine Corps, snipers, and competitive shooters.

The RWVA also teaches a slice of Revolutionary War history to illustrate the importance of marksmanship in American culture. Modern day politics are a forbidden topic within this organization. We stick to the politics of 1775.

It is my understanding that, last year, the RWVA held more than 1,000 training events spread across all fifty states. All instructors are volunteers. Thanks to them, I have known the satisfaction of repeatedly hitting a standard NRA target at 800 or 1,000 yards. It is an interesting skill to have mastered.

The Delta

Chapter Twenty-Three

Returning Home

Hayah

The Swamp
*I have a friend who has been mucking around
in a swamp for some time
She has been up to her thighs in thick, stinking slime
Dark, obscured creatures were seen to dart and slither
She kept at it.*

*Then, the other day, she offered a pure, refreshing
glass of water to our circle of friends
She was also wearing some fragrant blossoms
On closer observation I saw a stream
And,
A garden taking root in firm, moist soil
She had found the spring under that swamp,
cleared a channel for it to flow,
and,
the
swamp*

A Second Look at Jesus

Drained.
Hallelujah

John

Several years ago, I accepted an invitation from Alice to go to church. She joined a small Church. They provided her with a rich, loving context she had been craving for some time. This was an arrangement she simply would not live without. I enjoy relationships, but have always been somewhat more aloof. For me, the monk's cave always beckons.

I was willing to try church, but there were a few barriers to my joining. Foremost among them was a lingering awkwardness between myself and the theological assumptions of the modern church. I simply had good reason to follow my own counsel on certain matters. I did not want to quarrel, but I was resolved to be true to my own experience. The next Sunday, I was invited by the Senior Warden of the Church Vestry to become a member of that church. I spoke frankly with her, explaining that I held some dissenting views and I did not intend to renounce them simply to get along. If she and the church could accept me on those terms, I was in; otherwise, I was out. She said, "Come in." I did.

This contrasted with my father's experience. His father was a Baptist of Welsh and Anglo-Saxon origin. My grandmother was an Irish Catholic. My grandfather had to promise his fiancée's priest that all of his children would be raised under Catholicism. He kept his promise. My father told me only once had he tried to opt out of Sunday mass. Grandfather delivered some rapid and skilled attitude correction of the type that left bruises. My grandfather was a rough, tough man. On the positive side, my father always considered himself fortunate to have received training from the Jesuits in nearby Brighton, New York. He credited the intellectual rigor he learned from them as an advantage that served him well his whole life.

Returning Home

Having been raised as a Roman Catholic, I know their ways reasonably well. I have since come to view the Church of Rome as a respected mother with some traits that are particularly hard for me to live with. In particular, I have found she has a somewhat expansive view of her authority and the prerogatives that come with her seniority. Although the church where I am presently residing is a younger and more genial "aunt," I honor the good that the Church of Rome has accomplished. I value the hard-won lessons of her two thousand year history.

In 2014, the Catholic Church elected a promising new leader, Pope Francis. I wish him well in what appears to be a sincere attempt to refocus his church on those values that matter most.

My life, as I have come to live it, could not have been possible without the cultivation of friendship, social tenderness, and delicacy learned from my church friends and my wife. As I see it, Christ's message is the unreserved affirmation of life, calling for the free, intelligent, and voluntary sharing of every resource likely to advance the cause of good. What is good? It is full and free communion with the Source of Life. To accomplish this, we must make an uncompromising commitment to serve the most low and degraded as a willing tool of the most high. This is relationship writ large. In all of this, the example of Jesus is foremost. For me, the church family has provided a practical context for fresh beginnings and an opportunity to put spiritual insights into practice.

The overall approach of my particular church has been personally helpful to me. Institutionally, my church is confident enough in the values they love that they allow respectful latitude for their members to reach their own conclusions, in their own time. We know our church is not responsible for our relationship with God. *Each of us is individually responsible.* The church just helps. Faith, experience, and knowledge are allowed to grow slowly and organically over time. As a result, members tend to have a highly personalized and resilient belief structure. Checking every box in the doctrinal list is not required on a moment-to-moment basis. A few elements of Christianity thoroughly incorporated into

A Second Look at Jesus

our lives are considered better than a superficial assent to all expectations at once. In sum, because this church is patient, I have been able to grow. Because they are humble, I can become bold. This has been my experience.

I have found that when experience rather than doctrine leads, our lives can become like a living work of art. Scripture and tradition are competent to inform, but not control life. Only the Spirit of God is qualified for that job. Effective prayer helps opening to that Holy Spirit. *Discovery prayer* offers a venue for the innocent, pre-human impulses that nourish our existence to interface with our conscious mind. With regular experience of these realms, their influence will be felt more directly and with increasingly clarity within our daily lives. We and those we touch will be transformed as the impressions of this world are systematically exposed to the divine perspective. I have found that, with *Discovery Prayer*, I am progressively rendered more thoroughly and joyfully subservient to the Author of Life.

With this spiritual updraft from our relationship with our Creator, we are uplifted. We have more inner resources to meet challenges in our lives. We become naturally more sober regarding worldly circumstances and more joyous regarding spiritual existence. We enthusiastically come to accept our own part in a lifelong cooperative enterprise with our Creator.

One problem with religion based on an imposed belief structure is that it can produce a brittle faith and personality. If some element of the belief structure cannot be adequately supported, the whole structure is prone to shatter like a tempered glass window. I know this first hand by the way I thought and interacted, when I was fully programmed as a youth. I have since concluded that this is, unfortunately, true among many believers. It appears they are convinced that on spiritual matters, *belief* is superior to *experience*. Is this really the best way to approach the subject of God? The distrust of personal insight assumes genuine experience is either unobtainable or inferior to a doctrine. It is not. With a more

Returning Home

flexible, experience-based approach, challenges are more likely to be an occasion for adjustment and growth rather than breakage.

To be fair, I need to acknowledge a very thorough and faithful reading of traditional scriptures can be a reliable way to stimulate insight into the character of God. This study narrows the focus of what God *must be like* to have left such signs as He did.

As I understand it, the best method of reading scripture is in a manner called *lectio divina*, or reading with the soul oriented to recognize the Bible as the expression of God. Regarding the mind, the result of this method is like using a surveyor's transit to take a fix and a bearing from one example of divine expression after another. This approach to scriptural study is an answer to the question: What perspective is Spirit of God making intelligible through this Bible author? If done properly, the lines of insight intersect in scripture, and us, to locate and define the divine potential inherent in the *Bible* and in the human condition.

For example, Jesus is quoted as saying, "My father and I are one," and "No man is good, only God." If both of these quotes are reliable, and I believe they are, then a true reading of the stature of Jesus will include both his complete identification with the Source of Creation and a radical personal humility. In other words, the reality of God was fully present only when the personality of the man, Jesus, was fully absent or transparent. He affirmed there is no existence apart from God. We cannot confirm this however, until our inner life begins to function in a manner like that of Jesus. Until then, these words reflect only abstract concepts and speculative thought.

Enlightened reading of scripture requires having at least a glimmer of insight into God's perspective before we look for meaning. If we begin with this insight, scripture opens before us because the same divine spirit that inspired the authors is interpreting the work for us. Therefore, when relevant scripture is available, there is no good reason to reinvent the wheel. We should use it! Seekers have been finding God since the beginning of time and traditional religious testimony should not be neglected.

A Second Look at Jesus

However, unenlightened scriptural reading leaves a big footprint. In the past, a heavy Christian tread has crushed many. For example, the church once persecuted scientists who believed the Earth was round or revolved around the Sun. Narrow reading of scripture also causes many to make erroneous assumptions about the spiritual lives of Christian dissenters and non-Christians.

Consider the matter of blaming the all Jewish people for the execution of Jesus. At a critical moment, according to the Bible, the crowd of Jews present at the trial of Jesus called upon Pilate to crucify Jesus. When he hesitated, the crowd of Jews before him are reported as saying in Matthew 27:24 "And all the people answered and said, His blood be on us, and on our children." Regrettable results followed from the perverse and misguided doctrine followed from *that* verse. I observe two thousand years of bullying for the simple offense of refusing to be convinced about Christian doctrine.

The long-running ill will cultivated by our church against Jews culminated in the murder of millions during WW2. Yes, the Nazis did the actual acts of murder, but we Christians are responsible for the cumulative effects of this malicious Christian doctrine that set the stage for those murders. Our failure to use discernment and kindness in writing and reading scripture can lead to disaster. We are generally better off if we grant others the benefit of the doubt. Of course, for this to work, we need to be capable of doubt.

Scripture depends upon the insights and deeds of our predecessors. We are always playing catch-up with scripture. For some believers, if the Bible does not require something, it is more or less *forbidden*. For others, spiritual life becomes interpreted as *perfect emulation* of the written word. When that turns out to be unobtainable, we are disappointed.

Scripture is a description of reality. It is one-dimensional if it is without an echo from our own soul. If we can find a way, we must, at any price, access the reality itself. Then, the same power responsible for writing the scripture will inform us what the original intent was. We must *not* be satisfied with the description alone.

Returning Home

Genuine spirituality includes incorporation of spiritual dynamics into human life.

Some might argue that a religious system that depends upon limited human understanding is lacking in scope. In the first place, I have found this not to be true in my own life. We can only know God as "He" is knowable through humanity. The sun the earth, the stars and the galaxies have their own experience of their creator. Their scope of life dwarfs our own. I imagine their appreciation of God is very great indeed. Human claims to an ability to make comprehensive and perfect judgments concerning the definitive nature of God are just the product of hubris wrapped in scripture. We can speculate but there is no substitute for direct experience. Even then, it is *just human* experience.

Is there something wrong with Biblical speculation or action based upon that speculation? Not really. Sometimes, that is the best we can do. However, we need to know when to leave aside emulation of the past and act with faith in the authority of what we ourselves have experienced and what we truly are. I did not begin to own the teachings I had received until I was able to express them in my own words, and actions. I did not truly appreciate the degree of perfection found in Biblical expressions until I tried to interpret or improve upon them.

We cannot become Jesus Christ. He used the eternal offer of God to meet the exact need of his time and place. We can, however, discover within ourselves the power and wisdom to become "George Christ" or "Jennifer Christ", and meet the need of our own time. Of course, we may want to consult scripture to be as sure as we can that we do not wander into mediocrity or grandiose self-deception. Jesus set a clear standard and the *Bible* shows us a very good picture of what the genuine article looks like. What I am suggesting is that we follow his historic example with fresh, original, and inspired action.

Until 1968, it was possible to go to any American bank, present a dollar bill and receive a U.S. silver dollar. That coin has real heft and its substance has inherent value. The dollar bill was known

A Second Look at Jesus

as a promissory note; it was simply a receipt for the silver equivalent safely stored for us at the bank. The law promised it would be redeemable upon demand for silver. In the same way, genuine scripture should be redeemable for direct experience. Otherwise, the scriptural claim for Biblical authority is of questionable value.

My Church has developed a helpful approach to scripture and Christian education. It is based upon their historical experience. When they declared their independence from the Church of Rome in 1534, a path was chosen that steered a middle course between the conservative, traditional teachings of the Roman Church and the fresh beginnings of the Protestant Reformation movement. Guided by such theologians as Richard Hooker (1554-1581) and their philosophy of reasonable, charitable moderation, the Church of England avoided the worst effects of intolerance and violence that tore at the fabric of Europe during that time. We believe this *middle path* has served us well.

Today, our approach to scripture honors both tradition and fresh, insightful Bible scholarship. We like to describe our religious approach as a stable, three-legged stool supported by tradition, scripture, *and* reason. Reason, at the time of our formation, was considered the best possible human resource for understanding of spiritual matters. More broadly, this may also be called discernment, insight or revelation. Members of my church are encouraged to think for themselves and do their best to discern what valuable truths can be found in scripture and traditional teachings. All are welcome to participate. Dissenting views are largely respected and/or tolerated.

In truth, all beliefs follow our experience, *not vice versa*. We all "cut our coat" of theology to fit "our cloth" of experience. I believe this is likewise true for life perspectives in general. Spiritual poverty (a scarcity of direct experience of God), yields miserly judgments in every part of our lives. Fear necessarily prevails. Spiritual abundance (a persistent and firm spiritual connection with our creator) finds numberless opportunities to see and apply the grace of God. In this condition, joy always abounds.

Returning Home

I recently attended a half-day seminar on Centering Prayer at a local church, offered by two charming and effective women who proceeded to tune up my meditation practice. I found it very helpful. The teachers reminded me I needed to treat my ongoing inner experience like any other distracting thought. (I had been clinging to my inner experiences.) When I simply turned back to my meditation practice, I found *new* insight and *fresh* experience. The Centering Prayer Organization is inspired and led by Father Thomas Keating. He was well represented that day by Judi and Claudia. His teaching can be found at; *centeringprayer.com*

I acknowledge that the path I have been taking can also have pitfalls. The mystical path cultivates innocent exploration, which *can* result in a certain habitual naiveté and gullibility, at least in the early days of practice. Mindless devotion to, and even subjugation by, domineering leaders is an example of exploitation of this vulnerability. We also tend to be, or at least appear to be, somewhat lawless. This tendency bears watching. Are we consistently following the higher law we perceive, or do we follow it only when it is convenient and comforting? Even if we *are* diligent, do our insights have an ephemeral, impractical and an unrooted quality? To be masterful or even competent we need to develop our personality so that it incorporates the whole reality of God. Can we effectively convey the subtle experience we first discover, under optimal inner conditions, intact and functional? Do our insights take practical form within the challenges of our daily life? If not, we must mature until they do!

All of the errors that mystics are prone to come from a failure to properly integrate our human condition into our spiritual evolution. The ordinary, daily experience of being held accountable to those I meet has been helpful and necessary to keep me balanced as I have grown. My wife is especially diligent in trying to guide me away from trouble with a runaway ego. She nudges me away from my tendency to lecture and toward a more respectful, helpful, and practical application of insights I come across. She tells

A Second Look at Jesus

me when I start to get too full of myself. We can all benefit from someone like Alice in our lives!

Traditional/scripture-based religion and mysticism can be useful in balancing and guiding each other. For that reason, I hope we will always have healthy examples of each approach in our culture.

For my part, I know Jesus has revealed God to me more perfectly than I knew Him before. I welcome the chance to join with him in an ongoing effort to "be perfect even as my Father in heaven is perfect." I accept His offer of help. Who would not if they properly understood the opportunity that he offers?

I have found nurture with a small, weekly Christian breakfast group I meet with on Friday mornings. Little by little, they have coaxed me further out of my shell. I have learned to listen as everyone tells their story about the spiritually significant events over the past week. I listen more than I talk. Week by week I try to tell my story in a way that is intended to be clear and useful.

Another major avenue in my growth with Christianity has been a four-year Bible study program offered through the seminary at the University of the South at Sewanee, Tennessee. Known as Education for Ministry (EFM), this program parallels the curriculum offered in their seminary. Year one is *Old Testament* studies year two is *New Testament*; while years three and four are *Church history* and *Theology*.

Throughout the EFM program, the designers of the course have clearly tried to present a broad spectrum of the various facts and theories as they are found within genuine church history. There was a minimum of editing and shaping to reach predetermined conclusions. This was my introduction to academic Biblical scholarship. It was, for me, a very good and rare opportunity to gather quality information. More importantly, it encouraged me to think for myself on spiritual and religious matters.

Under the guidance of our teacher, Andy Atkinson, we were expected to absorb this material. By listening, private reflection, and discussion in an intimate group we explored for useful truth.

Returning Home

In this way we were able to individually formulate a more mature and informed view of God and the church. We tried to make it consistent with our personal experience, known history and scriptural integrity. This course of study proved to be a perfect opportunity for me, with the help of Alice, to sift through centuries of interesting material to determine what seemed helpful and what did not.

One of the conclusions I reached as a by-product of this process of examination is that it is best to insist on examining the most important questions in our lives for ourselves. If we accept this responsibility, our own lives will be both interesting and consequential.

It has long been the habit of many Christians to criticize those who differ from their understanding of God. A certain amount of debate may be necessary to clarify what innovators intend and to judge the consequences of such innovations. However, I consider the value of condemning those who differ from us overrated. The people who actually try it in their lives best judge the value of innovative religious thought. It has not been necessary for me to buy into the doctrine of the Mormon Church to see they are good people with valuable qualities. This is likewise true for Jehovah's Witnesses, Unitarians, Apostolics, Fundamentalists and others. It is not my job to judge them.

In general, the subject of Christ is much too big for human understanding. Most of the various creeds and sects that developed over the past two thousand years are best examined for the germ of truth and useful insight contained within them. These innovations developed within the context of their times and usually for good reasons. Of course, they all fall short. This is inevitable. However, they also advanced our human repository of experience and wisdom. It is up to us, in our own time, to do something useful to improve our generation's ability to grasp the reality of God.

If we want to do justice to the reality of God working through man and woman, we will benefit by looking at the big picture

A Second Look at Jesus

presented by this evolving aggregate of spiritual history. *All* this diversity is a human attempt to do justice to the vast subject of Christ. This view respects both the human factor in our church's history and God's part in guiding the unfolding of His message.

Over the past five hundred years or so, the institutional church has gradually been weaned off most of its coercive prerogatives. As a result, the church has had to fall back on charm and persuasion, where once it had other options. It has also fallen into a virtuous competition based upon love in action to see who, among religious institutions, is able to do the most good in this world. Thank God for that!

It is my hope that the institutional church is now ready to begin the process of re-joining with its more spiritual roots that preceded the various schisms that have distorted our birth right. Some of the practices of those early Christian seekers might seem odd today. However, much of what they taught and did, would likely advance the lives of Christians individually and Christianity as a whole. We need to reclaim *all* of our spiritual inheritance. We will just need some courage and discernment to accomplish this project.

In spite of all obstacles, the Christian movement has produced some wonderful saints. I have been deeply moved by Thomas Aquinas, Augustine, Frances of Assisi, Meister Eckhart, Nicholas De Flue, Catherine of Sienna, Theresa of Avila, John of the Cross, John of Damascus, as well as many others who deserve our careful attention. These saints have greatly enriched my life.

Some caution and discernment is required. The official biographies of the saints are often used as an endorsement of standard church doctrine. They tend to be quite saccharine and without wholesome nourishment. Opening ourselves to the influence of these saints is best begun by reading what these lovers of God had to say for themselves. The most original and unfiltered material should be sought out to get a meaningful result in this kind of study.

Here is an example of what such inspired people can do for us today. One day, Pir Vilayat taught a group of us his rendering

Returning Home

of the form of meditation St. Nicholas De Flue used daily. We were told to close our eyes and turn our attention upward while envisioning the Word of God dwelling with God. Then we slowly turned our heads and our attention in a descending arc past our left shoulder and toward the base of our spine. While doing this we called to mind and heart the essence of events that formed the turning points of the life of Jesus: The annunciation, conception, birth, youth, ministry, death and descent into hell. As we did this, we were told to exhale in one long, continuous breath.

At the low point of our descent we paused briefly. Then as we inhaled, we continued the arc of our attention upward and around the right side of our body. While doing this we recollected the resurrection, the appearance of the resurrected Jesus to the disciples, his ascension to heaven, the emergence, and multiplication of the Holy Spirit experience among the disciples and the expanding Christian community. With this up draft of the Spirit, we ascended back to resume our attention to the Word and God as we gazed upward and briefly held our breath.

This practice is a succinct recapitulation of the love of God expressed through the life of Jesus. Each repetition is exactly one breath long. We breathe out the incarnation of God's love and breathe in the return to intimacy with our Creator. This is *not* a good form of meditation for beginners. To be truly effective we need to already be attuned to the elements that make up the reference points of the life of Jesus, so we are not hung up in the details. For me it is a wonderful way to clarify and concentrate the impact of Jesus upon our lives and the world in which we live.

I would like to revisit an important point here. A God-realized person *can* accomplish *anything* because of the power of God that one can draw upon at the root of their existence. In contrast, God *does* accomplish *everything*. This is the difference between being a fully realized *child* of God and the *being* God. We can optimize the function of our human existence through good spiritual and personal practices, but in the end, our physical form is

A Second Look at Jesus

mortal and limited in scope of understanding and action. Jesus expressed this by his personal humility.

The Wave
I am beginning to crest.
The wind has stirred me into a building wave with
suggestions of intimacy.
Now the bottom has crowded me upward,
concentrating my force.
From the surface I may not appear to be much;
just another wave in an endless series.
I know better.
My being is indivisible.
I am equally present in the China Sea and the Atlantic Trench.

All of my resilient, fluid wisdom is expressed in every gesture.
The daring and vitality of numberless beings of fin and tooth in-
form and enrich my every impulse.
This shrug onto a Carolina beach is of one piece
with all my watery substance.
My withdrawal will be of no less value for the observant.
When I recede, observe the rich collection of plunder and delicate
life tracings that litter the shore.

John

What is my view of the Bible in the form we commonly have it today? I see plenty of evidence of editing and revision of the Jesus stories before and during its composition. A certain amount of editing has also been detected in later years too as the books of the Bible were copied and replaced. I am convinced certain passages are very close to what Jesus actually said, while others reflect varying degrees of creative revision to reflect the evolving views of Christian authors and the challenges they faced.

Returning Home

Initially, there was an attempt and a failure to convert the Jewish people en masse to the message of Jesus. Soon, there was a more successful attempt to adapt the message to the non-Jewish world. Over time, the Jesus movement adapted as necessary, adjusting his message to meet and overcome developing conditions. A discerning reading of scripture shows indications of all this.

There was also an apparent effort to add some gilding and embellishment of the simple teaching of Jesus that had the effect of obscuring his humanity. I consider this regrettable because I believe Jesus is a more effective agent of change when both his humanity and divinity are viewed simply and clearly. We could have had the simplicity of a religion based upon a Jesus fully explained within his Jewish context. Instead, the Greco-Roman tendency to create a myth out of the lives of exceptional people was given full scope especially after our adoption by Constantine in 313 CE.

At the same time, I believe some important elements of the teachings of Jesus are not found in our scripture. Both Paul and Jesus reveal hints here and there that they possessed significant knowledge and personal experiences they would make available only to the mature Christians who are ready for the deeper mysteries of God. This is what Jesus was referring to when he made his cryptic warning about not "casting pearls before swine," (Mt 7:6) and Paul referred to people not ready to go from spiritual "milk" to solid food (1Cor 3:21). Unfortunately, it appears this toward secrecy has gone too far. As a result of concealment and then neglect, this knowledge of deeper teachings has appears to have been reduced to a small, distorted remnant, or lost altogether.

What might have been the content of this deeper teaching? Here are a few examples: Paul refers to "the fourth heaven" in second Corinthians 12:2 and then says that "that no one is permitted to tell of such things". This leads one to ask; how many heavens are there? Also, why were such things kept secret? Why was there a mention in Mark 14:51-52 of a young man clad only

A Second Look at Jesus

in a linen cloth at the Garden of Gethsemane? Is there significance in the appearance of this, the traditional garb of candidates initiated into the mystery schools of that time? What did Jesus mean when he said, "If your eye is single your whole being will be flooded with light" in Matthew 6:22? What exactly is the name of God Jesus taught his disciples and referred to in his prayer to God in John 17:26? I am confident that it was *Yahuweh* and/or *Yehuwah* or some version of it.

As discussed earlier, the sequence of vowels found in *Yahuweh* reflects the "upward" aspirations of humanity. If one wanted to reflect the "downward" aspiration of God it would be necessary to reverse sequence of the vowels. This may be the true state of affairs. The actual name of God revealed to Moses on mount Horeb was *Eh Yeh*, literally "I AM." Therefore, God's perspective of manifesting from essence toward creation would likely begin with Yeh. If I am correct, the "secret" name of God would be fully expressed as *Yehuwah*.

There is one more indicator that *Yahuweh/Yehuwah* is a correct understanding of the full, Hebrew name of God. The name Moses reported from his experience on Mount Sinai was EH YEH. If you look at *Yahuweh/Yehuwah*, you with find that same Name I AM Is embedded there.

The expression of the concept of the Trinity finds application here as well. The vowel sounds found in *YaHuWeH* or *Yehuwah* have the intrinsic capacity to stimulate, in sequence, the spiritual centers found in the heart, throat and crown of the human form. Therefore, it would not be inaccurate to say that the full name of God has three elements that it calls upon, (Y*a*) recalls perfect our origin at the opening of creation. *Weh* calls upon our emergence into diversity. *Hu* calls upon the intimate connectedness between these two extremes. *Yehuwah* would have a similar significance from the opposite perspective. In other words, both *Yahuweh* and *Yehuwah* embody the names of the father, the Son and the Holy Spirit. All three perspectives are expressed simply and efficiently in a compact and efficient expression. When fully

Returning Home

functioning within our lives, both of these names of God guide us into a functional reality that replicates a clarified perspective of God and his creation within the human form. With correct use of *Yahuweh* and *Yehuwah* we can also prepare ourselves to become more efficient vehicles for God's expression. There are numerous indications that these names of God were used in this way by the Hebrew community from the time of Moses until a few hundred years before the time of Jesus.

If the apostles on Pentecost and we in our own lives, function as originally designed by our Creator and demonstrated by the example of Jesus Christ, our unlimited spiritual legacy will become active within our daily lives. Certainly, this is much to be desired. We only need to follow all of the prescriptions Jesus gave us.

This also touches upon the name of Jesus. As I mentioned earlier, the Church of Rome teaches that the name of Jesus should be pronounced *Yesu*. Consider the sequence of vowels here. They are e and then u. Consider further the statement of Apostle Paul when he said "therefore God exalted him to the highest place and gave him the name that is above every name," in Plillipians 2:9. The early Christians believed that the name of Jesus was powerful. A name that was comprised of the first two syllables of the Hebrew name of God would fit this definition. I am therefore of the opinion that, at least among his closest disciples, Jesus would have been known as *Yehu* or *Yehushuah*. Therefore, when I want to explore the essence of the person we commonly know as Jesus, I *use* the name *Yehu* or *Yehushuah*.

This passage raises various important questions. Why *would* Jesus teach his disciples the name of God if he did not intend for them to use it and pass it on? This leads inevitably to another question. Why did this very important word and a thorough understanding of its proper use not show up in the Baltimore Catechism of my youth? I would genuinely like to hear a justification from those who confidently claim that Christianity is ideally formulated as it is commonly found today.

A Second Look at Jesus

What I am advocating is a return to the situation that existed with the Apostles in the early days of our church. Those apostles had the person of Jesus both before and after his resurrection. They trusted and had faith in him (at least part of the time). The Apostles also had and used the name of God as a spiritual aide. The Apostles had both faith in Jesus and the name of God. Why should we not have both? I am not claiming that Discovery Prayer is necessary to receive the Holy Spirit. I am saying that the use of a Sacred Name as I suggest will help us to become a better vessel for the Holy Spirit. This is our heritage and we would do well to claim it.

It is important to note that this name of God is a verb, not a noun. It is not an object suitable for objective worship. It is only knowable as a mode of function. Unless we come to function as God does we will have no participation in the reality of God.

I have my own guess about how the actual name of God was ended within Christianity. In their enthusiasm to dispense with the numerous constraints of Hebrew heritage, early Gentile Christians apparently abandoned the use of the Hebrew name of God along with the other Jewish practices associated with the life of Jesus. The struggle between Apostle James, the brother of Jesus and Apostle Paul may not have been as innocuous at it is depicted In Acts. Luke, the writer of Acts was a close ally of Paul.

Early on, the prevailing influence of the presence of Jesus was so powerfully intoxicating that his presence alone could and did animate many early Christians. The story and the personality of Jesus, as revealed by the Apostles like Paul, was so appealing and the rewards of attunement to him were so evident, that I can understand why our predecessors might have chosen as they did. Why bother with the name when you had the reality?

Given his conversion experience, for example, Paul had little choice. He represented Jesus as he discovered Him. He encountered Jesus by being a world-class sinner. He his acts against the church of Jesus were so cruel and evil that it was necessary for the risen Christ to personally whack him off his horse on that road

Returning Home

to Damascus. The context of this encounter with Jesus differed from that of the other apostles. He said as much in Corinthians 15:9. "For I am the least of the apostles and do not even deserve to be called an apostle, because I persecuted the church of God."

Thereafter Paul was utterly faithful to his conversion experience. He honestly differed with the other disciples about what mattered in gaining reconciliation with God. In these sense we should all emulate Paul. In order to be effective, *we must be true to our conversion experiences as well.*

In time, Christians came to call exclusively upon God in the name of *Jesus* and neglect *Yehuwah* entirely. I doubt that Jesus would have approved of this. He is on record declaring otherwise. However, the early disciples did what seemed best at the time. Since I was not there at the time, my judgement is lacking some perspective.

Later, some of the more mystically oriented gentile Christians came to focus on the Gospel of John and certain aspects of Paul's teaching. Many from this group later became involved in a project to intellectualize the mystic journey and harmonize it with Greek philosophy. These religious philosophers came to be known as *Gnostics* for the great emphasis they laid upon *knowledge*. (*Gnosis* means knowledge.) As part of this and other expressions of Greek acculturation, the Aramaic and Hebrew relics such as *YHWH* were likely shown the back door.

In any case, the most important teaching of this kind would not likely have been committed to writing. As an esoteric teaching, it would only be given to qualified candidates, in private and under an oath that it was to be kept private. This kind of teaching was usually whispered mouth to ear or passed silently from heart to heart. It was a privileged initiation for the worthy alone. To varying degrees, this has been my consistent experience with *all* my spiritual guides.

The Christian communities that would most likely have kept and faithfully used the sacred name *YHWH* were those centered in Jerusalem. They were led not by Peter or Paul, but by Saint James, the brother of Jesus. At that time, he was popularly known as James the Just and was widely respected among both Jews and Christians.

A Second Look at Jesus

He was also enough of a threat to the established Temple leaders that the Jewish High Priest, Hanan ben Hanan, took the unusual step of executing him without Roman permission in 68 CE. This occurred during the brief period when one Roman procurator had been recalled and his replacement had not yet arrived. It was widely seen as a judicial murder at the time.

Then, in 70 CE and again 130 CE the Jewish nation rose in revolt against The Roman Empire. The savage Roman response devastated the Jewish-Christian church. The 4th century Church historian, Eusebius, reported that forewarned by prophecy, the Jewish Christians had fled Jerusalem eastward via Pella, east of the Jordan River just before the siege of Jerusalem began February of 70 AD.

There, beyond the wrath of the Roman Empire, these original Christians found refuge among the Arabs. In addition, for centuries thereafter, all who differed with the established Roman Church and escaped death were exiled. Among these refugees, many likely found refuge east of the Roman Empire. Years later, some form of their teaching likely inspired and influenced Mohammed's grasp of Jesus. It also informed the Sufi appreciation of Christian mysticism.

Here is a poem by Rumi, a famous Muslim Sufi.

The Body is Like Mary

The body is like Mary and each of us has a Jesus inside.
Who is not in labor, in holy labor? Every creature is.
See the value of true art when, the earth or a soul is in
the mood to create beauty;
For the witness might then for a moment know that, beyond
any doubt, God really is there within,
So innocently drawing life from us with Her umbilical
universe – infinite existence...
though also needing to be born. Yes God also needs
to be born!
Birth from a hand's loving touch. Birth from a song,
from a dance, breathing life into this world.

Returning Home

The body is like Mary and each of us, each of us, has a Christ within.

Rumi[11]

The original Jewish-Christian church that was centered in Jerusalem never recovered from this devastation and eventually became nearly destroyed as an alternate point of view. Their favored *Bible* text, in Aramaic, was known as "The Gospel of the Hebrews" and has been lost as well. With this turn of events, the Christian use of sacred name prayer likely tapered away and ended.

The Eastern Church carried on certain aspects of their unique perspective but the western churches in Constantinople and Rome were enduring adversaries against "the Judaizers" and did their best to distort and destroy their legacy. This is an important part of my perspective concerning the course of Christian history. It explains the dilution of spiritual clarity and potency that we witness from the time of Jesus until today. From the perspective of the standards set by Jesus, Christianity today under-delivers. This need not remain so.

This retelling of history could help to explain why Christianity has turned out as it has. The major Christian establishments claim that they hold intact the entire legacy of Jesus. Considering the uneven performance that we have seen in the Christian movement over the centuries, I wonder about the validity of their claim of infallibility. We have tried to be worthy disciples but we have failed to measure up to the standard set by Jesus. With this deficit in mind, I suggest that we be open minded about what we can possibly do to improve our fidelity to Jesus.

As taught by some, most notably Paul, Christianity went from the teachings *of* Jesus to the teachings *about* Jesus. This is a critical distinction. It was as though Jesus was teaching us to *become the sun* of God's luminous power of creation, just as he had. He

A Second Look at Jesus

advocated his personal own credo for our use: "Be yea perfect, even as your God in heaven is perfect."

In contrast, the followers of Jesus came to worship Jesus himself as a sacred object. We were taught to be illuminated in the reflection of His light. This is like the illumination of the moon, not the sun. This regression from the direct interaction with God "The Father" has progressed to a great degree in present day Christianity. Today, expectations of direct experience are much reduced and yet even *they* are often not met!

The early church was obsessed with an expectation that God was about to intervene decisively in the affairs of humankind. A dominant theme running through the teachings of John the Baptist, Jesus, the original disciples *and* Saint Paul, was the expectation that God would utterly destroy the evil world order built upon coercion and replace it with one based upon Godly love yielding a perfect, resonant and nourishing for all life.

Jesus was considered the leading edge of this divine tsunami of Godly revolution. His death and resurrection were identified as the events that would trigger the final countdown that was fully expected to reach its conclusion within the lifetimes of the original disciples. A divine upheaval was considered inevitable and imminent. In this context, it must have seemed the entire past, which included such elements as the Sacred Name of God, was simply irrelevant. It was as though Christians were just waiting, in an orderly and loving manner, near the emergency exits of a building scheduled for demolition. Years or even decades might be needed to get a strong result from traditional sacred name prayer. However, if the **Big Event** was about to unfold, if the time of a decisive Godly cleansing was nearly at hand, why would one even start such a practice?

In fact, history has *not* recorded a single and decisive act by God to finish extinguishing evil in this world. We commonly see evidence of evil around us. If the events described in the Book of Revelation have already happened in ordinary history, no one has noticed them. Truly, Jesus *had* and indeed *was* the antidote

Returning Home

for the poison of sin. However, history shows that this cure has been absorbed into humanity *gradually* and its *evolutionary* effect has been taking some time to unfold. The result is clearly Incomplete.

Perhaps, what we actually *need* and have needed for a long time is a personal approach for the long haul. I believe we need a reliable spiritual catalyst that helps us grow steadily throughout our lives. With this in mind, I consider it desirable that we take up, as best we can, the abandoned practices Jesus himself used to become such a superlative Son of God. This will allow us to repower and optimize our ability to conclude the work of Jesus within our lifetime.

Because of the abandonment of Sacred Name Prayer, the witness of Jesus has fallen upon less and less well-prepared ground over time. Therefore, because we Christians are less rooted in the subtle, inner firmament of life, we tend to have a poor focus on the reality of Christ, the intersection of Creator with creation. Instead, we focus on the circumstantial aspects of the Christian story: the words, the images and the subtle but elusive spiritual perfume that persists in the wake of our history and rituals. Lacking a thorough and firm grounding in deeper dimensions of our souls, we also tend to blunder past the truly important turning points of our lives. Do we have the capacity to notice "burning bushes" as we pass nearby? If not, we need to take corrective measures.

At the same time the Jerusalem church was in distress, the form of Christianity advocated by Paul was propagated very effectively among Gentiles. It presented the gist of the Christian insight, but with a minimum of the traditional Hebrew context and methods. The conversion story for Gentiles offered Jesus not exactly as Jesus described it. Instead, it became a sophisticated form of idolatry with Jesus as the object of worship. Is this really what Jesus intended?

The challenge with this westernized approach to the message of Jesus is the uneven quality of the representatives. If spokesperson was a very worthy vicar (substitute) of Christ like Saint

A Second Look at Jesus

Paul, then all is well. If the representative did not have a very good personal grasp upon the true stature of Jesus, that would be reflected too.

Too often, we followers of Christ have only an intellectual or emotional grasp of what Jesus was trying to convey. Moving with confidence and competence beyond the borders of our individuality is precisely what the effective use of a Sacred Name accomplishes. In order to arrive at our true destination, talk, even the inspired talk, must be left behind.

History shows that Paul's followers grew in numbers and influence with the aid of an efficient organization and an effective political strategy. Later, when Roman Emperor Constantine reconciled with the church in 313 CE, he chose and enforced a simplified form of Paul's approach to Christianity. In doing this, Emperor Constantine chose a religious profile that best met his need for an effective religious partner to strengthen his empire. The mystics were probably considered too independent and not reliable team players. Thereafter, the power of the Roman government aided the established church in the suppression of alternative forms of Christianity.

For these reasons, among others, Christianity evolved into the form we commonly observe today. I need to be very clear. Christianity, as we commonly experience it today, is very good. I simply believe that it can be better. Why hsould we not thoughtfully reclaim more of what has been left behind.

When viewed objectively, Christian history strongly resembles a battle of brands, not unlike the ongoing struggle of various fast food enterprises in our own time. Ray Kroc has made McDonalds the most profitable restaurant company of all time by quickly providing a broadly desirable product at an affordable cost. A carefully defined mission, superior management and an efficient operation all play a part in their success. McDonalds and those who have emulated their business model, dominate their market. However, no one would expect to have a superlative dining experience at one of these establishments. That would not

Returning Home

be reasonable. If you want *that quality of experience,* you need to take some initiative and make a larger and more thoughtful investment in cost, care and time. Likewise, in our prayer life, if we want different results we need to try different methods.

The Protestant Reformation movement was all about fresh starts. Martin Luther's central insight was that saving grace was not earned; rather, it was the free gift of God. Since the time of Luther, he and those he inspired have cultivated a resurgence of fresh, sincere scriptural analysis. This was a largely intellectual project in support of spiritual freedom. Luther himself was an accomplished scholar and he encouraged all Christians to explore scripture for themselves.

For those who want intellectual help in discerning and exploring the more authentic and original message of Jesus, as found in scripture, I recommend the work of Bart Ehrman, Professor at University of North Carolina, Chapel Hill. I consider him a worthy successor to the five hundred year enterprise begun by Martin Luther early in the 16th century. A good place to start might be one of Dr. Ehrman's books such as *Misquoting Jesus* or his introductory college level textbook, *The New Testament*. All his books offer a very readable summary of current academic scholarship on various biblical topics. He strikes me as an honest man and I have found his work useful in clarifying the message of Jesus.

I must add something here. Scriptural scholarship is the process of using the written records at hand to reveal truth. There is no guarantee that existing doctrine will be reaffirmed in this process. In fact, the initial result may be that the working assumptions of our theological view are upended. It is not uncommon for scholars to follow evidence faithfully and reach conclusions that conflict with their personal beliefs. As a result, their previous concepts, and ours, may be shaken. Sometimes they even collapse into ruins. When this occurs, it is sometimes part of our job as Christians to reconceive a functioning and whole faith that is more consistent with evidentiary truth. A mature relationship with God should be able to sustain us during such intervals of

A Second Look at Jesus

faith reformulation. Faith in our concept of God is not the same thing as faith in God.

Years ago, I read a news report about the photographing of a top-secret Russian submarine in a concealed, concrete berth. One of the guards was willing to take some pictures. The most interesting part of the story was the American agent gave his spy a common, disposable camera. That camera was made to be opened and discarded by the developer when he retrieved the film. In this case, the spy was instructed to turn over the *entire* camera to his handler, not just the film. The CIA lab was then able to produce excellent images because, after analysing the imperfections of the *lens*, they could make the necessary corrections to the *images*. A study of Church history, archaeology and modern bible scholarship can perform this clarifying role for us, if we participate.

Even if the Holy Spirit inspires us, we, and the writers of the Bible, leave traces of our writing craft and our limitations. This is inevitable, as our lenses have features. We unavoidably distort and diminish the truth we are trying to express.

Examination of the historical context of the *Bible*, the editorial priorities of the authors of the *Bible* and other factors can be detected with careful examination of the scripture. When we take these elements into account, and make the corrections necessary to correct the distortions of the authors, it is possible to discern with greater clarity what was and is the most original and authentic message of Jesus. We cannot entirely subcontract this discernment to our leaders. We must make it our own. This is part of our personal responsibility.

Some Christians might not consider this a helpful perspective. They do not want any further clarification outside of a copy of their favorite translation of the Bible. I understand and respect this as a personal choice. For my part, I would prefer to know relevant truth, whatever its source. Truth is always helpful, even if it makes us temporarily insecure or uncomfortable. First, it allows us to focus more accurately on the actual *intention* of Jesus.

Returning Home

Second, acknowledging a certain amount of ambiguity in the meaning of scripture might be a very good thing. It reminds us that the whole purpose of the religious enterprise is to discover what we can verify *in our lives*, not on paper or in theory. This forces us to move from theory to accomplished fact, if we want to actually *be* Christians. If we cannot make a certain doctrine function in our lives, we have a responsibility to question its authenticity.

This same ambiguity has created a need for what has become the true genius of the Christian contribution to the world's spiritual treasury. What Christians have learned to do is inspire an *intuitive leap of faith* based upon partial information. Making the best of our scriptural heritage, we identify and focus upon examples of enduring truths. This addresses a perennial human condition. Is information ever complete? If not, do we dare act? The answer is that we <u>must</u> act and do so decisively. Life is short and we need to make the most of it. Where information ends, spiritual intuition <u>must</u> lead the way.

Having sampled the other world's religions, I can testify that Christian scriptures have nowhere near the precision and completeness of other faiths. This may be a good thing. Cultivating a constant inclination toward God may be far better than exhaustive and precise instruction. Facts, details and insights follow a genuine encounter with God. However, they are surprisingly unhelpful in the lead-up to such an event.

For example, Muslims claim that nearly every prophetic word that Mohammed spoke was recorded soon after he expressed it. He then verified the accuracy of everything written. After Mohammed's death all of his close disciples gave sworn depositions concerning the other significant words and acts along with his personal history. All of this is recorded in Arabic, which is well understood today. Collectively, these first-hand testimonies are known as *Hadith*. There are about 500,000 *Hadith* of various types and grades of reliability. Because of all this, Islamic traditionalists have much more material to work with than Christian

A Second Look at Jesus

conservatives do. Their orthodoxy is much more thoroughly supported by their written records.

By creating and maintaining such a strong system, Mohammed in his time and Islamic conservatives today have also created a disincentive for fresh spiritual insight. In theory, such a thorough system has the virtue of ensuring that error and failure are rare so long as one submits to the system. Today, many Islamic conservatives have come to view the innovations Mohammed established to raise the *minimum standards* of ethical behavior and spiritual aspiration of his day as more than an ideal. They enshrine them as *the best and only acceptable standard.*

While working within the society of his birth was a practical and wise strategy for Mohammed, I do not believe that this was the only way to organize a spiritual society. If, for example, Mohammed had been born to Chinese, American or African parents, he would have worked within *those* cultures and tried to perfect *those* social ideals.

I believe that a case can be made for viewing Mohammed's teaching as an effort to encourage an evolving standard of higher spiritual, ethical and personal values. During Mohammed's time, he had to find a way to survive and thrive in an extremely harsh and cruel society. I am confident that, given a more friendly and accommodating social environment, Mohammed could have and would have adopted a more peaceful and kind message. It is possible that if Mohammed lived today, he would do a first class job of making peace with the other nations and religions and guiding Islam to adapt and improve in the face of the more benign challenges it faces in the world today. The world today offers fresh opportunities.

In contrast, Islamic conservatives, *salafis*, emphasize conformity to their own historic ideals. To these Islamic conservatives, western religion and society appears dangerously free and chaotic. Westerners also appear weak, undisciplined and irresolute. These Islamic conservatives are poorly prepared to see the possibility that freedom works very well to guide society

Returning Home

as a whole in spite of the individual examples of foolishness and decadence.

Many Islamic conservatives have also managed to justify a suppression of the counsel and initiative of women. There is even a tolerance of genital mutilation of women. They do this in defiance of scriptural records that reveal the clear intent of Mohammed to respect and empower women. If Mohammed were alive today, I am confident that he would lament the widespread waste of feminine talent within Islamic culture.

Islam, which means *submission* in Arabic, is a perfectly correct and necessary response when God's angelic messenger is directly pressing upon you. This "pressing" by the angel Gabriel is how Mohammed described his spiritual experience that resulted in his prophetic gift. However, submission is less appropriate or helpful when uninspired and opinionated human beings are doing the pressing. In my opinion, the best and primary mission of Islam is to bring us to a direct encounter with the same spiritual source that stimulated Mohammed's wisdom and prophetic guidance. With genuine prophetic insight, human opinion and tradition become subordinate, as they should.

Having said all of this, I acknowledge that my understanding of traditional Islam is weak. If I had a good opportunity to learn more about mainstream Islam, I would gladly act upon it.

Compared to Islam, the claim of Christian fundamentalists for a comprehensive scriptural guidance system is actually quite weak. The words of Jesus were not recorded during his time and he did not verify their accuracy. The choice of items to be recorded and the editorial choices of organization and emphasis were made anonymously and long after Jesus had passed from the scene. There is not even an indication that Jesus wanted to leave a written record. I believe that he was aiming for transformed disciples to record of his teaching within their humanity.

Just before the period of Bible composition, there was a brutal Roman invasion followed by widespread genocide within Israel. This chaotic environment would have made accurate

A Second Look at Jesus

and thorough collection of original testimony about Jesus much less efficient. In spite of this shockingly loose conveyance of the words and deeds of Jesus within the Bible, the intent and flavor of the life of Jesus has come through to our day. I credit the striking originality and authentic power of the witness of Jesus for the survival of his teaching in spite of very adverse conditions.

The witness of Apostle Paul is the first and best example of this innovative tendency in the Jesus movement. We, and our entire western society, are the products of the legacy of his great spiritual creativity. We need to both appreciate this fact and place it in context.

Because of the lack of verifiable information, Christians have been forced to exercise a more intuitive and personal grasp of the true intent of Jesus. This has allowed for both excellence and evolutionary innovation alongside the potential for spiritual misunderstanding. More than Islam, Christianity requires an intuitive leap to grasp the intent of Jesus and the ways of God. As a result, a certain amount of original thought and innovation is required within Christianity. . This gap in orthodoxy has served us well. It has helped us escape stagnation again and again.

I understand the desire of many to accept the writings of the Gospel as literal truth. On the face of things, there might seem to be no other way to take the teachings contained in the Bible seriously and allow them to have a powerful impact upon our lives. Suppose, for example, someone accepts the notion that walking on water, the miraculous birth, or the physical resurrection of Jesus might not be literally accurate. Might he then be more likely to reinterpret other teachings in a way that make him more emotionally comfortable and *not* spiritually challenged? If we take the path of indiscriminate doubt, would not the entire scriptural record be of no practical use to us?

Acknowledging this risk, the details of our beliefs are something we each need to work out individually. If it seems that this approach creates a greater burden of personal responsibility and

Returning Home

dynamic tension upon an individual believer, you are right. As adults we *should* be willing and able to embrace and use valuable spiritual essence from scripture while not allowing interference from unhelpful material.

Furthermore, I consider the particulars of our faith are best respected, as a private matter, if we want to listen most clearly to the testimony of our soul. We should be allowed to adjust our understanding as we mature and grow in actual spiritual experience. Genuine evolution of our faith needs space to grow. Constant pressure to conform is not helpful. Therefore, if we want to compare differing interpretations of the Bible, it might best be done with a friendly kindness, a respect and a desire to be helpful to those who differ from us. Easy does it. Only when inspiration from the speaker meets genuine experience from the listener does meaningful learning occur.

In any discussion concerning biblical scripture, I value the ability of my counterpart to paraphrase whatever text they quote. This shows me that I am speaking to a thoughtful person, not a parrot. I also appreciate an attempt to place that understanding within a broader context of what God and the Bible author are trying to express. The importance of this display of understanding is similar to the value my teachers once placed upon "showing the math" on tests. Having a correct answer without the ability to explain how one arrived upon it is rightly considered suspect.

A local minister once told me, unless I would agree with him, in advance, that the entire *Bible* was the *inerrant word of God*, he would not discuss spiritual matters with me. I like and respect this man. We have broad agreement on many personal and social issues. We simply disagreed on the best use of the Bible. It seemed to me that he glossed over much of the legitimate complexity of the scriptural witness and then conflated the incompatible material he drew upon to create the illusion of uniformity. He also seemed to depend heavily upon circular logic. However, in our discussions, he would hear none of this. He simply would not,

A Second Look at Jesus

perhaps could not, venture into the unknown without the very close support of the *Bible as he understood it*.

This expresses, briefly, where some doctrinaire "fundamentalists" seem to reside. This path can lead to isolated and highly defensive positions, defined more by the contradictions ignored than the positive values affirmed. On certain topics, it may be helpful to accept that some answers are not clear. That they are, at least for now, mysteries.

I repeat, occasionally doubting our *understanding of God* is not the same as *doubting God*. It is just a natural element of growth and *should not be* suppressed.

In the coastal area where I live, there are a number of stunningly elegant birds such as the Egret and the Blue Heron. When I encounter them going about their business I usually pause for at least a few moments and marvel. I imagine that one day I might show one of these magnificent creatures to a visitor from another area. If those visitors are excessively bookish and closed-minded they might balk when I told them that, they were looking at a Blue Heron. They might doubt that I am being accurate since many of these birds, at least those examples found locally, are not even slightly blue. They are grey.

This is often the case when a highly doctrinaire person is exposed to a genuine truth or spiritual experience. There is often some dissonance and confusion while the genuine is compared with the theory. For comfort's sake, a poorly prepared seeker might even develop a habit of avoiding the possibility of all *contradictory* experiences by avoiding *all* experience. This is commonly accomplished by resorting to an entirely intellectual and literal use of the Biblical. I recommend that we learn to accept the discomfort associated with an honest attempt to reconcile theory and experience. In this way, our truths will become larger and more potent.

Often, the important truths are simple, once we learn to recognize them. The tangles surrounding these truths are of human origin. Overcoming the mystery of obscure passages with

Returning Home

excessive indoctrination is just a vain attempt to negate the innocent wildness of God. Perhaps we should be less willing to ascribe the significance of Divine Reality to our limited understanding.

What was my conservative Christian friend afraid of? He may have thought I wanted to interfere with the truths he held dear, to rob him of his literal truth. No, I respect his right to draw his own conclusions. I am just concerned, since he used so many of his faculties defending the *literal word*, he will have scant capacity to appreciate the *more than literal truth*. He is so intent upon filling the vessel of Christian literature that he has come to believe that there is eternal virtue in taking the shape of a doctrinal container.

Much of what my friend believes, the most important parts, are truer than he seems to suspect. What I want to offer is a way of exploration I am familiar with and he is not. It is also a way to more completely *live* those truths we both admire. Sometimes, such conversations with the opinion-bound are like offering a fresh, ripe fig to someone who has never tried one before. A fig *does* look somewhat plain or even disreputable. My friend is suspicious. He will not taste my fig. If I can introduce the practice of sacred name prayer without triggering his "orthodoxy alarm", so much the better. Nonetheless, I intend to set forth an experience-based spiritual option with all possible clarity.

A prudent Christian might want to ask, "What is the likely result of result of using the practices I advocated here?" Of course, we are all unique and come with our own "baggage" but I can confidently make a general summary of what would be a likely income. If spiritual experience becomes an increasing quotient in our lives, we can expect:

1. A decrease of motivation based upon fear and insecurity. Instead, we will become more personally animated with insight and love.

A Second Look at Jesus

2. A firmer, more supple and more discerning faith that focuses on the "big picture" on the reality of God rather than detailed opinions about God.
3. A stronger and more intimate appreciation of both the Divinity and the humanity of Jesus.

If I *am* persuasive, could my fundamentalist friend go about incorporating these practices without losing his friends and associations? Perhaps. Perhaps not. First, there is no reason why we should rush right out and contradict everyone in sight as soon as we start to see benefits from a new approach. Simply adding richer content to truths he and his friends already agree upon could fill a lifetime. Then, if someone asks him directly, "What is your secret? What makes a difference for you?" He can begin to explain, but with humility and discretion.

Several times in my life, I have had to endure the anxiety and the pain of following my conscience beyond the groups I had come to depend upon for fellowship and inspiration. I went from an all-inclusive association with the Catholic Church, to a longhaired orientation in the late 60's and early 70's, to explore broader options in my life. I cut my hair and became a disciple of Maharishi so that I could better plumb the depths of my soul. I left the TM organization in order to act more freely and responsibly, to trust and honor what I found within. I joined a Fundamentalist church to explore Christianity and left to respect the personal testimony of the Holy Spirit and my life experience in general. Further changes have been necessary; I have tried to be brave about them. I still suffered when I was unable to maintain those relationships. I always avoid such losses if I can. However, in some cases, I found change preferable to smothering in place and I did what I had to do.

These comments about the *Bible* notwithstanding, my soul unambiguously affirms that the authors of the Bible knew quite a lot about the nature of God. The Bible also chronicles the historical challenge of bringing the spirit of God to bear upon our human

Returning Home

condition. The *Bible* and church history are a condensed collection of thousands of years of inspiration, experience, and practical wisdom. I am thankful the message of Jesus has survived in *any* form. Under no circumstances will I dispense with what the Bible has to offer. That would be too foolish.

It is not my intention to state that traditional Christian teaching is wrong. Even if I could present an argument to that effect, I am not sure that it would be ethical to do so. I only hope to show that the practice of verification by direct experience is *plausible* so that some will "give it a fair try." Then, they can see for themselves if the results they find justify that venture.

In fact, my own critical analysis of the scriptures has left me closer to and more respectful of the core of traditional Christian values than I expected to be. I find the spiritual, ethical and social lessons that traditionally flow from them are a reliable source of sound guidance in human affairs. I also find the basic truths about God and humankind reasonably accessible in the canonical scriptures, so long as we are open to surprise.

For example, the concept of Trinity is a useful description of an underlying reality. Here is how I see it. Jesus, through the connection afforded by the Holy Spirit, expressed the fullness of God the Father, our Creator. This relationship began in earnest with the descent of the Holy Spirit as depicted in all the Gospels. The saving power of Jesus is based upon the full and normal functioning of all these elements commonly known as Father, Son and Holy Spirit. We can and should function likewise.

When the apostles on Pentecost and we in our own lives, function as originally designed by our Creator, in the manner of Jesus Christ, our unlimited spiritual legacy becomes accessible within our mundane lives. This is much to be desired.

The whole point of the gospels and the mission of Jesus is to bring us to the point that we know the Holy Spirit, our Creator as Jesus did. Jesus led the way. We need only follow. The true mission of the church is to facilitate the initiation of this experience

A Second Look at Jesus

for each of us and then to support us, as necessary, while our transformation unfolds.

I have my differences with the religious *status quo*, too. I have little interest in making religion the servant of government or cultivating a religious monoculture. I have found it desirable to respect and heed the counsel of women and of my Jewish heritage more closely than the early church fathers did. That does not mean everything they did was defective. That is far from true. I see no point in disputing with the Christian tradition excessively. Instead, I am trying to raise expectations of what we can each discover and embody. Then, I would like to set in motion a process to help fulfill those expectations as widely as possible. In this way, I hope to play a role in reanimating the best of our traditional values. If I can accomplish this, I will be well satisfied.

The Shop
Our Lord runs a garage.
Just give him a call
and
he will tow away
your defective heap of junk.
In due course,
it all gets stripped to the frame
and rebuilt.
In the mean-time, we customers
hang around the waiting room
munching popcorn and killing time.
Now and then, the proprietor asks
for a volunteer
to run an errand.
Then, one of us,
itching for a little adventure,
steps up.
Next, invariably, He says:

Returning Home

"Here, check this out,"
as he flings a key ring
across the room.
Outside is a vehicle with my plates on it.
My key fits and the engine rumbles to life.
The paint, the interior, the stereo system are all first class.
Man o man,
what an upgrade!

John

My personal approach to God has been quite simple. It has been essentially top down. I was blessed and challenged with a strong spiritual experience at the early age of nineteen. Since then I have been busy coping with the aftermath. In essence, life has placed in my path a succession of teachers, friends, and situations all helping me to come down to earth as an improved human being.

When I left the TM movement, I was stiff, spiritually reserved and emotionally inaccessible. I was also something of "a know-it-all." Further, I was also somewhat reluctant to participate in ordinary human life, even when the situation in front of me was unjust and needed correction. I have since spent much of my life trying to live more artfully and responsibly.

Maharishi was in the habit of describing his meditation system as the Science of Creative Intelligence. In truth, the path to discovery of the divine dimension of life *can* be most efficiently revealed by a simple and systematic approach. What is needed next, however, is not science, but art. We might call it the art of personality. How *can* we best express God's bounty? This is what I have found among my Christian friends; Christians share freely, even when they are suffering from spiritual poverty. Whatever they have is freely available to all. This is what Jesus and the Christian witness has cultivated within my life. Without the preparation of the spiritual *science* of inner discovery, my *art* would have been lacking in purity of materials and scope of expression. Without

A Second Look at Jesus

art, the expression of *science* would have been as beautiful and useful as seeds in a bottle.

I have not lost contact with the practice I learned from Maharishi. One cannot un-ring a bell. Its effects are unalterably a part of my life. Neither is anything good wasted in our lives. I have taken on other teachings and meditation practices not for a *deeper* experience, but for a *broader* experience. This approach has worked well for me. First, I was transformed by the unity of *singularity* made possible by turning away from perishable values. Later, I was able to appreciate the hidden *unity* within creative diversity. This is what the Christian way has shown me: the discovery of Christ *within* creation as a whole. I am further informed that truly loving God means loving everything in creation, *including* the mess.

Over time, my mentor, Robert Pritchard, my wife, Alice, my Sufi Pir and my Christian friends, convincingly demonstrated the significance and potential of the human condition to me. Little by little, they humanized me. Throughout this process, as I attempted to make sense of life, I have also tried to be useful to my fellows.

You may ask what all of this has to do with salvation through Jesus. My answer begins with this question; exactly what it is about Jesus that made him an irresistable, reliable template to prepare us for a reunion with our Creator. For me the lively, radiant and natural connection Jesus maintains with both his Creator and us attracts. It was not just a matter of being rooted in the divine; it was both his mastery and his humble, approachable personality that makes Jesus attractive to me. I want to embody as much of this type of personality as I can. This is the kind of Christian I want to be.

Jesus could probably have lived a long, comfortable life if he had adjusted his message a little to avoid direct conflict with worldly power. Instead, he chose to remain true to his transforming encounter with the Holy Spirit. The aftermath redirected the course

Returning Home

of humanity. He set a dynamic, living standard that is very high and yet obtainable, <u>if we use His methods</u>.

Some of the distinctions I have made may seem no more plausible than any other explanations that are offered in the marketplace of spiritual ideas. There is a reason for this. At some point in our lives, it is as though we are well out at sea and viewing our docking place at a distance through binoculars. Everything appears to be flat and one-dimensional. As we come closer and then dock, our space perception begins to function better. Life takes on a three dimensional aspect. Then, as we move about and interact with the people and environment of our destination, the truths that were so hard to discern at a distance become obvious. The qualities of the people and their environment are fully appreciated only with close examination and direct experience. We all need to get to port and experience life there. Then discussions will be more meaningful. It is the direct experience that comes with Discovery Prayer that brings us up close to the qualities that really matter.

This brings us more or less up to date. I make friends whenever and wherever I can. I take time for daily spiritual practice. I use scripture as an aid to spiritual growth, not a substitute. I also consider the lessons of history and tradition. The opinions of profane "religious lawyers" and politicians I routinely discard. I likewise ignore the counsel of those who are not spiritually generous and joyous in their personal lives.

Finally, I consult my own connection with my Creator. God is my Senior Advisor and Guide. I would never take the biblical interpretation of a stranger if it violated the historical record, common sense, or my own spiritual counselor. After all, I am responsible for the consequences of my choices, not my associates.

Poetry of Motion
*Like an aircraft that skips and kisses the ground
when taking off or landing.*

A Second Look at Jesus

Poetry is the language of transition between
the mind and the eternal soul.
Some religious aviators re-enact the flights of others with
descriptive prose and static displays that shine brightly.
Others can even make their engine roar while the rudder,
aileron and elevators move
But ropes and chocks make it all an empty gesture.
The description of flight and the ability to make it
happen are separate endeavors.
They always have been.
Actual flight is individual, solitary.
There is risk.
There is cost in time, love, and wealth.
My advice is to pay the price and learn to actually
skip into the eternal sky.
Then you will know what all the fuss is about.
If your chosen guide doesn't speak poetry
it's not likely that he has flown,
even as a passenger,
and
cannot know what it takes to help you soar.
I advise you to find an experienced pilot
and
pay the price.
You won't regret it.

John

Therefore, you might ask, "What is the point of all these words?" There is a fascinating passage in the Gospel of Luke Chapter 24, verses 13 through 35. Soon after the crucifixion, some Jesus lovers met a man on the road to Emmaus. He appeared to be a stranger. Later, they realized they had been in the company of the risen Christ. They had not recognized the physical face of Jesus. Apparently, he appeared like someone else

Returning Home

entirely. His companions did not recognized until he was leaving. In retrospect, they reported, "Were not our hearts burning within us as we walked on the road, and he opened the scriptures to us." It was not the appearance of Jesus that remained unchanged in resurrection, but the power of his presence that continues. *Their hearts burned.* People come and go. The presence of Christ is all that endures and the kingship of God, in our lives, is all that matters.

A Taste of Salt

Chapter Twenty-Four

Answering the Cynical Revolt

Hayah

As I write this book, I have an unusually large amount of time on my hands. The demand for my skills as a developer and general contractor has been very modest. I have also "benefitted" from a severe financial humbling in this recent recession. I have a mountain of debt and my income is slight and erratic.

At one point, I even tried to find work at the local, manual labor pool, but I somehow failed the prequalification test. Every mortgage payment or tank of gas is a small miracle. In sum, I am much more aware of my human vulnerabilities than I was a few years ago. Because of all this, I am in a more reflective state of mind, motivated to recall what I *have* found true. I *want* to tell this story and I will try to finish it well.

The effect of writing this book has already been a great blessing for me. The process of identifying and organizing the elements of my inner life for coherent expression has triggered a

A Second Look at Jesus

reorganization in fact. I have never been better able to perceive and function. I consider myself already well compensated, even if not one person buys this book.

Low Pressure System
Yesterday I developed a low-pressure system in my heart
I had shrugged off a whole crop of foolish, conflicting aspirations
Then this capacity,
a vacuum in the center of my being,
began to attract.
and
A swirling vortex formed.
Voluntary replacements from the far corners of creation
presented themselves
Poised and ready
These were a superior sort of desire
The type that does no harm,
and
always comes to fruition.
Interesting.
Very interesting.

John

After more than forty years of regular meditation, I have a much clearer understanding of what is available within. When I started, I was thrilled to find a whisper or a glimmer of genuine spiritual experience. It was like listening for a tiny little bell in the middle of boisterous traffic. Over time, these inner experiences have intensified, as I have become more able to bear them. As you might expect, my particular manner of experiencing my source is conditional upon my original makeup and the various meditation practices I have embraced. Nonetheless, my human composition is about like anyone else's. I am only reorganized somewhat from the way

Answering the Cynical Revolt

I was before. As a result, my perception and interests have changed.

The Art of Life
We are a brush in the hand of our Creator
Touching this canvas at birth, it advances under us
Vast numbers of hollow filaments convey our essence into this world drawing, even now, from the dawn of creation
That elixir flows, according to our nature and capacity, bright or pastel, thick or thin, broad or narrow, straight or complex as we leave our mark
Do yourself a favor
Find an instructor, a good one
He or she will help you open to your original promise
There is so much to learn:
Vision
Technique
Mixing solvent, binder and pigment
Cleaning your tools
Studying the classic artists Rembrandt, Da Vinci, Jesus, Buddha, Moses, Elijah, Hafiz and others
Exploring and cultivating enlightened imagination
And finding that sweet friction where our freedom meets divine guidance
In due course our stroke will be complete and we will back up to see the full perspective
But, for now, let's just enjoy the job at hand

John

When I look within, I perceive that I am like a bundle of hollow filaments that resonate and convey an indescribable flow of vitality and intelligence. One end of these filaments is very broad and diffuse, like a gossamer funnel or flower. Their edges are indiscernible within the immovable solitude of the Creator. The

A Second Look at Jesus

other end of these fibers is narrow and compact. They are the ultimate narrow path. They are attached to this world through my human frame. The creative process percolates through and out of these filaments. At the broad end of each filament is the mere suggestion of a divine quality that gestates, develops and emerges, making itself felt through me and into this world. The first Divine Quality I followed to its source was the sacred word I was given in 1970. This strengthened me and showed the way. Many others followed since then. Sacred names from Christian, Jewish, Islamic and Hindu traditions have all found a home in my life. I have also gratefully listened to the testimony of these other traditions. This has been true wealth to me and I wish to share a portion of it with you in a form you are willing to accept.

A degree of tension exists between the two poles of my existence; the inner and outer. The resonance of these fibers, the music it creates animates what I call my life. Lately, however, the sense of distance between the poles of my life seems to be collapsing. The whole mystery is becoming nearer and more intimate. In the beginning, I sensed a great distance between my inner and outer life. Now, I more accurately described this experience as stretching from *here to here*. I have the sense that my skin only marginally covers the wonders of the universe.

In spite of the lofty perspectives I have described, I am not always *on* to the same degree. Often, there are significant parts of my being that are "closed for renovation." If I am running my life inartfully or with inadequate love, my peripheral abilities become inactive, as necessary. Some of my attributes have been decades in preparation before emerging. All of this growth happens on its own schedule. I have only limited ability to influence the details of my unfolding. For the most part, I simply feed the process with regular prayer and meditation.

Nonetheless, there is an absolute floor and base to my inner life. I am always aware that I am present as an extension of the one and only Being who makes up and animates this entire creative enterprise. It really is very simple. This fact supports

Answering the Cynical Revolt

all of the other phenomena. The tricky part is making sense of and choosing action to deal with the worldly tangle I see around me. This outer world takes much love, patience and understanding.

I am mindful that many do not participate much in their inner life. There are a number of reasons why this is the case. They coalesce into one. The values of this world, as it is presently constituted, have a nearly uniform effect of distracting and coarsening those who participate in it. Becoming an exception to this rule requires wise, skilful action. This is what I am trying to convey, what it takes to be an exception.

A living membrane that starts as a subtle, selective barrier can become a calcified armour shell in the face of predation. Joints can become arthritic and stiff through assumption of a single, rigid posture of resistance. Spiritual practices are a skilful means of using the intelligence, force and structure that underlies our lives to break shells when they constrain and flex stiffened joints to allow freer movement. No one should leave childhood without such skills. However, it is never too late to benefit from them.

Religious and non-religious people have been wrangling about the merits of their points of view for most of human history; I propose they should instead spend some more time considering the merits of the other's point of view.

The non-religious have a number of valid points to make. They should be recognized and acknowledged. In the first place, they have correctly identified a long history of shortcomings associated with organized religion. There have been many wars over the years associated with religious rivalry and many individual acts of murder and cruelty to enforce doctrinal conformity. There have also been long stretches of time when religion was widely misused as a vehicle to gain worldly security, wealth, and power. The more common experience of simple religious pretention and hypocrisy is repulsive as well. By disassociating themselves from religion's troubling amalgamation, non-religious people are showing a laudable instinct for spiritual hygiene. These people

A Second Look at Jesus

should be appreciated for their independence and willingness to accept responsibility for their inner life.

Many who are nominally non-religious are devoted believers in science and technology. In this, they are sons of Plato and his Christian student, Thomas Aquinas. There are important benefits to this approach to life. The mind is respected. Experience is respected. Expression of opinions is respected. As a practical result of these values, we are blessed with the many practical miracles that flow from scientific knowledge and technology.

I see no reason to give up rational thought for religious hocus-pocus. The practices I advocate will not hamper any of the valuable scientific attributes in our modern society. What Discovery Prayer *does* offer is an opportunity to escape from limitations of the mind and a path to its unlimited source. It helps us to develop the more fluid and subtle mental function that are needed to explore and inhabit the frontiers of the rational mind. This mode of function accommodates all aspects of the mind within a context of nourishment, dignity, and love found within spiritually oriented friendships. It is also a first step away from a life held in suspense by an ethic of dithering when faced with the unknown.

This is not the "magical thinking" that we Christians sometimes engage in to the annoyance of our rational friends. I propose that we develop of a state of being that bridges the gap between mundane reality and the mysterious origin of life. Then, we can grow to embrace that mystery where it is found, and on its own terms.

As for atheists, they are putting up a clear sign that the various religious formulas they have encountered have not worked for them. They have given up on *pie in the sky* belief systems. Instead, they have decided to focus on what *is* within their purview. They just want to be good and successful human beings. There is nothing wrong with this as a working hypothesis. However, if such a person is approached with an opportunity to find the source of his humanity without the usual claptrap of organized religion, perhaps he might be privately willing to try it. There is no reason not to do so.

Answering the Cynical Revolt

Agnostics have shown an inspiring honesty by admitting they do not know God. I have news for them. I am right there with them. Ultimately, God is not knowable. The human configuration is wholly inadequate for knowing much about the reality of God. We are simply outclassed. The most dangerous and profane people in the world are those who think they know **the** truth about God. Instead, agnostics can set that question aside and seek an expanding experience of their own source. Nothing exists without a source. With a little time in skilful observation, we will open up and enrich our lives from that source. The question of what to call that source can be deferred until another day.

In my experience, nominal believers can be the most difficult people to approach. Sometimes, I think of them as *soft focus* Christians. On the one hand, their profession of belief is a useful shield against the incessant marketing of the various Christian franchises. On the other hand, a generalized estimate that God, in some form, exists is a comfort. Many view a serious attempt at a spiritual life as too risky. For them it seems too much investment in spiritual matters just seems to set us up for disappointment, which brings discomfort. All that I can say is the failure to take full advantage of this gift of life is a sure loss. Therefore, why not take the risk on something truly grand before it is too late?

Many of the non-religious are dedicated to finding a fresh start, a spiritual rebirth. They are doing research. Truly, they often *"look for love in all the wrong places."* Nonetheless, they are trying to find a better way. Properly approached, hardly anyone is uninterested in spiritual life. They just do not want to repeat proven mistakes within their own lives.

Many life choices reflect true insights that find less than ideal application. Some have correctly identified the truth that we often weave our own confining bonds within our assumptions and thought processes. We create our own chains. Sometimes, drugs and alcohol are used to relax these bonds. Of course, to the extent that our brains are not actually destroyed by these substances,

A Second Look at Jesus

the bonds are still present when we become sober again. A better way is to disassemble the tangle that has caged us in. This will take some time and skilful practice, but it is worth the effort to effect a lasting solution to this universal human problem.

The immersion of our individual lives into the collective of our society is a common way to attempt an escape from our inner problems. Collectivism is a distraction from inner conflict, but does not heal the soul. To the extent that group thought helps us cope, we become dependent upon it. However, a society or a church of weak and spiritually crippled individuals is necessarily unhealthy. A system, like socialism, that caters to and rewards our infirmities will encourage us to cultivate them. On the other hand, a system like fascism, that worships strength alone, will consume the society in which it grows.

Establishing and maintaining a society that balances the needs of the weak and the strong, along with the individual and group concerns, is a symptom of a healthy society. It is not a solution achieved by political action alone. The proper balance that makes for an optimal society is variable and elusive unless the members of that society have a strong spiritual quotient with the resulting abilities of regeneration and self-regulation.

Many find inspiration by observing the Creator through His work in nature. They correctly observe that most human problems are made more intense by close association with other human beings. Dysfunction reacts to dysfunction in a perverse manner like a critical-mass nuclear reaction. Experience shows that inhumanity comes mostly from other humans, not the challenges of nature. In fact, nature has a bracing cleanliness and vitality that brings out those same virtuous elements within us. Nature is a most subtle and ancient religion. However, living in nature is not, in itself, enough to bring satisfaction. Unless we resolve our inner conflicts, we will bring them with us into a pristine environment and spoil it too. Still, I have found that whatever spiritual practices I use, they are most effective if I combine them with regular access to nature.

Answering the Cynical Revolt

There was a time when the self-improvement and human potential movements tended to be bourgeois in their goals and trite in their methods. Those days are over. There has long been a vast field of human aspiration that religious leaders have either mismanaged or left unaddressed. Many churches have long been more skilled at filling pews than doing something spiritually useful with their members. Secular teachers have now stepped into some of these areas, often using methods and philosophy borrowed from traditional religions and accomplishing a great deal of good. In fact, there is now a significant amount of overlap and synergy between religious and self-help teachings. Secular teachers are taking on some important topics and they *are swinging for the fences.*

Religious people likewise deserve respect. By making a public declaration of their faith and intent, they are opening themselves up to closer public scrutiny and an objective standard of behavior that *appears* to limit their options in life.

To a much greater degree than most people appreciate, the popular culture has been informed and shaped by religious principles. One will not have much insight into civilization without understanding church history.

In fact, non-religious people would most likely not like this world very much in the absence of religious influence. The horrors of the 20th century wars have offered a glimpse of a world further loosened from their mooring in God. They vividly demonstrated that the religion of self-gratification is at least as dangerous as all the others. The 20th century was a bloody one and the 21st could be worse. Proceeding wisely would be worth the effort. We need to bring fresh ideas to life, but it is also necessary to consult the accumulated wisdom of human experience. Human life is not just about pleasure. We are all trying to find our way to a better mode of existence and no one has a monopoly on truth. For this reason, we would all be well advised to listen more carefully to each other, both believers and non-believers.

Much of the criticism people have against religious institutions is out of date. There is a powerful, worldwide religious evolution

A Second Look at Jesus

going on. Fresh, practical insights are emerging with increasing strength and frequency. Many, many wonderful teachers in the spiritual market have beautifully adapted the essence of their faith and practice to meet current conditions in this world. They have found various ways to apply a more spiritual approach to modern life. Before we give up on spiritual life, we should broaden our search.

Then, there are the people, like me, who have taken refuge with spiritual paths outside of the way of Abraham. We did not want to give up on experiencing God, even if our early religious teachers disappointed us. When we have verified to our satisfaction that we have grasped the fundamentals of our adopted spiritual path and we have confirmed, to our satisfaction, that our experience of God is genuine, we wonder, what could be next?

The path we took to our inner realization still leaves us somewhat alienated from the culture of our birth, our families, and the other sources of our worldly identity. For those of us who want to thrive where we live, I recommend a second look at our environment: natural, human, social, cultural *and* religious. These elements are all at hand. Perhaps, when we are ready, we should work within our culture to embrace its virtues and reject its vices. Why not be useful?

So, what do we want? What do we all want? Life. Jesus once addressed his mission with great clarity by saying, "I come that you may have life and have it more abundantly" (John 10:10).

With this in mind, I have one more sacred word to offer in this book. I recommend *Hayim*, or more correctly, *Chayyim*. *Hayim* means "Life." Like *Hayah*, it evokes the vitality of the heart and the crown areas with the "*a*" and "*e*" vowel sounds. It also begins with an "*h*" sound that enlists the assistance of the breath. Actually, the first letter of *Hayim* is a special kind of consonant called a voiceless pharyngeal fricative. This sound is made by slightly constricting the throat just behind the tongue when you make an "h" sound. This creates a slight *friction* as the air passes through the throat. Spiritually, this makes sense to me, as the

Answering the Cynical Revolt

human form does tend to have this effect of *friction* upon the Holy Spirit.

The final syllable, *im* is significant. The "*i*" is brief, almost like an apostrophe. The *m* lingers according to our taste. It has the effect of completing and regulating the opening of our crown area with a resonant, accommodating punctuation. This gives scope the human quality of reflective consideration. Overall, it is a wonderfully engineered word.

Before we close this chapter, I would like to share another delightful poem by Theresa of Avila.

Not Yet Tickled
How did those priests ever get so serious?
And preach all that
gloom?
I don't think God
tickled them yet.
Beloved – Hurry

Theresa of Avila[12]

Like most innovators, Theresa of Avila had some powerful enemies among men in the church hierarchy. They were determined to silence and control her. At a certain point, she and her nuns were even forbidden to read. In response, she turned to God and asked that he teach her about love. Her mystic poems record the result. What a blessing she became. We could follow her example. Is that not better than being mired in this world or endlessly disputing theology and other trivia?

Regarding religious institutions, the challenge is to eat the sweet, juicy part of their fruit and not the fibrous, bitter peel. Let us all feast together.

Chapter Twenty-Five

Something Old, Something New

Hayah

Stirring Ember

Stirring ember, drawing on formlessness, thank you for thawing to this humble creature. I regret that I have made such a mess of your joyous art. I was insane, drunk with the lusty splendor of your creation. I confess that I lost contact with the sobriety of your formless dignity and eternal perspective. Please guide me now, so that I can do my part, to make your work complete. Help me to be a blessing to every atom of your creation so that, in your time, we can all come home to you, whole and full of joy.

John

So, you might ask, what now? I reply, what do you truly want to do with your life? Do you feel a restless longing for more? Only you know if you are ready to try something new in order to

Something Old, Something New

get a new result. If you *are* ready to find more of what a human being is capable of, read on.

For spiritual growth, I recommend a focused approach. A spiritual endeavor is like digging *one* well, fifty feet deep and reaching water at forty-five feet rather than digging *five* wells, each ten feet deep. For this reason, it is likely wiser to focus primarily upon one well-chosen spiritual path until a decisive break-through is achieved. I have found that doing the same spiritual practices every day for long stretches of time will yield the best results. Any changes or adjustments should be done only sparingly and with good reason.

The whole point of the practices that follow is to re-establish a deeper and resilient relationship with our Creator. We need a repeatable and persistent access to that grace so we can move with more confidence and ability into the murky and messy particulars of human life where spirituality is truly tested.

What follows are several of what I call Discovery Prayer practices. They should be helpful for readers who are at home with Judeo/Christian teaching and want to venture more deeply into spiritual life. These spiritual tools date from our movements' youth, four thousand years ago, before we became so sophisticated and full of words. These practices free us from a word-bound relationship with God and help us to create a reliable pathway of continuity between our outward and inner lives. They are as potent today as during the times of Moses, the Prophets, and Jesus. They give us a direct way to escape the tyranny of our intellectual concepts and personal feelings. They help us to participate directly in the "peace that passes all understanding."

Often, our prayer life is altogether too crowded with extraneous thoughts and concepts. We have all sought more simplicity in our inner lives. Even a single preconceived concept is a barrier to a direct encounter with God's perspective. The following practices are intended to bring us that final step from the extreme simplicity of a single thought to the unity of perfect attention to the Author of Life. These sound-based prayers differ from the

A Second Look at Jesus

wordy, meaning-oriented prayers to which we have long been accustomed. Sacred word prayers are precise tools that stimulate inherent capacities rather than application of those capacities. Such prayers also open us to the opportunity to more simply and effectively "Be still and know that I am God" (Psalm 46:10).

Since you have gotten this far in my book, I believe you are serious about making some spiritual progress with no further delay. Therefore, I am going to treat you like an adult by giving explanations that are more full than usual in a book of this type. There is little choice if we want to have a strong result.

If I read the times correctly, our societies will be dealing with some challenges that can best be answered by widespread spiritual resourcefulness. Usually, the details of spiritual practices of the nature we are examining are only offered to those proven worthy and the prepared. Dilettantes waste the time of their teachers. Furthermore, the hostile will use detailed information to attack. Jesus warned us about this in Matthew 7:6 when he said; "Give not that which is holy unto the dogs, neither cast ye your pearls before swine, lest they trample them under their feet and turn again and rend you." This reserve is responsible for the fact that the widespread receptiveness to spiritual growth has not being properly met and served in the past. In my opinion, this conservative approach has proven to be unequal to the scope of our world's challenges and it is even less likely to meet our needs in the future.

There is another reason to spread quality seed far and wide along effective planting instructions. Today, people are increasingly willing to change *if* they are given a proper explanation up front. I have tried to offer a sufficiently detailed set of explanations to meet this challenge. I am not entirely sure how this will work out. I just thought that someone should try it. The more traditional approaches are already doing the best they can.

Now, there are some choices for you to make. I am offering a variety of spiritual practices. I cannot be with each of you personally, so I leave it for you to select among them and choose the one or ones that seem most meaningful to you at this time of your life.

Something Old, Something New

Use the spiritual practices I describe here with care and moderation and they will help you. If you act without moderation and wisdom, you alone will be responsible for unbalancing your life.

I have found all of the spiritual practices I describe below or have outlined earlier in this book to be safe, balanced and wholesome. Not only have I used them personally, they have also been tested by generations of spiritual seekers and have proven their worth over time.

First, whatever else you do, I recommend that you begin with a breathing practice. Here is a good, beginning method:

1. Sit comfortably and close your eyes.
2. Pay attention to your breath.
3. Lengthen and deepen your breath by beginning with a long, slow, and full exhalation. Do not strain yourself.
4. Next, allow your inhalation to be effortless and also long, slow, and full.
5. Do not pause more than a moment between breaths.
6. Make this conscious effort to lengthen your breath several times. Thereafter, breathe naturally for the balance of your sitting.
7. You will inevitably become aware of thoughts, bodily sensations or activity in your surroundings.
8. While you are aware of these thoughts sensations or sensory stimulations, simply add awareness of your breath.
9. It will come to feel as though you are *breathing through* these other experiences.
10. Follow this routine for several minutes before Discovery Prayer then do it again ending with several deep breaths.

So far, I have proposed a number of sacred words as worthy aids to prayer. They are: *Ah, Aha, Abba, Abwoon, Amma, Hayah, Hayim, Yahu, Yehu, Yahushua, Yehushuah Yahuweh and Yehuwah*. If you choose one or more of these sacred word practices you should use then as follows:

A Second Look at Jesus

1. First, sit in a comfortable and stable position.
2. Close your eyes.
3. Pronounce the word gently and clearly.
4. Say it more and more softly until it is no longer audible and only detectible as a silent, breathy whisper.
5. Carry on silently without controlling your breath. Repeat your sacred word as naturally as any other thought.
6. If you are distracted by other thoughts, noises or sensations simply return to your sacred word.
7. Do this twice a day for about fifteen or twenty minutes, morning and evening.

If we want to take on a sacred word for Discovery Prayer, we need to be careful to use it as a simple collection of sounds. Some of these words carry a great deal of doctrinal and historical baggage. I recommend we leave such considerations outside the door of your personal practice. With all spiritual practices, if we do not approach them with a freshness and innocence, we will render the entire exercise confused and useless. We will all be better off if we just do the practices and stay away from spiritual argument as much as we can.

In fact, having heard all of these explanations about how and why Discovery Prayer works, we would be well advised to forget them entirely while we actually use these practices to explore the hidden nature of God. Otherwise, we will complicate the simplicity of our practice and render it much less effective.

A light touch with scripture and doctrine in daily life is also a good idea. The tendency to politicize our relationship with God was widely indulged in the past. The evil harvest of these policies is painfully obvious today. Please do not make this bad situation worse.

I recommend these spiritual practices be done twice a day, morning and evening, for up to thirty minutes. It would be unwise to overdo their use, especially in the beginning. Later, you might consider a spiritual retreat from time to time or some of the

Something Old, Something New

other enhancements I have in mind. However, from the beginning to the end we need to establish a liveable pace in our spiritual endeavours.

Due to the ambitious goals associated with these spiritual practices, it may seem we should all try very hard, all the time. This is not the case. Gentle, simple, persistence is all that is required for success. In this way, we will steadily build up spiritual competence and reserves for natural application, as we need them. A leap ahead in spiritual perspective happens on its own schedule. We cannot force it.

We are not starting a marathon or a sprint. What I am proposing a short walk, to a spring, that is on our own property. We will not be exhausted. We gain vitality along the way.

Afterwards, we should just go about our normal daily activity, trying to make the best decisions we can as situations present themselves. If you like, you may keep a journal to record what strikes you as interesting or important.

Yahuweh/Yehuwah is something of a special case. It is somewhat large and hard to digest in the beginning. So, when first learning *Yahuweh* and *Yehuwah* I suggest a gradual, progressive approach. Begin with the *Ya* syllable and practice it alone for four months. Then add *Hu* to make *YaHu* and do this combination for an additional four months. Next add the final syllable *Weh* for an additional four months. In this way, work your way through the entire YaHuWeh/YeHuWaH Name over a two-year period. Then, once fully internalized, carry on with the entire practice as part of your daily routine.

While exploring, we may find our attention drawn to sensations in various parts of our body. The sacred words we are using may even seem to resonate here or there. Underlying this is a natural affinity between certain vowel sounds and the spiritual sensitivities and capabilities associated with the heart area, the throat, the crown of our head etc.

For example, the *aaa* sound has the effect of opening and this is most obviously and reliably found in the heart area. This is the

A Second Look at Jesus

primary effect of the use of *Ah, Aha, Abba, Amma,* and plays a part in *Yahushua* or *Hayah.* The *u* or *oo* sound found in, *Hu, Yahushua* and *Abwoon,* acts upon the throat area. The *eee* sound *of* the second syllable of *Hayah, Hayim* and the third syllable of *Yehuwah* and the last syllable of *Yehuwah* enliven the crown area. The effect is like the relationship between the changing tone of a flute and the skilful use of our fingers to open and close the openings on the body of any instrument to create an inspiring melody.

A Hole In a Flute
I am

A hole in a flute
That the Christ's breath moves through-
Listen to this music.
I am the concert
From the mouth of every
Creature
Singing with the myriad
Chords

Hafiz[13]

The heart is the center of the human experience. The crown area is the edge of our individuality as it emerges into diversity. The throat area supports the experience of intimacy, continuity and sacred communication between the heart and crown centers. When mature, these practices affirm the underpinnings of our humanity. They open us to the genesis of the creative process that is unfolding as our lives and they bring these elements in a balanced and harmonious interrelationship. The result of an efficient spiritual practice is like a well-tended fire.

Something Old, Something New

Spiritual Fire
*We were conceived as temples
With an altar,
and a hearth
for the primal, white-hot flame of life.
When we embrace this holy fire,
all we are
all we touch
all we perceive
is consumed, transformed
into an essence
and
rises as a fragrant perfume,
sweet and intoxicating,
inflaming the love,
and
the passion
of the most high.*

John

Collectively, the effect of awakening these three centers of spiritual attunement is to tune up our higher functions. The lower functions (between our heart and the base of our spine) are not directly part of this book's work. However, they will naturally strengthen and realign themselves under the systemic influence of the upper spiritual centers and ordinary human life.

Breath awareness has a generalized effect of highlighting the connection between our breath, our mind and the spirit. The experience of breath compliments all of the other practices.

Likely, by natural inclination, one or more of these practices will appeal to you more than the others will. I see nothing wrong with giving those practices more attention. Reinforcing success is usually a good idea. Focusing on a single, simple practice is the most rapid way to achieve a meaningful result.

A Second Look at Jesus

I suggest you not neglect the other practices all together. It is a good thing to keep our base of experience somewhat broad too. However, Choosing one sacred word and using It alone for an indefinite time is a perfectly valid way to proceed too.

I recommend that you choose what sacred word to focus upon based on how well you respond to it at this time. To this end, I recommend that you try each of these words for at least a week. A month might be better. I propose that you trust your instincts alone as to which one is most helpful to you at this time.

There may come a time when the result of spiritual practice peaks in a very strong effect. This is a good outcome and accommodating such a result is an essential art unto itself. In this circumstance it is natural to "back off" and asses what is taking place. Take the time to do so. Simply "breathing through" emerging sensations can be helpful. I have also found the sacred word *Shalom* to be helpful in these circumstances. Gentleness and patience should be the watchwords as turning points in our spiritual maturity emerge.

The sacred words I have identified can be organized into a sequence from the most subtle and least specific to the more detailed and contextualized. Expressed this way our list of sacred words would read like this: *Ah, Aha, Amma, Abba, Hayah, Hayim, Yahuweh and Yehuwah.*

I have given my opinion about the "meanings" of these various sacred words. Religious and academic writings offer other opinions. It would be a serious mistake to choose your meditation on the basis of only descriptions by others. You are not ordering a something over the internet. Try the products before buying! We all need to begin "where we are" and find a practice that feeds our present needs. We must trust that our appetite for God will grow and guide us as necessary.

I acknowledge that, at first look, this proposal for the use of multiple sacred names appears to be contrary to early Judaeo/Christian practice. Yes, *Yahuweh/Yehuwah* was clearly at the center of their entire sacred name program. Yet, I suggest some

Something Old, Something New

diversity within our practices. The name *Yahuweh/Yehuwah* provides a path for the human approach to the Divine perspective. The ability to appreciate it is my goal. Still, I consider the simpler practices that precede it to offer a better beginning. Then we will better appreciate what comes later.

I am not alone in advocating a variety in our spiritual consumption. Moses and Jesus seem to have had a similar opinion on this subject. In Deuteronomy 8:3, we find "He humbled you, causing you to hunger and then feeding you with manna, which neither you nor your ancestors had known, to teach you that man does not live on bread alone but on *every word* that comes from the mouth of the LORD." In Matthew 4:4, we read "Jesus answered, 'It is written: 'Man shall not live on bread alone, but on *every word* that comes from the mouth of God.'" We would all do well to consume a varied diet of sacred words. It is my desire to do my part In presenting a buffet. Feel free to sample as you see fit.

In fact, no single word or action is adequate to express the entire reality of God. A doctrinaire intrusion into this tender area of inner growth is quickly counter-productive. I propose that we simply expose ourselves to sacred words and have faith in the ability of God to influence us as necessary! There is reason to trust your judgment in this matter.

Some of what I just conveyed might seem a little too direct and explicit. It might also be a little complex and detailed. Perhaps you find it somewhat like learning about sex from the school nurse. All that I can say in response is that some occasions benefit from metaphor and others require plain talk.

Some might also find what I have written a little far-fetched. I understand. I assure you that I have actually been somewhat reserved and understated in my claims and descriptions. In order to make everything more plausible I have tried to add context to my claims. I have shown how this approach to spirituality has worked in my own life. I have also tried to show that something similar may have been near the basis of our faith tradition.

A Second Look at Jesus

However, *your* proof of what I am describing resides within *you*. If, and only if, *you try* Discovery Prayer, will you have some idea how valid my descriptions and suggestions are. A few months of regular practice should give you an idea of what Discovery Prayer can mean for you. If you must judge, please try it yourself first, so you can form a valid opinion. Then you can judge the fruits within your own life.

Not all progress feels flashy or profound. In the beginning, and perhaps for a long time, the effect of Discovery Prayer may not produce a vivid inner experience. Instead, we will enjoy the generally refreshing effect that these intervals have on our daily life. It is like finding damp soil and a cooler environment as you dig, long before you get to a drinkable pool at the bottom of a new well. For much of our spiritual journey we are refreshed as we progress, but not fully satisfied. To reach our goal we must be as patient as necessary. No time spent in this endeavor is wasted.

It has taken us a long time to get ourselves into the constraints that we experience now. Even an effective and direct pathway to a restoration of our innate liberty will need a certain amount of time to have a clear effect. It is something like paying off a mortgage, only we are overcoming a deficit of a spiritual nature. I suggest you be patient and stick to a schedule of twenty or thirty minutes of spiritual practices, twice a day. In the meantime, just keep making the best life choices you can on a day-to-day basis. These practices are a supplement to, not a substitute for, a wholesome life.

As you progress, please feel free to contact me from time to time at my web site *asecondlook.org*. Tell me how you are doing. I will be adding some sound files to help everyone get their pronunciations right. I will also respond to some questions with the blog found there.

If you ever find yourself in Wilmington, you are welcome to stop by Good Shepherd church and chat with me about God.

Those are my thoughts, for now. I hope that this has been helpful. I wish you well.

John

Index of Key Terms

Aramaic, 128-132, 137, 172, 251, 253
Breathing, 35-36, 39, 48, 172-173, 211, 253, 291, 296
Delhi, 81-82, 84-85, 87-88, 94
Dhkr, 166
Discovery Prayer, 45, 61, 136, 143, 236, 250, 271, 282, 289, 291, 298
Ganges/Ganga, 97-98, 101
Greek, 122, 128-130, 134, 143, 172, 251
Guru Dev, 47, 63, 65, 73, 90, 98-99, 102
Hafiz, 159, 212, 279, 294
Hazrat Inayat Kahn, 152, 157, 159
India, ix, 31, 82-83, 86, 89, 91, 94, 96, 103, 125, 132, 156
Jesus, iv, vii-x, 2, 4, 39, 54, 55, 61, 71-72, 110, 112, 116, 120, 123-129, 133-135, 139, 141-144, 154, 156-157, 167-168, 172, etc.
Kabir, 102-103
Kumba Mela, 101
Latin, 55, 128, 130, 172
Lord's Prayer, 130
Pir Vilayat, iv, 152, 157, 160, 162, 165, 176, 182-183, 196, 214, 244
Pir Zia, 214
Madras, 91-94, 96
Maharishi, iv, 41, 47-52, 59-69, 73, 74, 84-87, 89, 96-100, 102-105, etc.
Mantra, 29-30, 36, 59, 60, 63-64, 69, 76, 88, 100, 183
Noor, 160-162
Ruah, 172-173

A Second Look at Jesus

Rumi, 143, 252-253
Sacred Words:
  Ah, 70, 291, 294, 296
  Aha, 70, 291, 294, 296
  Abba, 71, 291, 294, 296
  Abwoon, 130, 291, 294
  Ahad, 171
  Alim, 171
  Amma, 72, 291, 294, 296
  Azim, 171
  Hayah, 45, 58, 75, 81, 91, 97, 105, 120, 133, 136, 146, 151, etc.
  Hayy, 171
  Hu, 144, 171, 293-294
  Shalom, 296
  Ya, 171, 293
  Yahu, 144, 291
  Yahushua, 144, 291, 294
  Yahuweh, 136-137, 248-249, 291, 293, 296-297
  Yehuwah, 248-249, 251, 291, 293-294, 296-297
  Yehushuah, 249, 291
  Yehu, 249, 291
  YHWH, 134, 136, 142, 168, 251
  Yesu, 249
Rishikesh, 96-97
St. Paul, viii, 71, 124, 126, 224, 245, 247, 249-256, 262
St. Nicholas De Flues, 245
St. James the Just, 251
Transcendental Meditation, 29, 59, 64, 85
TM, 29, 49, 52, 59, 61, 63-66, 68, 70, 73, 76, 84, 96, 100-102, etc.
Theresa of Avila, 45, 47, 151, 244, 287
Wazaif/Wavzifa, 69

Index of Key Terms

Poems by various Saints:
10,000 Idiots, 212
The Sad Game, 212
The Body is Like Mary, 252
Until, 143

The Smart Dogs Ran Off, 103
Every Prophets Name, 46
Not Tickled Yet, 287

Poems by author:

Restless, vi
Striking Sail, 2
A Good Hunter Knows, 13
The Rabbit, 40
You and I, 49
A Poem Is, 77
Resonance, 79
Delhi 1972, 87
The Lord in Rags, 92
A Tryst with Ruah, 172
My Daughters, 210
I was Wrong, 211
The Beginning, 213

A New Product at the Kiosk, 215
Burnt Sacrifice on Oleander
Drive, 215
Omnivore, 217
The Swamp, 233
The Wave, 246
The Shop, 268
Poetry of Motion, 271
Low Pressure System, 278
The Art of Life, 279
Spiritual Fire, 295

Ecstatic prose by the author:
Intention, 218
Stirring Ember, 288
The Archer, xi
Owner, 38

References

1. Love Poems from God Translated by Daniel Ladinsky, Published by Penguin Compass, New York, 2002, Reprinted by Permission
2. Love Poems from God Translated by Daniel Ladinsky, Published by Penguin Compass, New York, 2002, Reprinted by Permission
3. Prayers of the Cosmos, Neil Douglas Klotz, Published by HarperCollins, New York, 1990, Reprinted by Permission
4. Dictionary of Deities and Demons in the Bible edited by Karel van der Toorn and published by, Published by Brill, Amsterdam, 1999
   I have reprinted, with permission, the portion of this publication that summarizes current academic research on YHWH. It is found at the end of this book.
5. Love Poems from God Translated by Daniel Ladinsky, Published by Penguin Compass, New York, 2002, Reprinted by Permission
6. The Sources of Islam; A Persian Treatise, William St. Clair Tisdall, General Books LLC, 2013
7. I Heard God Laughing Translated by Daniel Ladinsky, Published by Penguin Compass, New York, 1996, 2006, Reprinted by Permission
8. I Heard God Laughing Translated by Daniel Ladinsky, Published by Penguin Compass, New York, 1996, 2006, Reprinted by Permission

References

9 The Subject Tonight is Love Translated by Daniel Ladinsky, Published by Penguin Compass, New York, 1996, 2003, Reprinted by Permission

10 The Gift Translated by Daniel Ladinsky, Published by Penguin Compass, New York, 1999, Reprinted by Permission

11 The Purity of Desire Translated by Daniel Ladinsky, Published by Penguin Compass, New York, 2012

12 Love Poems from God Translated by Daniel Ladinsky, Published by Penguin Compass, New York, 2002, Reprinted by Permission

13 A Year with Hafiz Translated by Daniel Ladinsky, Published by Penguin Compass, New York, 2011, Reprinted by Permission

A Bibliography of Suggested Readings

for <u>A Second Look at Jesus</u>

Jewish and Christian resources
1. <u>Ecclesiastical History</u>
Eusebius Pamphilus
Translated by C. F. Cruse
Published Henderson Publishers, 2000

    This important reference book cannot be entirely trusted. Eusebius, is clearly cherry picking his resource material to sustain his opinions. Nonetheless, many of the reference materials that are quoted no longer exist. This book is also a clear portrait of how the church wanted to be seen during the critical time of its incorporation into the Roman State.

2. <u>Reading the Bible Again for the First Time</u>
Marcus Borg
Harper Collins, 2002

A Bibliography of Suggested Readings

Marcus Borg shows us how to use modern scholarship to strengthen our faith and understanding of the Christian message.

3. A People's History of Christianity
Diana Butler Bass
Harper One, 1989
Diana Butler Bass gives us a glance at the long sweep of Christian history.

4. Love Wins
Rob Bell
Harper One, 2011
Here, Rob Bell helps us to face our fears of the threatening side of our Christian heritage.

5. Zealot
Reza Aslan
Random House, 2013
Resa Aslan shows us how to use original source material to gain a closer look at the original message of Jesus.

6. Bad Religion
Ross Douthat
Free Press, 2012
Ross Douthat effectively makes the point that cherry picking our Christian tradition seriously diminishes its power to transform us. At the very least, we should become aware of what Christianity has been if we want to avoid loss of important teachings.

7. EFM Program Study Materials
University of the South
http://www.sewanee.edu/EFM/
EFM is a serious and yet accessible four year survey course in Jewish and Christian teachings using original source materials.

A Second Look at Jesus

We read during the material individually and then the implications are talked out in small groups. The result is that everyone has an opportunity to digest and use material, as necessary to advance his or her lives.

8. The New Testament
Bart D. Ehrman
Oxford University Press, 2012
    Bart Ehrman is a gifted scholar and teacher of many original and courageously honest books.

9. Prayers of the Cosmos
Neil Douglas-Klotz
Harper Collins, 1990
    Dr. Klotz has dedicated his life to making the insights of Aramaic language understanding of Jesus more available. It is a lonely, neglected field that deserves more of our attention.

10. Archeological Study Bible, New International Version
Zondervan, 1984
    I use this bible for my own studies. Its language is clear and modern and the numerous mini-articles on history and archeology have helped me to appreciate the text more.

11. Strong's Exhaustive Concordance of the Bible
James Strong
Hendrickson Publishing
    This is an irreplaceable Bible research tool that gives an inquisitive mind of any sophistication access to the deeper meanings of any word that catches their interest.

12. The Fathers of the Primitive Church
Herbert A. Musarillo
Mentor Omega, 1966

A Bibliography of Suggested Readings

This book lets the early church leaders speak for themselves on a wide range of religious topics that they considered important in their time.

13. The Phenomenon of Man
Teilhard de Chardin
Harper Colophon, 1975
　　This book shows how an original mind can take a fresh look at the Christian faith. He was both respected and feared by the orthodox of his time. Today his vision is receiving increasing recognition as his detractors sink into obscurity.

14. The Book of Legends, *Sefer Ha Aggadah* (Selections from the Talmud with Midrash)
Trans. William Braude
Shocken Books, 1992
　　The study of the oral tradition (Talmud) of the Hebrew people is famously subtle and inaccessible to those who are not willing to learn Hebrew and Aramaic and devote a lifetime to its study. Midrash, the traditional system of analysis used in interpreting the written and oral traditions is also hard to access for outsiders. This book is an exception to the rule. Is shows a plain English sampling of that world. I am thankful for it.

15. Rabbis and Wives
Chiam Grade
Shoken Books, 1987
　　This book is a fun read that gives ordinary readers a bite-sized sampling of traditional Jewish thought.

16. The Cost of Discipleship
Dietrich Bonhoeffer
Touchstone, 1995
　　At a time when the institutional churches of Europe were granting concession left and right to the fearsome Nazi regime,

A Second Look at Jesus

Bonhoffer found the courage and the theology to fight back. To his eternal credit, Bonhoffer died for all the right reasons. This pivotal book reveals those reasons. We should learn to do likewise.

17. **YaHuWeH,** Exposition of the Name of *YaHuWeH*
NO MANS ZONE, 2012

18. The Sacred Name of Yahweh (Available on-line only)
http://www.yahweh.org/publications/sny/sacrednm.pdf
R. Clover
Qadesh La Yahweh Press, 2002

I regard these books as a beginning attempt to come to grips with the question of what the theological consequences might be if use of the name *Yahuweh* was important to the teaching of Jesus and the early church. I have not used these books to develop my ideas on this subject. I found them just as I neared publication. Nonetheless, I intend to examine them moreclosely.

19. CHRISTIANITY, The First three Thousand Years
Diarmaid MacCulloch
Viking, 2009

This is a long book but it is well written so it moves along well. This would be a good choice for someone who is interested in church history but does not feel ready to take on something as demanding as the EFM program.

20. The Cathars
Sean Martin
Chartwell Books Inc., 2005

If we want a mature love of Christianity and the church, we should be willing to see it clearly with both its virtues and defects in view. This book will give us a front row seat to observe of some of those defects in action.

A Bibliography of Suggested Readings

21. Servanthood, Leadership for the Third Millennium
Bennett J. Sims
Crowley Publications, 1997
   This may be the most important book on leadership I have ever read. It shows how to wield great power while keeping to the spiritually and psychologically safe perspective of a servant.

Other Religious and Spiritual writings

1. Thinkers of the East
Indres Shah
Penguin Books Ltd., 1971
   Indres Shah has written many books that make the best of eastern though; accessible, and fun. This is one of his best and it is a perfect starting point if you are new to this subject.

2. Awakening
Pir Vilayat Inayat Kahn
Tarcher/Putnam, 1999
   Pir Vilayat has only written a few books. His words are well chosen to give a clear and experience oriented introduction to Sufi thought and practice. Spirituality really is about awakening. Read and understand why.

3. The Call of the Dervish
Pir Vilayat Inayat Kahn
Sufi Order Publications, 1981
   This book talks about the rewards of drawing back from our ongoing social context to enable an encounter with the divine. We all need to recognize genuine "voices in the wilderness." It is a prelude to discovering our own voice.

4. The Ecstasy Beyond Knowing
Pir Vilayat Inayat Kahn
Suluk Press, an imprint of Omega Publications, 2014

A Second Look at Jesus

Pir Vilayat was working on when he died this book. It represents his best and most mature understanding of the art of the possible in the path of spiritual transformation.

5. Personality, The Art of Being and Becoming
Hazrat Inayat Kahn
Sufi Order Publications, 1982
   Pir Vilayat's father, Hazrat Inayat Kahn, did not lead a long life. He was sent from India to the West to introduce eastern spiritual thought. While here, he soon met some dedicated students who transcribed his many lectures into lucid English prose. These lectures were very diverse and amounted to an encyclopedia of accessible spiritual knowledge. Much of this material has been reorganized into books like this one. The art of personality in the backdrop of deep spiritual resourcefulness is an important topic and this book provides a viable framework for us to understand it.

6. Mastery Through Accomplishment
Hazrat Inayat Kahn
Sufi Order Publications, 1978
   Mastery through accomplishment is about being both spiritual and effective in this world. Nothing could be more important.

7. Saracen Chivalry
Pir Zia Inayat Kahn
Suluk Press, Omega Publications Inc., 2012
   Pir Zia is the son of Pir Vilayat and the grandson of Inayat Kahn. Pir Zia appears to be focused upon bringing authentic and timely Eastern spiritual culture to meet the specific needs of our time. If you are ready to move beyond the routine platitudes Islamic Spirituality endlessly repeated on television this book is a good place to start. It is about honor in war and peace.

A Bibliography of Suggested Readings

8. Caravan of Souls
Pir Zia Inayat Kahn
Suluk Press, Omega Publications Inc., 2013
    This is another book by the present leader of the Sufi order of the west. It is an overview of his grandfather's teachings.

8. Physicians of the Heart: A Sufi View of the 99 Names of Allah
Wali Ali Meyer, Bilal Hyde, Faisal Mukaddam, Shabda Kahn
Sufi Ruhaniat International, 2011
    Much of the Spiritual practice of Sufis involves the discovery of Divine qualities with the traditional names for those qualities. This book list those qualities and their significances.

9. The Hand of Poetry, Five Mystic Poets of Persia
Lectures by Inayat Kahn
Poetry translations by Coleman Barks
Omega Publications, 1993
    Sufi poetry is probably to best way to access to the deeper aspects of that path to understanding God. This book is a good way to begin to open yourself to that resource.

10. Bhagavad Gita, A New Translation and Commentary,
    Chapters 1-6
Maharishi Mahesh Yogi
Penguin Books, 1990
    This book was an important reference point in my youth. It expounds on the place of meditation using the classic Indian story of the Bagavad Gita, which means "The song of God."

11. Autobiography of a Yogi
Paramahansa Yogananda
Self-Realization Fellowship, 2007
    This book was important in my youth. Do you wonder how to be a God-realized person? This book will give you a reasonable idea what it will take from the Vedic perspective.

A Second Look at Jesus

12. Crest-Jewel of Discrimination
Shankara
Translated By Swami Prabhavananda and Christopher Isherwood
Vedanta Press, 1947, 1975
  This book summarizes the teachings of this important Spiritual reformer. This is advanced material. No one is talking down to you.

13. The Upanishads
Translated by Juan Mascaro
Penguin Books, 1965
  The Upanishads are a collection of the short and succinct teachings that make up the essence of Indian spiritual thought.

14. How to Know God: The Yoga Sutras of Patanjali
Translated By Swami Prabhavananda and Christopher Isherwood
Vedanta Press, 1953, 1981
  This sophisticated, concentrated material will only start to make sense after considerable spiritual attainment. It is nonetheless interesting to read and understand what spiritual masters are aiming to accomplish.

15. Tao Te Ching
Lao Tsu
Translated by D. C. Lau
Penguin Press, 1963
  This book will also make more sense as your spiritual life grows. It is at the center of much of the spiritual insight that has traditionally animated China and those who look to if for inspiration.

16. The Dhammapada
Buddha
Translated by Juan Mascaro
Penguin Books, 1973
  This is a good, traditional summary of the teachings of Buddha.

A Bibliography of Suggested Readings

17. The Vimalakirti Sutra
Translated by Burton Watson
Columbia University Press, 1997
 This was another important book in my youth. Is shows the kind of thought and action that is compatible with an ongoing spiritual life.

18. Zen Flesh, Zen Bones
A succinct collection of Zen & Pre-Zen writings
Compiled by Paul Reps
Charles Tuttle Company Inc., 1957
 This is a classic book that successfully highlights the unique flavor of Buddhism that flourishes in Japan.

18. The Tracker
Tom Brown Jr.
Berkley Books, 1979
 The is the first of a series of books about a man who met and learned from an authentic Native American medicine man and scout in his early youth. This man, who the author calls grandfather, learned his craft as an Apache youth in the closing years of the Indian wars. He then delivered his teaching intact to the author beginning at age 8. It is quite a story that smells of authenticity.

19. Fools Crow: Wisdom and Power
Thomas E. Mails
Council Oak Books, 1991
 This book gives a good taste of Native American Wisdom.

20. Das Energi
Paul Williams
Warner Books, 1973, 1978
 This odd and insightful book manages to talk about God and spirituality without using traditional religious words. It is likely to be interesting and inoffensive to atheists.

A Second Look at Jesus

21. The Hidden Origins of Islam
Edited by Karl-Heinz Ohlig and Gerd R. Puin
Prometheus Books

This book makes a fascinating and, if true, pivotal point that Islam began as a Christian reform reaction to the Western Churches. I did not use these books in developing my own Ideas in this area of inquiry. I found them just as I neared publication. Nonetheless, I intend to examine them closely.

Politics and Social Ethics

1. The Triumph of Liberty, A 2,000 year History, Told Through the Lives of History's Greatest Champions
Jim Powell
The Free Press, 2000

This Book delivers exactly what the title promises. It effectively makes the point that the American experiment was a long time coming and plenty of preparation was necessary.

2. The Road to Serfdom
F. A. Hayek
University of Chicago Press, 1944, 1994

Even if you were not interested in freedom, you would do well to read this classic book on the subject so that you would understand what the excitement is about..

3. Wealth of Nations
Adam Smith
Penguin Books Ltd. , 1776, 1986

This book was important to the political and economic of our founders of our country. Its principles have never been proven wrong. Watch the news. Further proof of the validity of the authors will arrive shortly.

A Bibliography of Suggested Readings

4. The Federalist Papers
Alexander Hamilton, James Madison, John Jay
Bantam Classic, 2003
 This book and the following one should be read together. The federalist papers were the essays written by those politicians who wanted to sell the American people on the idea of a more powerful national government with the passage of our current constitution. Promises and assurances were made that all would go well. The anti-federalist papers were the replies of the sceptics who thought that the whole enterprise was a bad idea. After reading these books, you will have a fresh and clear perspective on today's political drama.

5. The Anti-Federalist Papers and The Constitutional Convention Debate
Edited by Ralph Ketcham
Signet Classic, 2003

6. Notes on the State of Virginia
Thomas Jefferson
Edited by William Peden
W. W. Norton & Company Ltd., 1972
 This book goes far toward filling out the rest of Jefferson's political philosophy.

7. More Liberty Means Less Government
Walter Williams
Hoover Institute Press, 1999
 I simply love the witty and wise musings of this man.

8. Hologram of Liberty
Kenneth W. Royce
Javelin Press, 1997
 Warning! This is a "take no prisoners" book. The author gives a credible and succinct analysis of exactly how the and why the

original US government system "evolved" into the form we see today.

9. Hamilton's Curse
Thomas J. DeLorenzo
Crown Forum, 2008
 This book focuses upon the likely role that the brilliant Alexander Hamilton played in setting up the subversion and eventual eclipse of our early constitutional promises. This is original thinking from a skilled historian.

10. Original Meanings
Jack N. Rakove
Alfred A. Knopf, 1996
 This book plays the important role of reminding us what are the original meanings of the words and concepts of our constitution. These are important, necessary understandings.

11. A Nation of Sheep
Andrew P. Napolitano
Thomas Nelson, 2007
 This is a quality, contemporary diatribe against modern tyranny by a gifted author.

12. Radical Son
David Horowitz
The Free Press, 1997
 This book describes the American Left, as I knew them in my youth. The author tells about his personal journey back toward traditional American values. I found this book helpful.

13. The Law
Frederic Bastiat
Tribeca Books, 2007
 This is a seminal work on the immorality of tyranny.

A Bibliography of Suggested Readings

14. Moral Minority, Our Sceptical Founding Fathers
Brooke Allen
Ivan R. Dee, 2006
This book describes the religious beliefs of our country's founders as they were, not as we wish they were. It is fascinating.

15. Democracy in America
Alexis De Tocqueville
Harper Perennial, 1969
This book, written not long after the birth of our country, gives firsthand account of Early American life.

16. The Minute Men
John R. Galvin
Potomac Books Inc.2006
This book gives a detailed account of the people who were wise enough to pick the right fight and foolish enough to believe that they might win it.

17. A Hell of a Whipping, The Battle of Cowpens
Lawrence E. Babits
The University of North Carolina Press, 1998
This battle was the critical turning point in the war for our liberty. It is one of our few outright victories. The story of how it came to be is of enormous human interest to me.

18. Cape Fear Rising
Philip Gerard
John F. Blair, 1997
This is the story of a successful, white racist revolt in my hometown.
19. Holy War
Karen Armstrong
Anchor Books, 1988, 1991, 2001

A Second Look at Jesus

This book thoroughly and sensitively addresses crusade, Jihad and the challenge of Israel. It is especially important to have a grasp of these topics, as Crusading era history looms large in modern day Islamic political thought.

International Affairs

1. The Gathering Storm
Winston Churchill
Houghton Mifflin Company, 1948

Winston Churchill is one of the greatest men of the last century. He was brave, resourceful, clever, and in the run-up to WW2 right when nearly everyone else was wrong. This autobiographical book details those times. It is fascinating reading.

2. Endless Enemies
Jonathan Kwitney
Penguin Books, 1986

In post 9/11 America, the successes of the CIA in protecting our nation are universally recognized. This book addresses the cold war years when the CIA created many enemies around the world in order to win the cold war at any cost.

3. War is a Racket
General Smedley D. Butler
Feral House, 1935, 2003

This is a classic anti-war tract written by the former commander of the US Marine Corps. He was in a position to know that during that era the US military was often little but a bill collector or US financial interests. Here he lays out his gripes in the way only a Marine Officer can.

A Bibliography of Suggested Readings

4. <u>The Two faces of Islam</u>
Stephen Schwartz
Anchor Books, 2002
This fine book identifies an important divide within the Islamic culture.

5. <u>The Arab Mind</u>
Raphael Payai
Hatherleigh Press, 2002
This is a companion piece to the above work. Much of the upheaval of modern middle-eastern politics amounts to imposition of Arab values on non-Arabs. This book attempts to reveal the salient characteristics of Arab mentality while identifying the reason for those values. It is a truthful and respectful book.

6. <u>Al Qaeda in its Own Words</u>
Edited by Gilles Kepel and Jean-Pierre Milelli
Translated by Pascal Gazaleh
Belknap Press, 2008
This book is based upon the premise that too much reading between the lines is a mistake in understanding the motivations and goals of Al Qaeda. Their own words plainly reveal most of what we need to know.

7. <u>Jihad</u>
Ahmed Rashid
Yale University, 2002
Westerners have a hard time understanding Jihadi values and methods. This book explains what is really transpiring beneath the surface of Jihadi actions.

8. <u>Noor-un-nisa Inayat Kahn (Madeleine)</u>
Jean Overton Fuller
East-West Publications, 1952, 1988

A Second Look at Jesus

This book is the story of Pir Vilayat's sister who served with SOE in occupied France during WW2. She was a genuine hero.

9. The Art of War
Sun Tsu
Simon and Brown, 2012
   This ancient text on war-winning strategies is always timely.

10. The Ascent of Money
Niall Ferguson
Penguin Press, 2008
   Understanding money is key to understanding human motivation. This book has much to teach us.

Other Topics of Personal Interest

1. Rules of Civility and Personal Behavior
George Washington
Applewood Books, 1988
   This great man first set out to be a good man by writing his own book of dos and don'ts.

2. The Wit and Wisdom of Baltasar Gracian, A Practical Manual for Good and Perilous Times
Baltasar Gracian
Adapted and edited by J. Leonard Kay
Pocket Books, 1992
   This book is a treasure chest of wise counsel for all occasions. You will need to be thinking clearly throughout because the author clearly is.

3. The Wit and Wisdom of Winston Churchill
Edited by Carol Kelly-Gangi
Fall River Press, 2013

A Bibliography of Suggested Readings

There is plenty of wit and wisdom here and it is expressed in an appealing a playful manner.

4. The Truth About Self Protection
Massad Ayoob
Bantam Doubleday Dell, 1983
 If you are not a pacifist, you should read this book. It might save your life.

5. How to Spot a Liar
Gregory Hartley and Maryann Karinch
Career Press, 2005
 This book provides insights that will be needed in everyday life.

6. The Sociopath Next Door
Martha Stout
MJF Books, 2005
 This is a companion book to the previous one. According to this book, one person in 25 does not possess the ability to feel empathy or remorse. They are unable to care about anyone but himself or herself. They are also typically very charming and make superlative liars.

7. Things That Matter
Charles Kruthammer
Crown Forum, 2013
 This book is written straight from the heart. The author shows us what a person of stature and values sounds like. Reading this book renewed my faith in the human experiment.

8. The First American
H. W. Brands
Doubleday, 2000
 Benjamin Franklin has been an irreplaceable guide for me in my journey to become a well-rounded and responsible man. This

A Second Look at Jesus

book is the best I have found on the excellent qualities demonstrated by this great American.

9. Jesus and Muhammad
Mark Gabriel
Charisma House, 2004

Mark Gabriel is uniquely qualified to give an authentic view of Islam. He holds a PHD in Islamic studies from Al-Azar University in Cairo. His encounter with Jesus and everything about him strikes me as unusually authentic and truthful. All his books are worth reading in these troubled and confusing times.

10. The Tipping Point
Malcolm Gladwell
Little Brown and Co., 2000

Malcolm Gladwell Has written a number of fascinating books about how and why things happen. I recommend them.

11. The following excerpt from The Dictionary of Deities and Demons in the Bible is reprinted with permission from Brill publishing. It is intended to give my readers an overview of the scholarly work that has gone into reconstructing the correct and original pronunciation and use of *Yahuweh*, the primary Hebrew name of God.

Yehuwah

Reference Material

YAAQAN → YA'ÛQ

YAHWEH יהוה
I. Yahweh is the name of the official god of Israel, both in the northern kingdom and in Judah. Since the Achaemenid period, religious scruples led to the custom of not pronoucing the name of Yahweh; in the liturgy as well as in everyday life, such expressions as 'the →Lord' (*'ădōnāy*, lit. 'my Lord', LXX κύριος) or 'the →Name' were substituted for it. As a matter of consequence, the correct pronunciation of the tetragrammaton was gradually lost: the Masoretic form 'Jehovah' is in reality a combination of the consonants of the tetragrammaton with the vocals of *'ădōnāy*, the *ḥaṭēf pataḥ* of *'ădōnāy* becoming a mere *shewa* because of the yodh of *yhwh* (ALFRINK 1948). The transcription 'Yahweh' is a scholarly convention, based on such Greek transcriptions as Ιαουε/ Ιαουαι (Clement of Alexandria, *Stromata* 5, 6, 34, 5), Ιαβε/ Ιαβαι (Epiphanius of Salamis, *Adv. Haer.* 1, 3, 40, 5 and Theodoretus of Cyrrhus, *Quaest. in Ex. XV; Haer. fab. comp.* 5,3).

The form Yahweh (*yhwh*) has been established as primitive; abbreviations such as Yah, Yahû, Yô, and Yĕhô are secondary (CROSS 1973:61). The abbreviated (or hypocoristic) forms of the name betray regional predilections: thus *Yw* ('Yau' in Neo-Assyrian sources) is especially found in a North-Israelite context; *Yh*, on the other hand, is predominantly Judaean (cf. WEIPPERT 1980:247-248). The alleged attestation of *Yw* as an onomastic element on an arrowhead dated to the 11th cent. BCE on the basis of its script (F. M. CROSS, An Inscribed Arrowhead of the Eleventh Century BCE in the Bible Lands Museum in Jerusalem, *ErIsr* 23 [2992] 21*-26*, esp. n. 3), still maintained by J. C. DE MOOR (*The Rise of Yahwism* [2nd ed.; Leuven 1997] 165-166), is uncertain on epigraphical grounds (P. BORDREUIL, Flèches pheniciennes inscrites, *RB* 99 [1992] 208; A. LEMAIRE, Epigraphic palestinienne: nouveaux documents II - décennie 1985-1995, *Henoch* 17 [1996] 211). The form *Yhw* is said to be originally Judaean (WEIPPERT 1980: 247), but its occurrence in the northern wayfarer's station of Kuntillet 'Ajrud shows that it was not unknown among Northern Israelites either. In the frequently attested Nabataean personal name *'bd'hyw* (variant *'bd'hy*), the element *'hyw* (*'hy*) has been interpreted as a spelling of the divine name Yahweh (M. LIDZBARSKI, *ESE* 3 [1915] 270 n. 1); it is not certain whether it is a theonym or an anthroponym, though, and a connection with the tetragrammaton is unproven (KNAUF 1984). It is unclear whether an allegedly northern Syrian deity Ιευώ (Porphyry, *Adv. Christ.* fr. 41, apud Eusebius, *Praep. Ev.* 1, 9, 21; cf. Ιαώ in Theodoretus, *Graec. aff. cur.* II 44-45 and Macrobius, *Sat.* I 18-20) is related to the god Yahweh. In the Mishna, the divine name is usually written '' in combination with *šĕwā'* and *qāmeṣ* (WALKER 1951).

II. The cult of Yahweh is not originally at home in Palestine. Outside Israel, Yahweh was not worshipped in the West-Semitic world—despite affirmations to the contrary (*pace*, e.g. G. GARBINI, *History and Ideology in Ancient Israel* [London & New York 1988] 52-65). Before 1200 BCE, the name Yahweh is not found in any Semitic text. The stir caused by PETTINATO (e.g. Ebla and the Bible, *BA* 43 [1980] 203-216, esp. 203-205) who claimed to have found the shortened form of the name Yahweh ('Ya') as a divine element in theophoric names from Ebla (ca. 2400-2250 BCE) is unfounded. As the final element of personal

A Second Look at Jesus

names, -ya is often a hypocoristic ending, not a theonym (A. ARCHI, The Epigraphic Evidence from Ebla and the Old Testament, Bib 60 (1979) 556-566, esp. 556-560). MÜLLER argues that the sign NI, read yà by Pettinato, is conventionally short for NI-NI = ì-lí, 'my (personal) god'; it stands for ilī or ilu (MÜLLER 1980:83; 1981:306-307). This solution also explains the occurrence of the speculated element *ya at the beginning of personal names; thus ^{d}yà-ra-mu should be read either as DINGIR-lí-ra-mu or as ^{d}ili$_x$-ra-mu, both readings yielding the name Iliramu, 'My god is exalted'. In no list of gods or offerings is the mysterious god *Ya ever mentioned; his cult at Ebla is a chimera.

Yahweh was not known at Ugarit either; the singular name Yw (vocalisation unknown) in a damaged passage of the Baal Cycle (KTU 1.1 iv:14) cannot convincingly be interpreted as an abbreviation for 'Yahweh' (pace, e.g., DE MOOR 1990:113-118). Also after 1200 BCE, Yahweh is seldom mentioned in non-Israelite texts. The assertion that "Yahweh was worshipped as a major god" in North Syria in the eighth century BCE (S. DALLEY, Yahweh in Hamath in the 8th century BC, VT 40 [1990] 21-32, quotation p. 29), cannot be maintained. The claim is based on the names Azriyau and Yaubi'di, attested as indigenous rulers from north Syrian states in the 8th cent. BCE. The explanation of these names offered by Dalley is highly dubious; more satisfactory interpretations are possible (VAN DER TOORN 1992:88-90).

The earliest West Semitic text mentioning Yahweh—excepting the biblical evidence—is the Victory Stela written by Mesha, the Moabite king from the 9th century BCE. The Moabite ruler recalls his military successes against Israel in the time of Ahab: "And →Chemosh said to me, 'Go, take Nebo from Israel!' So I went by night and I engaged in fight against her from the break of dawn until noon. And I took her and I killed her entire population: seven thousand men, boys, women, girls, and maid servants, for I devoted her to destruction (ḥḥrmth) for Ashtar-Chemosh. And I took from there the '[r']ly of Yahweh and I dragged them before Chemosh" (KAI 181:14-18). Evidently, Yahweh is not presented here as a Moabite deity. He is presented as the official god of the Israelites, worshipped throughout Samaria, as far as its outer borders since Nebo (נבו) in the Mesha Stela, נבו in the Bible), situated in North-Western Moab, was a border town.

The absence of references to a Syrian or Palestinian cult of Yahweh outside Israel suggests that the god does not belong to the traditional circle of West Semitic deities. The origins of his veneration must be sought for elsewhere. A number of texts suggest that Yahweh was worshipped in southern Edom and Midian before his cult spread to Palestine. There are two Egyptian texts that mention Yahweh. In these texts from the 14th and 13th centuries BCE, Yahweh is neither connected with the Israelites, nor is his cult located in Palestine. The texts speak about "Yahu in the land of the Shosu-beduins" (t; š;św jhw;; R. GIVEON, Les bédouins Shosou des documents égyptiens [Leiden 1971] no. 6a [pp. 26-28] and no. 16a [pp. 74-77]; note WEIPPERT 1974:427, 430 for the corrected reading). The one text is from the reign of Amenophis III (first part of the 14th cent. BCE; cf. HERMANN 1967) and the other from the reign of Ramses II (13th cent. BCE; cf. H. W. FAIRMAN, Preliminary Report on the Excavations at 'Amārah West, Anglo-Egyptian Sudan, 1938-9, JEA 25 [1939] 139-144, esp. 141). In the Ramses II list, the name occurs in a context which also mentions Seir (assuming that s'rr stands for Seir). It may be tentatively concluded that this "Yahu in the land of the Shosu-beduins" is to be situated in the area of Edom and Midian (WEIPPERT 1974: 271; AXELSSON 1987:60; pace WEINFELD 1987:304).

In these Egyptian texts Yhw is used as a toponym (KNAUF 1988:46-47). Yet a relationship with the deity by the same name is a reasonable assumption (pace M. WEIPPERT, "Heiliger Krieg" in Israel und Assyrien, ZAW 84 [1972] 460-493, esp. 491 n.

YAHWEH

144); whether the god took his name from the region or vice versa remains undecided (note that R. GIVEON, "The Cities of Our God" (II Sam 10:12), *JBL* 83 [1964] 415-416, suggests that the name is short for *Beth-Yahweh, which would compare with the alternance between →Baal-meon and Beth-Baal-meon). By the 14th century BCE, before the cult of Yahweh had reached Israel, groups of Edomite and Midianite nomads worshipped Yahweh as their god. These data converge with a northern tradition, found in a number of ancient theophany texts, according to which Yahweh came from →Edom and Seir (Judg 5:4; note the correction in Ps 68:8[7]). According to the Blessing of Moses Yahweh came from Sinai, "dawned from" Seir, and "shone forth" from Mount Paran (Deut 33:2). Elsewhere he is said to have come from Teman and Mount Paran (Hab 3:3). The references to "Yahweh of Teman" in the Kuntillet 'Ajrud inscriptions are extra-biblical confirmation of the topographical connection (M. WEINFELD, Kuntillet 'Ajrud Inscriptions and Their Significance, *SEL* 1 [1984] 121-130, esp. 125, 126). All of these places—Seir, Mt Paran, Teman, and Sinai— are in or near Edom.

If Yahweh was at home in the south, then, how did he make his way to the north? According to a widely accepted theory, the Kenites were the mediators of the Yahwistic cult. One of the first to advance the Kenite hypothesis was the Dutch historian of religion Cornelis P. Tiele. In 1872 TIELE characterized Yahweh historically as "the god of the desert, worshipped by the Kenites and their close relatives before the Israelites" (*Vergelijkende geschiedenis van de Egyptische en Mesopotamische godsdiensten* [Amsterdam 1872] 559). The idea was adopted and elaborated by B. STADE (*Geschichte des Volkes Israels* [1887] 130-131), and it gained considerable support ever since, also among modern scholars (see, e.g., A. J. WENSINCK, De oorsprongen van het Jahwisme, *Semietische Studiën uit de nalatenschap van Prof. Dr. A. J. Wensinck* [Leiden 1941] 23-50; B. D. EERD-MANS, *Religion of Israel* [Leiden 1947] 15-19; H. H. ROWLEY, *From Joseph to Joshua* [London 1950] 149-160; A. H. J. GUNNEWEG, Mose in Midian, *ZTK* 60 [1964] 1-9; W. H. SCHMIDT, *Exodus, Sinai, Wüste* (Darmstadt 1983) 110-118; WEINFELD 1987; METTINGER 1990:408-409). In its classical form the hypothesis assumes that the Israelites became acquainted with the cult of Yahweh through Moses. Moses' father-in-law—Hobab, according to an old tradition (Judg 1:16; 4:11; cf. Num 10:29)— was a Midianite priest (Exod 2:16; 3:1; 18:1) who worshipped Yahweh (see e.g. Exod 18:10-12). He belonged to the Kenites (Judg 1:16; 4:11), a branch of the Midianites (H. H. ROWLEY, *From Joseph to Joshua* [London 1950] 152-153). By way of Hobab and Moses, then, the Kenites were the mediators of the cult of Yahweh.

The strength of the Kenite hypothesis is the link it establishes between different but converging sets of data: the absence of Yahweh from West-Semitic epigraphy; Yahweh's topographical link with the area of Edom (which may be taken to include the territory of the Midianites); the 'Kenite' affiliation of Moses; and the positive evaluation of the Kenites in the Bible. A major flaw in the classical Kenite hypothesis, however, is its disregard for the 'Canaanite' origins of Israel. The view that, under the influence of Moses, the Israelites became Yahwists during their journey through the desert, and then brought their newly acquired religion to the Palestinian soil, neglects the fact that the majority of the Israelites were firmly rooted in Palestine. The historical role of Moses, moreover, is highly problematic. It seems more prudent not to put too much weight on the figure of Moses. It is only in later tradition that he came to be regarded as the legendary ancestor of the Levitical priests and a symbol of the 'Yahweh-alone' movement; his real importance remains uncertain.

If the Kenite hypothesis is to be maintained, then, it is only in a modified form. Though it is highly plausible that the Kenites (and the Midianites and the Rechabites may be mentioned in the same breath) intro-

325

A Second Look at Jesus

duced Israel to the worship of Yahweh, it is unlikely that they did so outside the borders of Palestine. Both Kenites and Rechabites are mentioned as dwelling in North Israel at an early stage; so are the Gibeonites, who are ethnically related to the Edomites (J. BLENKINSOPP, *Gibeon and Israel* [Cambridge 1972] 14-27). Some of these groups were not permanent residents of North Israel; they came there as traders. Already in Gen 37:28 Midianite traders are mentioned as being active between Palestine and Egypt (KNAUF 1988:27). If Yahwism did indeed originate with Midianites or Kenites—and the evidence seems to point in that direction—it may have been brought to Transjordan and Central Palestine by traders along the caravan routes from the south to the east (J. D. SCHLOEN, Caravans, Kenites, and *Casus belli*, *CBQ* 55 [1993] 18-38, esp. p. 36).

III. Explanations of the name Yahweh must assume that, except for the vocalisation, the traditional form is the correct one. The hypothesis which says that there were originally two divine names, viz. Yāhū and Yahweh, the former being the older one (MAYER 1958:34), is now generally abandoned in light of the epigraphic evidence (CROSS 1973:61; pace KLAWEK 1990:12). The significance of the name Yahweh has been the subject of a staggering amount of publications (for an impression see MAYER 1958). This "monumental witness to the industry and ingenuity of biblical scholars" (CROSS 1973:60) is hardly in proportion to the limited importance of the issue. Even if the meaning of the name could be established beyond reasonable doubt, it would contribute little to the understanding of the nature of the god. The caution against overestimating etymologies, voiced most eloquently by James Barr, holds good for divine names as well. From a perspective of the history of religion, it is much more important to know the characteristics which worshippers associated with their god, than the original meaning of the latter's name. Having said that, however, the question of the etymology of Yahweh cannot be simply dismissed. The following observations are in order.

In spite of isolated attempts to take *yhwh* as a pronominal form, meaning 'Yea He!' (from **ya huwa*, S. MOWINCKEL, *HUCA* 32 [1958] 121-133) or 'My One' (cf. Akk *ya'u*, H. CAZELLES, Der persönliche Gott Abrahams, *Der Weg zum Menschen, FS A. Deissler* [ed. R. Mosis & L. Ruppert; Freiburg 1989] 59-60), it is widely agreed that the name represents a verbal form. With the preformative *yod*, *yhwh* is a finite verbal form to be analysed as a 3rd masc. sing. imperfect. Analogous finite verbal forms used as theonyms are attested for the religion of pre-Islamic Arabs. Examples include the gods →Yaʿūq ('he protects', *WbMyth* I 479) and →Yaġūṯ ('he helps', *WbMyth* I 478). Much earlier are the Akkadian and Amorite instances of verbal forms used as divine names: ᵈIkšudum ('He has reached', ARM 13 no. 111:6) and Ešuḫ ('He has been victorious', H. B. HUFFMON, *Amorite Personal Names in the Mari Texts* [Baltimore 1965] 215) are just two examples (CROSS 1973:67). Morphologically, then, the name Yahweh is not without parallels.

The interpretation of the theonym as a finite verb is already found in Exod 3:14. In reply to Moses' question of what he is to say to the Israelites when they ask him which god sent him, God says: "I AM WHO I AM", and he adds: "Say this to the people of Israel, 'I AM has sent me to you'". The explanation here offered is a sophisticated play based on association: the root HWH is understood as a by-form of HYH, 'to be' and the prefix of the third person is understood as a secondary objectivation of a first person: *yhwh* is thus interpreted as *'hyh*, 'I am'. Since the significance of such a name is elusive, the reconstructed name is itself the subject of a further interpretation in the phrase *'ehyeh 'ăšer 'ehyeh*, 'I am who I am'. Its meaning is debated. Should one understand it as a promise ('I will certainly be there') or as an allusion to the incomparability of Yahweh ('I am who I am', i.e. without peer)? Even in the revelation of his name, Yahweh does not surrender himself:

YAHWEH

He cannot be captured by means of either an image or a name. The Greek translation ὁ ὤν (LXX) has philosophical overtones: it is at the basis of a profound speculation on the eternity and immutability of God—both of them ideas originally unconnected with the name Yahweh.

Since the Israelite explanation is evidently a piece of theology rather than a reliable etymology, it cannot be accepted as the last word on the matter. Comparative material from Akkadian sources has been used to make a case for the thesis that *yahweh is in fact an abbreviated sentence name. Among Amorite personal names, there are a number in which a finite form of the root HWY ('to be, to manifest oneself') is coupled with a theonym. Examples are Yaḫwi-ilum, Yaḫwi-Adad (ARM 23, 86:7), and Ya(ḫ)wium (= Iaḫwi-ilum, e.g. ARM 23, 448:13). These Amorite names are the semantic equivalent of the Akkadian name Ibašši-ilum ('God has manifested himself'). The objection that these are all anthroponyms, whereas Yahweh is a theonym, is not decisive. Cuneiform texts also recognize a number of gods whose names are in fact a finite verbal form with a deity as subject: ᵈIkrub-Il ('El has blessed') and ᵈIšmêlum (= *Išme-ilum, 'God has heard') can be quoted in illustration. STOL has made a strong case for regarding these names as those of deified ancestors (M. STOL, Old Babylonian Personal Names, SEL 8 [1991] 191-212, esp. 203-205).

Some scholars believe that Yahweh, too, is the abbreviated name of a deified ancestor. Thus DE MOOR construes the original name of the deity as *Yahweh-El, 'May El be present (as helper)' (1990:237-239). In support of this speculated form he adduces the name Jacob (Ya'ăqōb), which is short for Yʿqb-ʾl, 'May El follow him closely' (cf. Yaḫqub-el, H. HUFFMON, Amorite Personal Names in the Mari Texts [Baltimore 1965] 203-204; S. AḤITUV, Canaanite Toponyms in Ancient Egyptian Documents [Jerusalem 1984] 200), and such names as Yaḫwi-Ilu in Mari texts. DE MOOR draws the conclusion that originally Yahweh was "probably the divine ancestor of one of the proto-Israelite tribes" (1990:244). Yet though theoretically possible, it is difficult to believe that the major Israelite deity, venerated in a cult that was imported into Palestine, was originally a deified ancestor. Though such gods are known, they are never found in a leading position in the pantheon. Their worship tends to remain local, as an ancestor is of necessity the ancestor of a restricted group.

There are admittedly ancient Near Eastern deities with a composite name who never were ancestors. Examples include rkb'l (traditionally vocalized as →Rakib-el) from Sam'al (KAI 24:16), and Malakbel, 'Aglibol, and Yarhibol from Palmyra. Morphologically, however, these names do not compare with a speculated *yahweh-DN, since the first component of the name is a substantive. The names just mentioned are best interpreted as 'Charioteer of El' (cf. TSSI II 70), 'Messenger of Bel', 'Calf of Bol', and 'Lord of the Source' (cf. J. HOFTIJZER, Religio aramaica [Leiden 1968] 32-38; for the interpretation of the name Yarhibol, cf. Akk yarḫu, 'water hole, pond', CAD I/J 325), respectively. In addition to the morphological difference with a hypothetical *yahweh-DN, Rakib-el and his likes are names of subordinate deities; there is no example of such gods heading the pantheon.

Related to the thesis that *yahweh is an abbreviated theonym is the suggestion that it is an abbreviation of a liturgical formula. The solution proposed by CROSS is an example. He speculates that the longer form of 'Yahweh' is extant in the title →Yahweh Zabaoth. The ṣĕbāʾôt (transcribed as Zabaoth in many English Bible translations) are the →host of heaven, i.e. the council of the gods. The name Yahweh Zabaoth is itself short for *Ḏu yahwī ṣabaʾôt, 'He who creates the (heavenly) armies', according to CROSS (1973:70). Since in his view this is in fact a title of El, the full name might be reconstructed as *Il-ḏu-yahwī-ṣabaʾôt. The analysis of Cross goes back to his teacher W. F. Albright (W. F. ALBRIGHT, review of B. N. Wambacq, L'épithète divine Jahvé Sebaʾôt, JBL 67 (1948) 377-381). D. N. FREEDMAN quotes from Albright's notes for an unpublished History of the Religion of

A Second Look at Jesus

Israel listing a number of reconstructed cult names such as **'ēl yahweh yiśrā'ēl*, 'El-creates-Israel' (on the basis of Gen 33:20) and **'ēl yahweh rûḥôt*, 'El-creates-the-winds' (FREEDMAN et al. 1977-82:547). Instead of a reconstructed form **yahweh-'el*, then, Albright reckons with a form **'El-yahweh*—which could be complemented by various objects. DIJKSTRA, too, argues that the original form is El Yahweh, 'El who reveals himself'—a form still reflected in such texts as Ps 118:27 (M. DIJKSTRA, Yahweh-El or El-Yahweh?, *"Dort ziehen Schiffe dahin...": collected communications to the XIVth congress of the International Organization for the Study of the Old Testament* [BEATAJ 28; ed. M. Augustin & K.-D. Schunk; Frankfurt am Main etc. 1996] 43-52).

Leaving aside for the moment the problem implied in the identification of Yahweh with El, the interpretation of Yahweh as an abbreviated sentence name (and possibly a liturgical formula) is not without difficulties. Since the idea that a human ancestor could rise to the position of national god flies in the face of the comparative evidence, a presumed El-Yahweh or Yahweh-El must of necessity be a divine name followed or preceded by a verbal form characterizing the deity. By implication, then, the proper name of the god has been replaced in the Israelite tradition by a verb denoting one of his characteristic activities. Such a process is unparalleled in ancient Near Eastern religions—unless one considers such Arab deities as Ya'ūq and Yaġūt, epithets of another deity, which would suggest a South Semitic rather than a West Semitic background for Yahweh. Isolated verbal forms such as proper names, however, are not uncommon in the Semitic world, as witnessed by e.g. the name **Yagrušu* of Baal's weapon. Solving the enigma of the tetragrammaton by positing another divine name is really a last option. A solution which explains the name in the form it has come down to us is to be preferred.

A problem hitherto unmentioned is the identification of the root lying at the basis of the form *yhwh*, and that of its meaning. Though some have suggested a link with the root ḤWY, resulting in the translation 'the Destroyer' (e.g. H. GRESSMANN, *Mose und seine Zeit* [Göttingen 1913] 37), it is generally held that the name should be connected with the Semitic root HWY. Also scholars who do not regard the tetragrammaton as an abbreviated theonym usually follow the Israelite interpretation insofar they interpret Yahweh as a form of the verb 'to be'; opinions diverge as to whether the form is basic or causative, i.e. a Qal or a Hiph'il. The one school interprets 'He is', i.e. 'He manifests himself as present', whereas the other argues in favour of a causative meaning: 'He causes to be, calls into existence'. The first interpretation has an exponent in VON SODEN. Adducing comparative material from Akkadian sources, he urges that the verb should be taken in its stronger sense 'to prove oneself, to manifest oneself, to reveal oneself' (VON SODEN 1966). A representative of the second school is ALBRIGHT. He takes **yahweh* as a causative imperfect of the verb HWY, 'to be'. Yahweh, then, is a god who 'causes to be' or 'brings into being'. In this form, the verb is normally transitive (W. F. ALBRIGHT, *Yahweh and the Gods of Canaan* [London 1968] 147-149).

A major difficulty with the explanations of the name Yahweh on the basis of HWY interpreted as 'to be', however, is the fact that they explain the name of a South Semitic deity (originating from Edom, or even further south) with the help of a West-Semitic etymology (KNAUF 1984a:469). The form of the name has the closest analogues in the pre-Islamic Arab pantheon; it is natural, therefore, to look first at the possibility of an explanation on the basis of the Arabic etymology. The relevant root HWY has three meanings in Arabic: 1. to desire, be passionate; 2. to fall; 3. to blow. All three have been called upon for a satisfactory explanation of the name Yahweh. The derivation of the name Yahweh from the meaning 'to love, to be passionate', which resulted in the translation of Yahweh as 'the Passionate' (GOITEIN 1956) has made no impact on OT scholarship. Hardly more successful was the

YAHWEH

suggestion that Yahweh is 'the Speaker', also based on the link of the name with the root HWY (cf. Akk *awû, atmû*; BOWMAN 1944:4-5).

A greater degree of plausibility attaches to those interpretations of the name Yahweh which identify him as a storm god. Thus the name has been connected with the meaning 'to fall' (also attested in Syriac), in which case the verbal form is seen as a causative ('He who causes to fall', scil. rain, lightning, or the enemies by means of his lightning, see BDB 218a). Another suggestion is to link the name with the meaning 'to blow', said of the wind (cf. Syr *hawwē*, 'wind'). This leads to the translation "er fährt durch die Lüfte, er weht" (J. WELLHAUSEN, *Israelitische und jüdische Geschichte* [3rd ed.; Berlin 1897] 25 note 1; KNAUF 1984a:469; 1988:43-48). Especially the latter possibility merits serious consideration. In view of the south-eastern origins of the cult of Yahweh, an Arabic etymology has a certain likelihood. Also, his presumed character as a storm god contributes to explain why Yahweh could assume various of Baal's mythological exploits.

The interpretation of the name of Yahweh is not entirely devoid of meaning, then, when it comes to establishing his character. If *yhwh* does indeed mean 'He blows', Yahweh is originally a storm god. Since Baal (originally an epitheton of →Hadad) is of the same type, the relationship between Yahweh and Baal deserves to be analyzed more closely. In the Monarchic Era, Baal (i.e. the Baal cult) was a serious rival of Yahweh. The competition between the two gods (that is, between their respective priesthoods and prophets) was especially fierce since the promotion of the cult of the Tyrian Baal by the Omrides. Because there was no *entente* between Yahweh and Baal, Yahweh could hardly have inherited traits of a storm god from Baal. Inheritance is too peaceful a process. Yahweh's 'Baalistic' traits have a dual origin: some are his of old because he is himself a storm god, whereas others have been appropriated—or should we say confiscated—by him. Examples of the latter include the designation of Mount →Zion as 'the recesses of →Zaphon' (Ps 48:3), the motif of Yahweh's victory over Yam (→Sea; for a thorough study see J. DAY, *God's Conflict with the Dragon and the Sea: Echoes of A Canaanite myth in the Old Testament* [Cambridge 1985]) and →Mot (W. HERRMANN, Jahwes Triumph über Mot, *UF* 11 [1979] 371-377), and the Baal epithet of →'Rider upon the Clouds'.

Owing to the emphasis on the conflict between Yahweh and Baal, it is insufficiently realized that Yahweh himself, too, is "a deity who is originally conceived in the categories of the Hadad type" (METTINGER 1990:410). According to the theophany texts, the earth trembles, clouds drop water, and mountains quake at the appearance of Yahweh (Judg 5:4-5). Though such a response of the elements to Yahweh's manifestation need not imply that he is a storm-god, the latter hypothesis offers the most natural explanation. When Yahweh comes to the rescue of his beloved, he is hidden all around by darkness, thick clouds dark with water being his canopy (Ps 18:12[11]). As he lifts his voice the thunder resounds (Ps 18:14[13]). Like Baal, Yahweh is perceived as 'a god of the mountains' (1 Kgs 20:23), a characterization presumably triggered by the association of the weather-god with clouds hovering above the mountain tops.

Though few scholars would contest the fact that Yahweh has certain traits normally ascribed to Baal, it is often argued that originally he was much more like El than like Baal. In the patriarchal narratives of Genesis, El names such as →El Olam and →El Elyon are frequently used as epithets of Yahweh. Various scholars have drawn the conclusion that El and Yahweh were identified at a rather early stage. This identification is sometimes explained by assuming that Yahweh is originally an El figure (thus, e.g. H. NIEHR, *Der höchste Gott* [BZAW 190; Berlin/New York 1990] 4-5). CROSS has argued that Yahweh is originally a hypocoristicon of a liturgical title of El. Yahweh Zabaoth, allegedly meaning 'He who calls the heavenly armies into being', is

329

A Second Look at Jesus

not a name but an epithet. According to CROSS, the god to whom it applies in the first place is El, since El is known in the Ugaritic texts as the father of the gods. The latter are conventionally referred to as 'the sons of El' (CROSS 1973). DE MOOR, who also holds that Yahweh is an abbreviated sentence name originally belonging to a human being, links Yahweh with El as well. Though *Yahweh-El was the name of an ancestor, the deified ancestor was also "an aspect of El" (DE MOOR 1990:244). In order to solve the apparent contradiction, DE MOOR explains that the deified kings of Ugarit, who 'joined' (šrk, KTU 1.15 v:17) El at their death, merged with the god (1990:242).

Speculations about the original identity of Yahweh with El need to be critically examined, however. There are problems concerning both the nature of the identification, and the divine type to which Yahweh belongs. It is insufficiently realised that, at the beginning of the Iron Age, El's role had become largely nominal. The process of El's retreat in favour of Dagan (the major god at Ebla in the late third millennium) and later Baal (the major god at Ugarit in the middle of the second millennium) had long been under way. By the beginning of the Iron Age, the cult of El survived in some border zones of the Near East. In most regions, however, including Palestine, El's career as a living god (i.e. as a cultic reality and an object of actual devotion) had ended; he survived in such expressions as 'dt-'l ('the council of El') and bny-'l ('sons of El', i.e. gods), but this was a survival only in name. This fact explains why there are no traces of polemics against El in the Hebrew Bible. It can therefore be argued that the smooth identification of El as Yahweh was based, not on an identity of character, but on El's decay. His name was increasingly used either as a generic noun meaning 'god' or, more specifically, as a designation of the personal god. In both cases, Yahweh could be called *'ēl* (on the identification of Yahweh and El see VAN DER TOORN 1996:320-328).

Along with the name, Yahweh inherited various traits of El. One of them is divine eternity. Ugaritic texts call El the 'father of years' (*ab šnm*) and depict him as a bearded patriarch; Yahweh, on the other hand, is called the →'Ancient of days', and also is wearing a beard (Dan 7:9-14.22). Like El, Yahweh presides over the →council of the gods. Compassion is another common trait: El is said to be compassionate (*dpid*), whereas Yahweh is called "merciful and gracious" (Exod 34:6; for these and other similarities see M. SMITH, *The Early History of God* [San Francisco 1990] 7-12). In some biblical passages, the parallels are consciously explored. Thus GREENFIELD has shown that Deut 32:6-7 applies to Yahweh various motifs and images originally associated with El. El (here Yahweh) is said to be Israel's 'father' and 'creator'; he is 'wise' and 'eternal' and has lived for 'the years of many generations' (J. C. GREENFIELD, The Hebrew Bible and Canaanite Literature, *The Literary Guide to the Bible* [ed. R. Alter & F. Kermode; Cambridge, Mass. 1987] 545-560, esp. 554).

An aspect of Yahweh that may be traced back to El, though only with great caution, is his solar appearance. Even though the theophany texts depict Yahweh primarily as a warrior storm-god, there are elements in their description which seem to assume that Yahweh is a solar deity. The Psalm of Habakkuk mentions God's 'splendour' (*hôd*), and possibly his 'shine' (*tĕhillâ*, v 3); God's appearance comes with brightness (*nōgah*) and rays of light (*qarnayim*, v 4). Likewise Deut 33:2 speaks about Yahweh 'shining forth' (ZRḤ) and lightning up (YPʿ, hiphil; for the terminology cf. F. SCHNUTENHAUS, Das Kommen und Erscheinen Gottes im Alten Testament, *ZAW* 76 [1964] 1-22, esp. 8-10). The closest extrabiblical parallel is found in a Hebrew text from Kuntillet ʿAjrud, in which the mountains are said to melt when El shines forth (*wbzrḥ .'l* [...] *wymsn hrm*, "when El shines forth [...] the mountains melt"; M. WEINFELD, Kuntillet ʿAjrud Inscriptions and Their Significance, *SEL* 1 [1984] 121-130,

YAHWEH

esp. 126; S. AḤITUV, *Handbook of Ancient Hebrew Inscriptions* [Jerusalem 1992] 160-162). Also outside the theophany tradition there is evidence of Yahweh as a solar god. Thus the word *'ôr*, →'light', is sometimes used as a divine title (Ps 139:11, cf. J. HOLMAN, Analysis of the Text of Ps 139, *BZ* 14 [1970] 37-71, esp. 56-58; for other solar language applied to Yahweh see M. SMITH, *The Early History of God* [San Francisco 1990] 115-124, Ch. 4: Yahweh and the Sun [but cf. the review by S. B. PARKER, *Hebrew Studies* 33 (1992) 158-162]; J. G. TAYLOR, *Yahweh and the Sun* [Sheffield 1993]).

A further link between El and Yahweh is the identity of their consort. Texts from Kuntillet 'Ajrud and Khirbet el-Qom refer to Yahweh 'and his →Asherah' (*w'šrth*). Though several scholars argue that this 'Asherah' is merely a cult symbol or a designation for 'sanctuary' (cf. Akk *aširtu*), the interpretation of the word as a divine name is to be preferred (*pace* J. A. EMERTON, New Light on Israelite Religion: The Implications of the Inscriptions from Kuntillet 'Ajrud, *ZAW* 94 [1982] 2-20; see M. DIETRICH & O. LORETZ, *Jahweh und seine Aschera* [UBL 9; Neukirchen-Vluyn 1992] 82-103). In the light of these data, the suggestion to emendate אשרה in Deut 33:2e into אשרה ('and at his right hand Asherah'; H. S. NYBERG, Deuteronomium 33,2-3, *ZDMG* 92 [1938] 320-344, esp. 335; see also M. WEINFELD, *SEL* 1 [1984] 121-130, esp. 124) remains a distinct possibility. Since Asherah is traditionally the consort of El in the Ugaritic texts, the pairing of Yahweh and Asherah suggests that Yahweh had taken the place of El (cf. M. DIJKSTRA, El, YHWH, and their Asherah: On Continuity and Discontinuity in Canaanite and Ancient Israelite Religion, *Ugarit: Ein ostmediterranes Kulturzentrum im Alten Orient* [ALASP 7; ed. M. Dietrich & O. Loretz; Münster 1995] 43-73, who finds here confirmation for the view that Yahweh is a particularized form of El).

Under northern influence, Yahweh came also to be paired with →Anat, possibly to be identified with the →Queen of Heaven mentioned in Jer 7:18; 44:17.18.19.25. Her link with Yahweh is evident from the name Anat-Yahu, attested in Aramaic texts from the Jewish colony at Elephantine (VAN DER TOORN 1992). Considering the fact that the only other male deities with whom Anat is paired are Baal and →Bethel (the deified baetylon, cf. also Sikkānu ['stone stela', Ug *skn*], a theonym surviving in the name Sanchunjathon = סכניתן), no influence from the cult or mythology of El is apparent here.

Though Yahweh was known and worshipped among the Israelites before 1000 BCE, he did not become the national god until the beginning of the monarchic era. Due to the religious politics of Saul, Yahweh became the patron deity of the Israelite state (VAN DER TOORN 1993:531-536; 1996:266-286). As David and Solomon inherited and enlarged Saul's kingdom, they acknowledged the position of Yahweh as national god. David brought the ark of Yahweh from Benjamin to Jerusalem (2 Sam 6); Solomon sought the blessing of Yahweh at the sanctuary of Gibeon, the national temple of the Saulide state (1 Kgs 3:4; VAN DER TOORN 1993:534-535). Evidence of the predominant role of Yahweh in the official cult during the Monarchic Era are the theophoric personal names, both the biblical and the epigraphical ones. The divine name Yahweh is by far the most common theophoric element (J. H. TIGAY, *You Shall Have No Other Gods: Israelite Religion in the Light of Hebrew Inscriptions* [Atlanta 1986]; S. I. L. NORIN, *Seine Name allein ist hoch. Das Jhw-haltige Suffix althebräischer Personennamen* [Malmö 1986]; J. D. FOWLER, *Theophoric Personal Names in Ancient Hebrew. A Comparative Study* [Sheffield 1988]).

The practical monolatry of Yahweh should not be taken for a strict monotheism. Not only did the Israelites continue to recognize the existence of deities besides Yahweh, they also knew more than one Yahweh. Though at the mythological level there is only one, the cultic reality reflected a plurality of Yahweh gods (MCCARTER 1987:139-143). Extrabiblical evidence from Kuntillet 'Ajrud mentions a 'Yahweh of

A Second Look at Jesus

Samaria' and a 'Yahweh of Teman'; it is possible that the two names designate one god, viz. the official god of the northern kingdom ('Samaria', after its capital). Yet the recognition of a northern Yahweh is mirrored by the the worship of a Yahweh of Hebron and a Yahweh of Zion. Though the constructions *běḥebrôn* and *běṣiyyôn* are normally translated 'in Hebron' and 'in Zion', a comparison of the name Milkashtart ('Milku of Ashtart') with the expression *mlk bʿṭrt* ('Milku in Ashart') suggests that such expressions as *yhwh běṣiyyôn* (Ps 99:2) and *yhwh běḥebrôn* (2 Sam 15:7) should be understood as references to local forms of Yahweh (M. L. BARRÉ, *The God-List in the Treaty between Hannibal and Philip V of Macedonia* [Baltimore/London 1983] 186 note 473; cf. 1 Sam 5:5 *Dāgôn bĕ'ašdôd*, 'Dagan of Ashdod'). The religious situation in early Israel, therefore, was not merely one of polytheism, but also of poly-Yahwism. The Deuteronomic emphasis on the unity of Yahweh (→One) must be understood against this background.

IV. *Bibliography*
L. E. AXELSSON, *The Lord Rose up from Seir* (ConB OT 25; Lund 1987); B. ALFRINK, La prononciation 'Jehova' du Tétragramme, *OTS* 5 (1948) 43-62; R. A. BOWMAN, Yahweh the Speaker, *JNES* 3 (1944) 1-8; F. M. CROSS, *Canaanite Myth and Hebrew Epic* (Cambridge, Mass/London 1973) 44-75 [cf. pp. 60-61 n. 61 for lit.]; M. DAHOOD, The God Yā at Ebla?, *JBL* 100 (1981) 607-608; O. EISSFELDT, El and Yahweh, *JSS* 1 (1956) 25-37; D. N. FREEDMAN, M. P. O'CONNOR & H. RINGGREN, יהוה *jhwh*, *TWAT* 3 (1977-82) 533-554; S. D. GOITEIN, YHWH the Passionate, *VT* 6 (1956) 1-9; R. S. HESS, The Divine Name Yahweh in Late Bronze Age Sources?, *UF* 23 (1991[1992]) 181-188; A. KLAWEK, The Name Jahveh in the Light of Most Recent Discussion, *Folia Orientalia* 27 (1990) 11-12; E. A. KNAUF, Yahwe, *VT* 34 (1984a) 467-472; KNAUF, Eine nabatäische Parallele zum hebräischen Gottesnamen, *BN* 23 (1984b) 21-28; KNAUF, *Midian* (Wiesbaden 1988) 43-48; R. MAYER, Der Gottesname Jahwe im Lichte der neuesten Forschung, *BZ* n.s. 2 (1958) 26-53; P. K. MCCARTER, Jr., Aspects of the Religion of the Israelite Monarchy: Biblical and Epigraphic Data, *Ancient Israelite Religion* (FS F. M. Cross; ed. P. D. Miller, Jr., P. D. Hanson & S. D. McBride; Philadelphia 1987) 137-155; *T. N. D. METTINGER, The Elusive Essence: YHWH, El and Baal and the Distinctiveness of Israelite Faith, *Die Hebräische Bibel und ihre zweifache Nachgeschichte* (FS R. Rendtorff zum 65. Geburtstag; ed. E. Blum, C. Macholz & E. W. Stegemann; Neukirchen 1990) 393-417; J. C. DE MOOR, *The Rise of Yahwism* (Leuven 1990); H.-P. MÜLLER, Gab es in Ebla einen Gottesnamen Ja?, *ZA* 70 (1980) 70-92; MÜLLER, Der Jahwenamen und seine Bedeutung. Ex 3,14 im Licht der Textpublikationen aus Ebla, *Bib* 62 (1981) 305-327; A. MURTONEN, *The Appearance of the Name yhwh outside Israel* (StOr 16/3; Helsinki 1951); M. S. SMITH, Yahweh and other Deities in Ancient Israel: Observations on Problems and recent Trends, *Ein Gott Allein* (eds. W. Dietrich & M. A. Klopfenstein; Freiburg/Göttingen 1994) 197-234; W. VON SODEN, Jahwe, 'er ist, er erweist sich', *WO* 3/3 (1966) 177-187 [reprinted in *Bibel und Alter Orient* (ed. H.-P. Müller; BZAW 162; Berlin & New York 1985) 78-88]; K. VAN DER TOORN, Anat-Yahu, Some Other Deities, and the Jews of Elephantine, *Numen* 39 (1992) 80-101; VAN DER TOORN, Saul and the Rise of Israelite State Religion, *VT* 43 (1993) 519-542; VAN DER TOORN, *Family Religion in Babylonia, Syria and Israel* (SHCANE 7; Leiden 1996); N. WALKER, The Writing of the Divine Name in the Mishna, *VT* 1 (1951) 309-310; M. WEINFELD, The Tribal League at Sinai, *Ancient Israelite Religion* (FS F. M. Cross; ed. P. D. Miller Jr., P. D. Hanson & S. D. McBride; Philadelphia 1987) 303-314; M. WEIPPERT, Semitische Nomaden des zweiten Jahrtausends, *Bib* 55 [1974] 265-280, 427-433; *WEIPPERT, Jahwe, *RLA* 5 (1980) 246-253.

K. VAN DER TOORN

www.ingramcontent.com/pod-product-compliance
Lightning Source LLC
Chambersburg PA
CBHW022058090426
42743CB00008B/640